TEST YOUR KNOWLEDGE OF
V. C. ANDREWS' WORLD
OF SHADOWS AND SHIVERS

—Why was V. C. Andrews compelled not to use her first name as the author of her books?

—How has V. C. Andrews continued to write novels from beyond the grave?

—Can you find your way through Foxworth Hall, Corinne's mansion, Whitefern, Cutler's Cove Hotel, and the other immortal manors of menace?

—Can you recall all the torrid scenes of temptation and forbidden passion?

—Can you answer the over 1400 questions designed to braintease and delight followers of the Queen of Dark Suspense?

You can do it all and much more with the help of—
THE V. C. ANDREWS TRIVIA AND QUIZ BOOK

Stephen J. Spignesi is the author of many books on popular culture, including the Stephen King quiz books (Signet Books), a Stephen King encyclopedia, a Woody Allen companion, and *The Official Gone with the Wind Companion* (Plume Books).

The Final & Ultimate V.C. Andrews Quiz Question

The hidden error can be found in the *Leafing Through . . .* section of Book 15, *Midnight Whispers*. The mistake occurs in the list, *"The 3 Questions Jefferson Cutler Asked About Dawn's Gold Watch."* The questions 9-year-old Jefferson asked are correct as listed, but he asked them about *his sister Christie's* watch, not his mother Dawn's. The watch was a birthday gift given to Christie at breakfast on the morning of her 16th birthday. The hint blatantly referred to "watch springs" (in the Spender quotation) and "Midnight" (in the Eliot excerpt), sending you to a list about a watch in a book with a reference to midnight. Of course, the hint could also have been referring to "hearts"; "love"; "memory"; "madness"; or "flowers"; but part of the fun lay in figuring out just what specific references in the hint were part of the clue, and which were decoys. (*Midnight Whispers,* 18.)

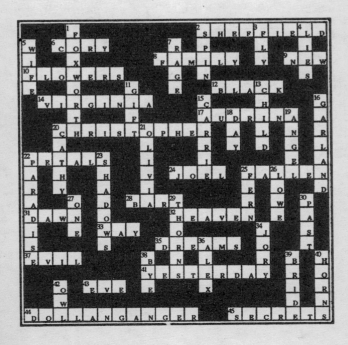

ABOUT THE AUTHOR

Stephen Spignesi is a writer and popular culture expert who lives in New Haven, Connecticut, with his wife, Pam, and their remarkable cat, Ben.

In addition to *The V. C. Andrews Trivia and Quiz Book*, Spignesi is also the author of the "Andy Griffith Show" encyclopedia, *Mayberry, My Hometown* (Popular Culture, Ink); *The Complete Stephen King Encyclopedia* (Contemporary Books); *The Stephen King Quiz Book* (New American Library); *The Second Stephen King Quiz Book* (New American Library); *The Woody Allen Companion* (Andrews and McMeel); and *The Official Gone with the Wind Companion* (Plume).

Spignesi was recently described as "The world's leading expert on Stephen King" by *Entertainment Weekly* magazine, and his work has appeared in *Harper's*, *Cinefantastique, Saturday Review, Midnight Graffiti*, and *Gauntlet* magazines, and *The New York Times*.

He is currently working on a number of nonfiction projects involving film, music, and popular culture, including the forthcoming *Encyclopedia of Odd* for Penguin USA, and a novel, *Amnesia*.

ANSWERS

(NOTE: The Answers section also provides the page numbers where answers can be found in the novels.)

Chapter 1. FLOWERS IN THE ATTIC

1. Multiple Choice
1. C. A blue Ford (17).
2. D. She got diarrhea (119).
3. A. Claustrophobia (142).
4. A. Jim Johnston used to call the Dollanganger kids "The Dresden dolls" (13).
5. B. Malcolm Foxworth tithed ten percent of his yearly income to the church (95).
6. A. "A woman who saves her favors for men of the aristocracy, or royalty" (212).
7. C. 8 (215).
8. B. 2½ (216).
9. A. It was two feet tall (216).
10. D. Tinkertoys (220).
11. B. From watching old Andy Hardy movies (222).
12. A. Switzerland (226).
13. C. 8 (259).
14. D. Cathy's intended stage name was "Catherine Doll." (It was later changed to

"Catherine Dahl.")
(109).

15. A. "Belated" (165).
16. B. Mary Lou Baker (257).
17. B. Thursday (288).
18. A. "Cindy Lou" (137).
19. A. "Charlie" (137).
20. B. They marked off the days with red X's on wall calendars (235).
21. B. They ripped pages from the oldest books in the attic and used them to wipe themselves (250).
22. C. South Carolina (311).
23. B. $396.44 (358).
24. C. Pneumonia (371).
25. C. Greenfield Highway (17).
26. A. The grandmother (385).

2. True or False
1. FALSE. Chris was two years and five months older than Cathy (8).
2. FALSE. He was 36 (13).
3. FALSE. He was driving a green Cadillac (15).
4. TRUE (16).
5. FALSE. He suffered from heart disease (32).
6. TRUE (95).
7. TRUE (99).
8. FALSE. They were married in church (101).
9. TRUE (137).
10. TRUE (157).
11. FALSE. It was a quarter moon (263).
12. FALSE. When Cathy asked him, he didn't

know which one lit up (263).
13. FALSE. One of his sisters lived in Vermont, the other two, down South (311).
14. FALSE. White chalk daisies kept them away (349).
15. FALSE. The paintings were by Goya (53).
16. FALSE. The Dollangangers' previous home was in Gladstone, Pennsylvania (5).
17. TRUE (5).
18. FALSE. Christopher Dollanganger's best friend was Jim Johnston (13).
19. FALSE. Alicia was 16 when she married Corrine's grandfather (96).
20. TRUE (96).
21. TRUE (133).

3. Bonus Questions
1. Two double beds, a highboy, a dresser, two overstuffed chairs, a dressing table and chair, and a mahogany table with four chairs (52).
2. She was nine (71).
3. He was 11 (71).
4. Six boxes (102).
5. He saw a tiger, an elephant, a grizzly bear, a brown-and-black bear, an antelope, and a mountain lion (214).
6. "[E]arth represents reality, and reality represents frustrations,

chance illnesses, death, murder, and all kinds of other tragedies." (According to Chris, that is.) (314).

7. (315).

8. "We lived in the attic/ Christopher, Cory, Carrie, and me,/Now there are only three" (402).

9. A photograph of her husband, Christopher, their marriage license, her wedding band (from her marriage to Christopher), and her engagement ring (also from her marriage to Christopher) (382).

10. A lizard-skinned wallet, a leather notepad and datebook, a wristwatch, his wedding band, two stuffed animals intended for the twins, and his clothes (19–20).

4. Who Said It?

1 D (53).
2 A (159).
3 E (300).
4 B (46).
5 C (175).

Chapter 2.   PETALS ON THE WIND

1. Multiple Choice

1. B. November, 1960 (4).
2. C. Henny was Paul's housekeeper–cook (11).
3. A. Cathy's middle name was Leigh (13).
4. B. 3 years, 4 months, 16 days (18).
5. D. Henny called Cathy "Fairy-Child" (26).
6. A. Paul's first wife's name was Julia (32).
7. B. Paul's son's name was Scotty. He was three when he died (32).
8. A. Twenty girls and three boys also auditioned for Marisha (56).
9. C. A gynecologist named Dr. Jarvis, a friend of Paul's, did the procedure (60).
10. A. Cathy was exactly 24 years and seven months younger than Paul (69).
11. C. Paul lived on Bellefair Drive (81).
12. B. "Hicktown" (83).
13. D. Julian hurt his back when he was young by trying to lift an engine (85).
14. D. Paul took the children to The Plantation House restaurant for Cathy's 16th birthday (103).
15. A. "Let me always succeed at what I set out to do" (105).
16. C. "Carrie had a strong dislike for the color yellow" (113).

17. C. Chris attended Duke University (136).
18. B. Cathy graduated from high school in January of 1963 (158).
19. A. Yolanda smoked grass (200).
20. D. Henny called Carrie "Tinkerbelle" (237).
21. C. Julian was buried next to his father, Georges (276).
22. D. Cathy gave up performing in 1972 at the age of 27 (308).
23. Chris was born in November 1942 (313).
24. B. Carrie was buried in August of 1972 in the Sheffield family plot (333).
25. C. Cathy used the expression "golly-lolly!" when she was a little girl (402).

2. True or False
1. FALSE. He played "Oh Susannah" (4).
2. FALSE. He had a wife and five kids (8).
3. FALSE. He hated working Sundays (8).
4. TRUE (11).
5. TRUE (15).
6. FALSE. Paul had *four* acres of garden and *two* gardeners (19).
7. TRUE (29).
8. FALSE. He originally told her that he had been a widower 13 years (30).
9. FALSE. Paul adopted Cathy, Chris, and Carrie at a hearing that Corrine did not attend (40).
10. FALSE. Cathy taught *herself* to go on *pointe* (48).
11. FALSE. Cathy first laid eyes on Julian in a performance of *The Nutcracker* (48).
12. TRUE (61).
13. FALSE. It was 10 miles outside the city (61).
14. TRUE (64).
15. TRUE (64).
16. FALSE. Paul smoked a pipe (68).
17. FALSE. Paul liked to drink "strong red wine" before he went to bed (71).
18. TRUE (78).
19. FALSE. Cathy's first ever date was with Julian Marquet (82).
20. FALSE. Cathy told Paul she hated her mother for "*ten million* reasons" (93).
21. TRUE (94).
22. FALSE. He took to drinking (95).
23. FALSE. It was three layers tall (105).
24. TRUE (106).
25. TRUE (107).
26. FALSE. Sissy Towers had brick-red hair and emerald eyes (113).
27. TRUE (113).
28. TRUE (113).
29. FALSE. The Rosencoff Ballet Company was planning to alternate performances of *The*

Nutcracker and
Cinderella (155).
30. FALSE. Cathy's
    nickname for Julian was
    "Jule" (210).
31. TRUE (239).
32. TRUE (311).
33. TRUE (313).
34. TRUE (322).
35. TRUE (327).
36. FALSE. Carrie
    committed suicide by
    arsenic poisoning (328).
37. TRUE (332).
38. TRUE (396).

3. Bonus Questions
1. Cathy and Bart's
   ancestors were both part
   of Virginia's Roanoke
   Island "Lost Colony"
   that vanished without a
   trace in 1591.
   Englishman John White
   returned to the island
   after an absence and
   found that the entire
   colony had vanished and
   that the only vestige of
   their existence was the
   word "Croatan" carved
   on a tree (137).
2. Jory had Chris's
   patience, Cory's quiet
   sweetness, and
   occasionally his father
   and mother's brashness
   (291).
3. He had six other
   attorneys besides Bart—
   Bart's only task was to
   make out Malcolm's
   wills (377).

4. Who Said It?
1 D (20).
2 A (48).
3 E (274).
4 C (75).
5 B (329).

Chapter 3. IF THERE BE THORNS

1. Multiple Choice
1. C. They visited Corrine
   in South Carolina once a
   year (5).
2. B. When the story
   begins, Cathy is 37, Jory
   is 14, and Bart is 9 (8–9).
3. D. Carrie and Cory
   were both born on
   May 5, 1962. The year
   was arrived at from
   Carrie's age (eight in
   1960) at the beginning
of Book 2 (16).
4. A. When the story
   begins, Bart is nine (16).
5. C. Jory's girlfriend was
   Melodie Richarme (22).
6. B. The Sheffields had a
   dog named Clover (28).
7. B. The door knocker on
   Corrine's house was a
   lion's head (41).
8. B. Janus. His full name
   was Jory Janus Marquet
   Sheffield (41).

9. A. Bart always wanted a pony that he would name Apple (48).

10. C. Malcolm Winslow's journal was red-leather-bound and began with the sentence: "I am beginning this journal with the most bitter day of my life: the day my beloved mother ran away and left me for another man" (51).

11. C. Simon Daughtry was the attorney who handled Cathy's adoption of Cindy (55).

12. D. In the fancy parlor with the concert grand piano, there was a long marble fireplace (64).

13. B. When Cathy first brought Cindy home, she was two years, two months, and five days old (65).

14. A. The parakeet's name was Buttercup (100).

15. C. Bart was born in July (115).

16. D. Marta often gossiped with Emma (138).

17. A. Bart claimed he had a fortune worth twenty billion, ten million, fifty-five thousand and six hundred dollars and forty-two cents. ($20,010,055,600.42). But he said he couldn't remember how much he had in stocks and bonds (158).

18. C. Bart's first psychiatrist was Dr. Mary Oberman (172).

19. C. Bart kept Malcolm's journal under his pillow (174).

20. C. Chris gave Cathy the figurine that Bart broke (180).

21. A. Cindy's favorite sandbox toys were a red pail and a red and yellow shovel (191).

22. D. Cathy, who was not supposed to dance anymore because of her trick knee, decided to play the mechanical doll, sitting in a chair, in the ballet, *Coppelia* (186), but she also ended up dancing the role of Swanhilda (195).

23. C. Bart read a passage in Malcolm's journal in which Malcolm talked about a girl he went to school with named Violet Blue. Malcolm shaved off all his hair the day she smiled at him, and the next day he cut off all of *her* hair (193).

24. B. Bart's second psychiatrist was Dr. Hermes (201).

25. A. Apple was killed by being starved and then stabbed with a pitchfork, apparently by John Amos (215).

26. B. John Amos assigned Bart to read 10 pages of Malcolm's journal every day (246).

27. A. Bart's favorite lollipops were cherry-flavored (252).
28. B. Cathy was born in April (268).
29. C. Chris was born in November (268).
30. A. Cathy's journal was blue leather (282).
31. B. Bart hid in a dumbwaiter (303).
32. C. Corrine's first words to Cathy in *If There Be Thorns* are, "Don't go in there!" (305).
33. D. They gave Bart a Shetland pony and a St. Bernard puppy (367).

2. True or False

1. TRUE (7).
2. FALSE. She had *two* twin beds put in the attic (9).
3. TRUE (12).
4. FALSE. Jory moved into junior year of high school with honors. Bart barely made it into fifth grade (25).
5. FALSE. She was two (26).
6. TRUE (32).
7. FALSE. He pretended he was *General* Winslow (41).
8. TRUE (43).
9. TRUE (47).
10. FALSE. She kept the name, the Marie DuBois School of Ballet (53).
11. FALSE. Chris talked Cathy into *being sterilized* after the birth of Bart (55).
12. FALSE. She had blue eyes (65).
13. TRUE (65).
14. TRUE (77).
15. FALSE. Bart had a fish tank in his room in which nothing would live. All he had in it was water and a toy pirate ship (83).
16. TRUE (92).
17. TRUE (97).
18. TRUE (102).
19. TRUE (102).
20. FALSE. John Amos lived in a room over the garage on Corrine's estate (115).
21. FALSE. He spent his tenth birthday on a hospital bed (134).
22. TRUE (136).
23. TRUE (137).
24. TRUE (142).
25. TRUE (150).
26. FALSE. He willed it to John Amos (152).
27. FALSE. He felt that way about John Amos (172).
28. FALSE. He forgot his *wallet* every day (187).
29. TRUE (230).
30. FALSE. Spaghetti was one of Jory's favorite dishes (262).
31. TRUE (262).
32. TRUE (331).
33. TRUE (345).
34. TRUE (371).

3. Bonus Questions

1. Bart once asked Corrine for cowboy boots, a cowboy saddle made of real leather, a hat,

buckskins, chaps, spurs, and beans to cook over a campfire (93).

2. Apple (his "puppy-pony"), his grandmother, Corrine, and John Amos (149).

3. Cathy indicated that she had come to the end of her book by putting her initials and address near the bottom of the page (284).

4. Corrine left the entire Foxworth estate to Jory

Janus Marquet, Bartholomew Scott Winslow Sheffield, and Cynthia Jane Nickols (Cindy). It was to be held in a trust for them until they were 25 (368).

4. Who Said It?
1 D (161).
2 A (21).
3 E (171).
4 B (115).
5 C (18).

Chapter 4. MY SWEET AUDRINA

1. Multiple Choice

1. A. Wars (3).
2. C. The River Lyle (5).
3. B. He had three framed pictures of Audrina on his desk (5).
4. A. None. He didn't have one picture of the Second Audrina on his desk (6).
5. Aunt Mercy Marie's "Teatime" was every Tuesday at four (6).
6. D. Aunt Mercy Marie had pale blue eyes (6).
7. C. The bed was 500 years old (11).
8. C. Everyone most favored The Roman Revival Salon (11).
9. B. She hid them in her bedroom closets (12).
10. D. He had dark black hair (13).
11. A. It was an octagon room (20).

12. C. He called her "Lucky" (25).
13. B. He called it a horned moon (30).
14. C. Because she never gave him a straight answer (34).
15. C. William Shakespeare (41).
16. B. It was bound in black leather (43).
17. B. Lana (50).
18. A. She loved cucumber and lettuce on thin slices of cheese bread (56).
19. B. Bourbon (59).
20. D. Horace (60).
21. A. Nelson (82).
22. A. She charged $50 per reading (88).
23. C. Her birthday was September 9, the date the "first" Audrina had "died" nine years previous (91).

24. D. D. J. Adare and Company (109).
25. A. She was 16 (112).
26. D. Audrina dropped it (128).
27. B. She had a bad heart (139).
28. A. It rained (140).
29. B. Elizabeth Taylor (152).
30. A. She was born on November 12th (161).
31. A. She had diabetes, which led to the amputation of both her legs (170).
32. C. She said it looked "gross" (173).
33. B. It was a wool periwinkle blue skirt that had to be dry-cleaned (179).
34. B. May (194).
35. B. She was eleven years and eight months old, as confirmed by Aunt Ellsbeth (195).
36. D. She experienced the "greatest passion of her life" when making love with Arden in a storm on the grave of the First Audrina in a "gotta-be-filmed-someday" scene (377).
37. B. She received electric shock treatments (382).
38. C. Vera (388).

2. True or False
1. FALSE. She was fat (6).
2. TRUE (11).
3. FALSE. It was royal purple (11).
4. TRUE (12).
5. FALSE. They visited her grave every Sunday after church (16).
6. TRUE (17).
7. FALSE. It was round (32).
8. TRUE (32).
9. TRUE (35).
10. TRUE (37).
11. FALSE (42).
12. TRUE (45).
13. TRUE (54).
14. FALSE. It held a ruby (54).
15. FALSE. She liked chicken liver pâté very much (57).
16. TRUE (59).
17. TRUE (63).
18. FALSE. According to Ellsbeth, Damian was a "Victorian at heart" (63).
19. TRUE (74).
20. TRUE (101).
21. TRUE (119).
22. FALSE. Aunt Ellsbeth didn't like any music that wasn't by Grieg (121).
23. TRUE (127).
24. TRUE (127).
25. FALSE. "Poor Aunt Ellsbeth couldn't cook worth a darn" (128).
26. TRUE (131).
27. TRUE (136).
28. TRUE (156).
29. FALSE. Her *left* leg was one inch shorter than her *right* (162).
30. FALSE. She used to be an Olympic ice-skating champion (167).

31. TRUE (178).
32. TRUE (229).

3. Bonus Questions

1. According to Aunt Ellsbeth, it meant "out of sync with the rest of the world" (8).
2. A one-pound box. He bought Vera a two-pound box (29).
3. Two (42).
4. The Bible told her (46).
5. "He liked it golden on the outside, tender on the inside" (105).
6. A cross of white roses with a violet ribbon. This arrangement was from Audrina (140).
7. "While the dew is still on the roses" (141).
8. A "better day tomorrow" (160).

4. Super Bonus Questions

1. The bodies were wishes that died; the bullets, words; the blood spilled, pride (3).
2. The completed rhyme goes as follows: "Step on black, live forever in a shack/Step on green, never be clean/Step on blue, work will never be through/Step on yellow, hear the world bellow/Step on red, soon be dead" (9).
3. The completed lines go as follows:. "Just a playroom, safe in my home,/Only a playroom, safe in my home" (45).

4. "[W]hen they are alone" (142).
5. Fate (172).
6. They were both into measuring penises. In *Flowers in the Attic*, Cathy once caught Chris measuring the length of his penis, and in *My Sweet Audrina,* Vera told Audrina that she measured Lamar Rensdale's erection and that it was "almost nine inches." She called Lamar's erection a "great gun cocked and aimed" (188).

5. Trick Questions

1. Twelve miles by car; five miles as the crow flies (7).
2. TRUE and FALSE. The answer is TRUE because that is the story that had been told for years and that had transmuted into a family myth for Audrina; and the answer is FALSE because we later learn that there was no First Audrina, that the "Second" Audrina was the *one and only* Audrina (31).
3. "Cook" (72).

6. Bonus Body Part Questions

1. She was born without hair, fingernails, and toenails (138).
2. Damian was livid that

Lucietta's nipples could be seen (123).

3. Eight inches (174).
4. They were "wine-colored and very large" (240).
5. She pinched her nipples (344).

7. Bonus Gross-Out Question

A "huge clot of blood" (224).

8. Who Said It?
1 E (63).
2 A (395).
3 D (82).
4 B (173).
5 C (173).

Chapter 5. SEEDS OF YESTERDAY

1. Multiple Choice
1. C 52. (3).
2. C 54. (3).
3. A. Green (3).
4. B. Seven years (6).
5. B. He gave them to the church to which he belonged (15).
6. A. He broke a leg (17).
7. B. Latin (17).
8. D. "What It's Like to Be a Monk in Today's Modern World" (18).
9. C. In a room on the second floor in the western wing (30).
10. C. Mainstream (31).
11. B. He was 26 (30).
12. A. One month (32).
13. C. Red (33).
14. D. The Source (41).
15. D. Respect (41).
16. C. "Turning on a light in a dark room" (44).
17. A. One year of bookings (52).
18. B. "Barbaric" (55).
19. D. Their muscles began to harden and become brittle as they approached 40 (56).
20. A. A straight scotch (60).
21. B. *Samson and Delilah* (74).
22. C. Marilyn Monroe (88).
23. C. Three times (95).
24. A. "Seasonless sawdust or shoe leather" (113).
25. B. Bary Boswell (140).
26. A. He was a "racehorse." This meant he was competitive and had to win to be happy (164).
27. B. An electric treadmill (180).
28. A. It was 12 feet long (180).
29. C. Jory's wife, Melodie (185).
30. C. He was able to sleep when she couldn't (195).
31. A. Yellow (203).
32. B. Sugar stiffening (213).

33. D. $10,000 or less (214).
34. B. South Carolina (218).
35. B. It took five people hours to decorate the tree (259).
36. A. On a tour around the world (407).

2. True or False
1. TRUE (4).
2. FALSE. It had stood empty for fifteen years (4).
3. FALSE. He *was* valedictorian of his class, but he graduated from Harvard Law School, not Yale (7).
4. TRUE (13).
5. TRUE. When it was necessary to address him, they called him "father" (14).
6. TRUE (17).
7. FALSE. He worked as a nightclub musician (17).
8. FALSE. He didn't speak a word of Italian (17).
9. TRUE (22).
10. FALSE. They descended the right staircase (29).
11. TRUE (29).
12. TRUE (31).
13. TRUE (31).
14. FALSE. He was *six* feet, three inches tall (34).
15. TRUE (38).
16. TRUE (38).
17. FALSE. He "didn't see anything wonderful about the 'Mona Lisa'" (41).
18. TRUE (42).

19. TRUE (50).
20. FALSE. There was an old-fashioned walnut tub in the bathroom (53).
21. TRUE (55).
22. FALSE. He cleared the floor by ten feet (55).
23. FALSE. She did not like the music room (60).
24. TRUE (68).
25. FALSE. Ice is best (72).
26. TRUE. She originally wore a red dress that Cathy felt belonged on a hooker (87).
27. FALSE. There was a huge ice sculpture of Foxworth Hall on the table (92).
28. FALSE. He broke his spine (110).
29. TRUE (148).
30. FALSE. She brought him roses (149).
31. TRUE (164).
32. FALSE. Cathy gave him the kit (166).
33. TRUE (180).
34. TRUE (180).
35. TRUE (189).
36. TRUE (192).
37. FALSE. He was a baritone (366).
38. FALSE. It was a black book (372).
39. FALSE. She was born in April (385).
40. FALSE. He was buried in the cemetery where Paul Sheffield, Corrine, Bart Winslow's father, and Julian were buried (402).
41. TRUE (405).
42. TRUE (406).

3. Bonus Questions
1. Five (31).
2. She wore blue panties and we were able to see them when Jory picked her up and spun her around and her blue skirt flew up (68).
3. The will stated that he would receive $500,000 a year until he was 35, at which time he would then receive the entire estate (168).

4. Mount Desert Isle (330).

4. Super Bonus Question
Because he knew she'd "say it was too soft and therefore useless functionally" (381).

5. Who Said It?
1 A (54).
2 E (55).
3 D (87).
4 B (225).
5 C (278).

Chapter 6.   HEAVEN

1. Multiple Choice
1. C. The Willies (2).
2. A. Shirley's Place (3).
3. D. He married Sarah two months after Angel died in childbirth (11).
4. C. They collected it in drainpipes and rain barrels (16).
5. A. They had one rooster (22).
6. A. They had thirty hens (22).
7. C. She was from Baltimore (27).
8. A. Miss Deale's hair was like Our Jane's: pale reddish blonde (27).
9. B. Atlanta (39).
10. D. Dark blue (44).
11. C. She believed in astrology (48).
12. A. He threatened them with 15 hours of detention if they spoke (53).

13. D. He gave her a gold bracelet set with a small sapphire (63).
14. A. She gave him a red cap she had knitted (63).
15. C. He gave her a "lovely" white sweater set (64).
16. B. The hound's name was Snapper (65).
17. A. His full name was Logan Grant Stonewall (76).
18. B. "In the hills, a girl who reached sixteen without being engaged was almost beyond hope, bound to be an old maid" (78).
19. C. He wanted to become a scientist, "a brilliant one, of course" (82).
20. C. There were three long rifles hung on the walls (86).

21. B. He contracted syphilis (92).
22. B. He couldn't see much past six feet away (118).
23. D. They used candles (123).
24. A. Granny taught them (124).
25. A. They used a wooden box on their porch (138).
26. C. She liked it medium rare (153).
27. B. Mushrooms (165).
28. A. They sold for $1,000; Luke got $500 each for them (173).
29. C. Mark (172).
30. B. Ellen (172).
31. A. He ran his own TV repair and sale shop (216).
32. B. McDonald's. Wendy and Cal Dennison took her there (222).
33. A. She owned and operated her own beauty salon and ceramics class (231).
34. B. She was born on February 22 (239).
35. A. She was "almost thirteen" (239).
36. C. She slept in between Cal and Kitty (250).
37. B. He said, "Jesus Christ" when he realized that Kitty was serious about having Heaven sleep in the same bed with him and his wife (252).
38. C. She had eight girls working for her (231).

39. A. She was a Baptist but she pretended to be of other religious denominations to try to find God (264).
40. A. He had six employees (274).

2. True or False

1. TRUE (3).
2. FALSE. Sarah was six feet tall without shoes (12).
3. FALSE. It was nicknamed Ole Smokey (16).
4. TRUE (18).
5. TRUE (23).
6. FALSE. She had nightmares every *Sunday* night (31).
7. FALSE. She was only 13 (45).
8. FALSE. He was only 15 (45).
9. TRUE (52).
10. FALSE. She pledged that she would not allow herself to fall in love until she was *30* years old (58).
11. TRUE (68).
12. TRUE (76).
13. FALSE. Heaven never daydreamed in school; only at home (81).
14. FALSE. The issue number was 1 (96).
15. TRUE (104).
16. TRUE (120).
17. TRUE (120).
18. FALSE. He felt that way about her blueberry pies (126).
19. TRUE (143).

20. FALSE. She reread *Jane Eyre* (181).
21. FALSE. He was a lawyer (172).
22. TRUE (186).
23. FALSE. She thanked him "*two* million times" (187).
24. FALSE. He was sold for $500, as were the other Casteel children (191).
25. FALSE. They were married five years when they bought Heaven from her father (220).
26. FALSE. She always wished she had been named Linda (223).
27. TRUE (229).
28. TRUE (235).
29. TRUE (237).
30. FALSE. Cal used black velvet towels and Kitty used pink towels (240).
31. TRUE (247).
32. TRUE (266).
33. TRUE (328).
34. TRUE (347).

3. Bonus Questions

1. A pot or other vessel used as an indoor portable toilet by mountain people who didn't have indoor plumbing. In the Casteel cabin, only Granny was allowed to use the indoor hockeypot. All others had to trek to the outhouse (3).
2. Her dead mother's special bride doll (10).
3. A nanny goat (23).

4. Tom and Heaven Casteel (36).
5. "Rock of Ages, cleft for me,/Let me hide myself in thee ..." (98).
6. "Satan's arms" (146).
7. Reverend Wayland Wise (186).
8. The Midnight Sun (286).
9. Sausage, fried eggs, and grits (346).

4. Super Bonus Questions

1. "Logan and Tom had the same kind of natural grace and ease with themselves that came from knowing who and what they were" (42).
2. A "board that dropped down and secured the door as a latch" (117).
3. "Devilishly" (66).
4. Guitars, banjos, and fiddles (91).
5. Maroon (189).
6. "And we walk with him" (201).
7. They were all blondes (260).
8. 210 Eastwood Street (270).

5. Grammatical Bonus Question

"Your" was pronounced as "yer," and "you" was pronounced as "ya" (116).

6. Epistolary Bonus Questions

1. It was written by Sarah

to Luke before she up and left (135).

2. Logan Stonewall (289).
3. The letter, which we find out much later was written by Rita Rawlings, was signed simply, "R" (297).
4. Tom Casteel (308).
5. Luke Casteel (428).

7. Disgusting Bonus Question

Our Jane once threw up on Miss Deale's wine-colored wool skirt (156).

8. The Abortion Question

Castor oil (162).

9. "Easy As It Seems?" Bonus Question

"Hell" (192).

10. Trick Question

We don't know, although the first movie she ever saw in *a movie theater* was *The Sound of Music* with Cal Dennison. Days earlier, on the way home to Candlewick after Heaven was bought by Kitty and Cal, Heaven told Kitty that she had seen a moving-picture only once, but didn't mention what movie. Later we're told that Heaven had "never been inside a movie theater before," with no explanation of the ambiguity/contradiction (285).

11. Who Said It?

1 B (60).
2 E (307).
3 A (81).
4 D (92).
5 C (436).

Chapter 7. DARK ANGEL

1. Multiple Choice

1. B. She had two blue suitcases when she landed (4).
2. C. "Townie" (6).
3. C. Jillian would not allow Heaven to address her as "Grandmother" (10).
4. A. Luke told Tony and Jill Tatterton that Leigh had died of cancer when the truth was that she died giving birth to Heaven (13).
5. B. Scuttles (17).
6. D. It was built by Tony's great-great-great-grandfather and improved upon by every first son who took it over (20).
7. A. He was only 18. (Smart boy, now, t'warn't he?) (24).
8. B. He was 17 (65).

9. A. Bridge (72).

10. D. It cost $1,000 (88).

11. B. He gave her $200, which was immediately confiscated by headmistress Helen Mallory (91).

12. D. The Red Feather (104).

13. B. Ten people attended (106).

14. C. He drove a Porsche (114).

15. B. A biochemist (115).

16. A. She wanted one of the club members to get a date with Troy Tatterton (127).

17. C. They ruined five sweaters, in addition to a wool skirt and a jacket (129).

18. Saturday (155).

19. C. It was in Chicago (157).

20. A. Chopin (211).

21. C. Bertie (242).

2. True or False

1. FALSE. She was wearing a *gray* fur coat (5).

2. FALSE. Jillian's first husband was Cleave VanVoreen (7).

3. FALSE. She pretended that Heaven was her niece (11).

4. TRUE (19).

5. FALSE. Farthinggale Manor's nickname was "Farthy" (21).

6. TRUE (25).

7. TRUE (63).

8. FALSE. Rye Whiskey was "stout" (74).

9. TRUE (76).

10. FALSE. Winterhaven was a church before it became a school (87).

11. FALSE. She hated it (104).

12. FALSE. They were seven years apart (128).

13. TRUE (135).

14. FALSE. They each wore what they wanted and Heaven thought that what most of them wore looked like it came "straight from Frederick's of Hollywood" (140).

15. FALSE. It was one of the haunts of the Boston University boys (159).

16. TRUE (172).

17. FALSE. The color scheme was red, *black*, and white, with *gold* embellishments (188).

18. FALSE. Troy Tatterton taught her (215).

19. TRUE (228).

20. FALSE. He hated it. It made him even *more* depressed (if you can believe it) than usual (229).

21. TRUE (231).

22. TRUE (244).

23. FALSE. His birthday was September ninth (247).

24. FALSE. They were Episcopalian (260).

25. FALSE. He was mauled to death by a circus lion (440).

3. Bonus Questions
1. The VanVoreen Steamship Line (8).
2. Eton (21).
3. Five years (26).
4. Two (29).
5. 7:30 A.M. (92).
6. 6:00 P.M. (93).
7. Mauve (125).
8. So that the building looked symmetrical from the outside (140).
9. The cottage was six times larger than the cabin (173).

4. Super Bonus Questions
1. Blue, red, and yellow (177).
2. She was eighth from the front girl (205).
3. He was 75 (224).
4. She got an A-minus (98).
5. Poverty in America (98).
6. Japanese pine trees (22).

5. Superstition Bonus Question
It prevented devils from following you inside (63).

6. Trick Questions
1. On page 87 of *Heaven,* we're told that Heaven would study English and literature in Beecham Hall, and then, on page 94, we're told that Heaven's English class was scheduled for eight o'clock in Elmhurst Hall.
2. Lunch was served at 12 noon for those in the lower two grades and 12:30 P.M. for the remaining students (92).
3. The fare was actually $12.50, but Heaven was so distraught (about seeing Logan with another girl) that she gave the guy $20 and didn't wait for change (169).

7. Prurient Interest Bonus Questions
1. Troy Tatterton. She was 18 years old (227).
2. Her legs (26).
3. Five boxes (busy girl, eh?) (309).
4. She was 14 (309).
5. She was 13 (378).

8. Epistolary Bonus Questions
1. Logan Stonewall (75).
2. Tom Casteel (156).
3. Troy Tatterton (392).
4. Her sister Fanny (399).

9. Gluttony/Conspicuous Consumption Bonus Questions
1. Ten pounds (318).
2. Nine carats (324).
3. A. He gave her a Rolls-Royce (203).
4. A custom-designed white Jaguar (324).

10. Who Said It?
1 D (44).
2 A (269).
3 E (71).
4 C (133).
5 B (413).

Chapter 8.   GARDEN OF SHADOWS

1. Multiple Choice
1. B. It was to be opened 20 years after her death (1).
2. A. Winfield (1).
3. D. It was made of oak (5).
4. B. Cigar smoke and whiskey (7).
5. A. She was six feet tall (8).
6. C. April (9).
7. C. She always brushed her hair 100 times after shampooing (9).
8. A. Her mother's blue sapphire pendant (10).
9. B. He was 55 (11).
10. C. Beef Wellington (11).
11. A. A Congregational church (31).
12. C. Over 150 years (36).
13. B. Benjamin Franklin (44).
14. C. Lamb (55).
15. B. Joseph (89).
16. A. April 7 (91).
17. B. Blue (105).
18. C. New London, Connecticut (107).
19. A. Richmond, Virginia (108).
20. B. She was 14 (Malcolm had been 53) (119).
21. C. Alicia's share of Garland's estate was $3 million in stocks (136).
22. C. Christopher's share of Garland's estate was $2 million in stocks (136).
23. B. Simon Chillingworth (142).
24. A. Malcolm and the maid who cleaned it once a week were the only people allowed in the study (192).
25. B. She insisted that he pay them each two year's salary as severance pay. She had originally asked for one year's salary for the departing servants, but when Malcolm whined and griped about the amount, she spitefully raised it to two years, knowing he had no choice but to obey her (197).
26. C. Olsen (197).
27. B. $1 million each (200).
28. A. Jazz (216).
29. A. Charleston (235).
30. B. Steak, ice cream, and cookies (239).
31. A. Twelve hours (242).
32. C. He invited close to 500 people to the party (245).
33. B. He had four fountains flowing (246).
34. A. He hired a ten-piece orchestra (246).
35. B. Corrine was 14 when she told Olivia, "Mama, I've become a woman!"; Olivia was sixteen (277).

36. C. Joel (289).
37. B. There were five others with him (302).
38. B. His name was Cruthers (359).

2. True or False

1. FALSE. She had a large bosom (8).
2. TRUE (9).
3. FALSE. He was a graduate of Yale (11).
4. FALSE. He was five (16).
5. FALSE. Her first time out riding alone with a man was with Malcolm (2).
6. TRUE (31).
7. TRUE (56).
8. FALSE. It was covered in rose-colored velvet (59).
9. TRUE (87).
10. TRUE (102).
11. FALSE. He died a month before the proposal (120).
12. TRUE (135).
13. FALSE. Once, when Alicia was swimming alone at the lake, Malcolm completely undressed and approached Alicia (who was also naked) in the water. She quickly delaked and fled (146).
14. TRUE (196).
15. TRUE (204).
16. FALSE. Olivia did the bob job (218).
17. FALSE. She found it in the parlor (235).
18. FALSE. John Amos believed that Malcolm had become Job (308).
19. TRUE (312).
20. TRUE (313).
21. FALSE. He believed that aviation was the transportation of the future (323).
22. TRUE (338).
23. TRUE (340).
24. FALSE. They took the name because Dollanganger was the real name of a Foxworth ancestor (366).

3. Bonus Questions

1. A blouse with a V-necked front. They were denounced as indecent when they first came out. They were thought to reveal too much bosom, but women continued to wear them (48).
2. Tamara Livingston's husband (80).
3. It means to dine out-of-doors (113).
4. Black, dark gray, or dark blue (164).
5. A red Oriental rug with gold fringe (214).
6. Mrs. Tethering. We don't know whether it was a sanitary napkin or a tampon (280).

4. Super Bonus Questions

1. When Olivia first met Malcolm Foxworth, she was planning to read "that new novel that was attracting attention,

Edith Wharton's *Age of Innocence*." In 1993, a film adaptation of Wharton's *The Age of Innocence*, directed by Martin Scorsese and starring Michelle Pfeiffer, was released in the United States (13).

2. She first met Malcolm in 1920, the year Edith Wharton's novel, *The Age of Innocence*, was first published (13).

5. Trick Question
1. No one. The book did not exist. After an evening during which Alicia Foxworth regaled Olivia and Malcolm with tales of her and Garland's escapades in Europe, Olivia sardonically thought to herself that she could easily describe the evening's complete narrative as *Tales of Garland Foxworth* by Alicia Foxworth (114).

6. Who Said It?
1 D (15).
2 A (177).
3 E (199).
4 C (117).
5 B (367).

Chapter 9. FALLEN HEARTS

1. Multiple Choice
1. B. She said she'd gain 300 pounds in an hour if she ate it (7).
2. C. *The Winnerrow Reporter* (9).
3. B. They were wed in June (11).
4. D. They gave her a needlepoint of Heaven's Willies cabin with "Home Sweet Home, from your class" stitched on it (13).
5. B. *The Wall Street Journal* (25).
6. A. He requested a highball, much to Heaven's surprise (28).
7. A. Tony offered Logan a vice-presidency in charge of marketing (52).
8. C. French Provincial (58).
9. A. Red and white (66).
10. B. At least 400 people attended (67).
11. D. "You Are the Sunshine of My Life" (67).
12. A. Tony Tatterton and Logan decided that Heaven should pick the spot (77).
13. B. He added $5,000 (88).
14. B. Wood (111).
15. D. Loneliness (118).
16. B. Logan (197).

17. B. Heaven (197).
18. A. She owned two Great Danes (213).
19. C. She agreed to pay Fanny $2,500 a month, but Fanny couldn't contact Logan in any way (217).
20. B. "Sonny" (223).
21. A. They were killed in a head-on auto accident (231).
22. D. He paid Tatterton one dollar—on the condition that Luke never contact Heaven again (246).
23. A. Maisie Setterton (307).
24. D. She paid Fanny $1,000,000 (394).

2. True or False

1. TRUE (8).
2. FALSE. She invited all the children in her class to the wedding (10).
3. FALSE. Her invitation to Pa Casteel was the last one she mailed (12).
4. FALSE. He had "sweet-potato red" hair (17).
5. TRUE (17).
6. TRUE (18).
7. FALSE. She had a diamond wedding band (22).
8. TRUE (40).
9. TRUE (47).
10. TRUE (64).
11. TRUE (64).
12. FALSE. Tony hated rock and roll and allowed only classics and easy listening music at Heaven and Logan's wedding reception at Farthinggale Manor (66).
13. FALSE. It was five tiers high (74).
14. TRUE (89).
15. FALSE. She committed suicide by swallowing an overdose of tranquilizers (171).
16. TRUE (173).
17. TRUE (180).
18. FALSE. She was not married (181).
19. FALSE. She had *gained* a tremendous amount of weight (190).
20. TRUE (222).
21. TRUE (229).
22. FALSE. "She was a tall, stout woman" (237).
23. TRUE (244).
24. FALSE. It was in the *Boston Globe* (253).
25. TRUE (270).
26. TRUE (363).
27. FALSE. It played a Chopin prelude (404).

3. Bonus Questions

1. Oil (59).
2. His children. Fanny didn't get a dime (214).
3. A black velvet smoking jacket, black slacks, and velvet slippers (223).
4. The 12th (244).
5. Ishtar (273).

4. Super Bonus Questions

1. Wilfred (230).
2. Horace (230).
3. The Eddington Funeral Home (247).

4. The Kingsington Cathedral in Atlanta (255).
5. It was a half moon (321).
6. A white carnation (65).

5. Epistolary Bonus Questions
1. Pa Casteel (16).
2. Troy Tatterton (175).

6. Conspicuous Consumption Bonus Question
A new silver Rolls-Royce (71).

7. The "Can It Be What I Think?" Bonus Question
Shaving (44).

8. The "You Can't Get There from Here" Ultimate Bonus Question
"And we are here as on a darkling plain ..." (The reason the question is called the "You Can't Get There from Here" question is because the answer to this question *cannot* be found in *Fallen Hearts*. Six lines of Arnold's poem are given in the novel, but the excerpt stops at the "Nor certitude ..." line. You would have to, first, track down the title of the poem, and then go find it and look up the next line in order to be able to answer this "ultimate" question. But that's exactly what you did, right?) (140).

9. Who Said It?
1 C (47).
2 E (136).
3 A (38).
4 D (53).
5 B (61).

Chapter 10. GATES OF PARADISE

1. Multiple Choice
1. B. Luke Casteel, Jr. (1).
2. A. He was studying for his M.B.A. (2).
3. C. Miss Marbleton (7).
4. A. It played "Memories" from *Cats* when it was opened (26).
5. C. She gave him his own color TV (26).
6. B. She gave him a solid gold, black onyx pinky ring (32).
7. B. Toby (44).
8. D. Jefferson Davis (68).
9. A. She was comatose for two days (69).
10. A. Her doctors believed it was caused by inflammation caused by

the trauma around her spine (92).

11. B. *People* magazine (103).
12. B. A pearl ring (115).
13. D. Dr. Malisoff (127).
14. A. It was built in 1850 by Tony Tatterton's great-great-great-grandfather (138).
15. B. He was sent to Eton because his father thought the English knew more about discipline than the American schools did (138).
16. B. Questions (158).
17. C. Boston (176).
18. D. The big toe on her right foot. It happened in the tub during hydrotherapy (235).
19. A. "Florence Farthinggale" (242).
20. C. She had nightmares (292).
21. D. Timothy Brothers (313).
22. B. It played a Chopin nocturne (320).
23. C. He had a stroke. Troy was with him at the end (424).
24. B. Drake Casteel (435).

2. True or False
1. FALSE. He had "dark sapphire" eyes (1).
2. FALSE. Annie's license plate said "ANNIE" (23).
3. TRUE (24).
4. FALSE. The room had blue satin drapes (27).
5. FALSE. He gave her a bronze picture of Farthinggale Manor (33).
6. TRUE (45).
7. TRUE. He was good at predicting the weather (55).
8. TRUE (71).
9. FALSE. She told him he looked like a banker (160).
10. TRUE (199).
11. FALSE. He bought her a black beret (278).
12. FALSE. Only her parents, her doctors, and the nurses had seen her naked (296).
13. FALSE. It only had two rooms (320).
14. TRUE (332).
15. FALSE. He was short and stocky (379).
16. FALSE. She loved roasted Cornish hen, but she liked it with cherry sauce, not mint jelly (406).
17. FALSE. Before he died, Tony gave Drake a large percentage of the stock in his corporation (428).

3. Bonus Questions
1. Drake was six feet two (8).
2. He gave her two weeks pay (194).
3. Three (24).
4. Dark green (25).
5. When Luke received notification of his acceptance and full scholarship to Harvard,

Fanny got drunk and
tore up the letter (45).

6. "Not once." This was
the lewdly suggestive
question a 20-year-old
"guest" at Fanny's 40th
birthday party asked
Fanny. She replied,
"Not once" (63).

7. Logan and Heaven
Stonewall (117).

8. Filene's (176).

9. Parson (278).

10. "Welcome Home Annie,
God Bless" (370).

4. Super Bonus Questions

1. Hickory (27).

2. "*Annie* ... Annie ...
Annie ..." (67).

3. Twice a day: once in the
late morning and once
in the early evening
(100).

4. It was Millie Thomas
(147).

5. Eggshell white (333).

6. She got her hair dyed
back to black; she had
her hair set into French
braid; she got a
pedicure; she got a
manicure; and she got
filled in on all the local
gossip (393).

7. The Winnerrow
Community General
Hospital (137).

**5. Epistolary Bonus
Questions**

1. Luke Casteel, Jr. (33).

2. Drake Casteel (38).

3. Luke Casteel, Jr. (190).

4. Luke Casteel, Jr. (263).

**6. Conspicuous
Consumption Bonus
Question**

A light blue new
Mercedes convertible
(23).

7. Trick Question

This question has two
answers: Yes, and we
don't know. Tony
Tatterton told Annie that
Luke told him that he
did receive a standing
ovation, but, of course,
Tony was making it all
up. So while it is
possible (and likely) that
Luke did receive the
ovation (from what we
were told of the address,
it was moving and
heartfelt), we can't
confirm it based on
Tony's fabricated
account (127).

**8. Boo-Boo Bonus
Question**

First, 24 karat gold is
pure, raw gold with no
strengthening alloys,
and it is rarely used (it's
almost *never* used in the
United States) for
jewelry. Second, if it
was used (as it is
sometimes in European
and Middle Eastern
countries), it would
likely *never* be used to
make a neckchain
because pure 24 karat
would be much too soft
to hang anything on.

And third, gold content is indicated by the word *Karat*. Gem weight (as in the weight of diamonds and precious and semi-precious stones like emeralds and amethysts) is denoted by the word *Carat*. I used to be a jeweler, so I know of what I speak (19).

9. Who Said It?
1 D (349).
2 A (349).
3 C (25).
4 E (427).
5 B (14).

Chapter 11. WEB OF DREAMS

1. Multiple Choice

1. D. It was called *Leigh's Book* (3).
2. A. It was four feet tall (6).
3. C. Rose-colored leather (7).
4. A. He was a foreman at an oil field (10).
5. C. 100 (10).
6. B. "Greensleeves" (13).
7. A. A bra (15).
8. C. Airline stewardess (23).
9. C. Abraham Lincoln (28).
10. B. A burgundy velvet smoking jacket and dark slacks (30).
11. A. The dining room (32).
12. A. A gold and diamond ocean liner pendant (40).
13. C. A rare blood disease (46).
14. C. A heart attack (46).
15. D. She told him she was only 28 years old. (51).
16. C. Andre's Boutique (116).
17. B. Lobster bisque (125).
18. A. Pink (125).
19. D. The great entry hall (127).
20. B. Her back (147).
21. D. A solid gold tie clip with diamonds, engraved "Love, Jillian" on the back (180).
22. C. An erector set (180).
23. B. Leigh VanVoreen (244).
24. C. He was eleven (245).
25. A. French kissing (248).
26. D. Accountant (273).
27. B. Maine (276).
28. C. "For my sister, Leigh" (301).
29. A. A music box that played some of *The Nutcracker Suite* (313).
30. C. "Mesmerizing" (315).
31. D. She had "barely twenty dollars" (362).
32. A. She took "nearly

two hundred dollars" from a desk drawer in Tony Tatterton's office (362).

33. B. Fullerton, Texas (367).

34. A. He changed a one-dollar bill into a five-dollar bill, and let her keep the five (372).

35. C. Ma's Place (388).

2. True or False

1. FALSE. A few employees remained on the premises and the grounds to look after things (1).

2. FALSE. She was wearing a cashmere sweater in the dream (4).

3. TRUE (6).

4. FALSE. He was only four years old (31).

5. TRUE (41).

6. TRUE (46).

7. FALSE. The luxury liner only had three pools (65).

8. FALSE. The name of the restaurant was The Casablanca (81).

9. TRUE (85).

10. FALSE. Tony Tatterton saw her naked in a tub—even her father hadn't seen her naked since she was ten (148).

11. TRUE (181).

12. TRUE (185).

13. FALSE. He took her to Leone's (197).

14. FALSE. Jennifer was at least three inches shorter than Leigh (209).

15. FALSE. He drew her from the top down (249).

16. FALSE. She detested traveling (265).

17. TRUE (296).

18. TRUE (296).

19. FALSE. It was a five-piece band (306).

20. TRUE (311).

21. FALSE. *Tony* Tatterton deflowered her by raping her after her 13th birthday party (329).

22. FALSE. It had broken down in the Pacific (355).

23. TRUE (378).

3. Bonus Questions

1. The "book of memories" diary given to her by her father (6).

2. He was only a year and a half old (37).

3. "The Princess Leigh" (40).

4. Green (53).

5. Jillian called Cleave "you fool" in front of Leigh (69).

6. Dresses and gowns sold for $800 to $10,000 (116).

7. Mildred was wearing a dark blue cardigan suit (272).

8. The memento was a globe in a glass cube

and on the cube was inscribed, "Leigh, we think the world of her" (307).

9. Light blue slacks and a white and blue short-sleeved shirt (332).

10. Lulu Belle (378).

11. Kasey and Brutus (405).

4. Super Bonus Questions

1. She was seven (7).

2. The guests were Tony and Troy Tatterton and Jillian and Leigh VanVoreen. Tony sat at the head of the dining room table, Troy and Leigh sat on Tony's left, and Jillian sat on Tony's right (44).

3. *The Jillian* (54).

4. By repeatedly listening to "Teach Yourself a Language" records (77).

5. A diamond tiara (122).

6. *"Jeunes filles!"* and *"Comment allez-vous?"* (292).

7. Angel, Leigh VanVoreen's Tatterton Portrait Doll (316).

5. The Kinky Bonus Question
She said it tasted salty (7).

6. The Prurient Interest Bonus Questions

1. Tony Tatterton (41).

2. Her favorite was Vladimir Nabokov's *Lolita,* "the story of an older man's love affair with a twelve-year-old girl . . ." (182).

7. The Prurient Interest "Which Twin Has the Toni?" Bonus Question
She had one under her right breast (241).

8. The Epistolary Bonus Questions

1. Raymond Hunt (115).

2. Her father, Cleave (157).

3. Her mother, Jillian Tatterton (402).

4. Tony Tatterton (424).

9. The Unkind and Heartless Bonus Question
Nancy Kinney (170).

10. The Arcane Reference Bonus Question
Aphrodite (171).

11. The "Who Could Possibly Know This?!" Bonus Question
It stated that in the second paragraph on the first page of the agreement (173).

12. Who Said It?

1 D (211).
2 A (59).
3 E (222).
4 B (392).
5 C (425).

Chapter 12.   DAWN

1. Multiple Choice

1. A. She was 14 years old (4).
2. B. Dark brown (7).
3. C. Richmond (10).
4. A. Frankie's Bar and Grill (14).
5. D. A strand of cultured pearls (28).
6. C. A yardstick (42).
7. D. Phys ed (44).
8. C. Mrs. Turnkey (56).
9. B. Mr. Moore (62).
10. A. Guitar (62).
11. C. "[H]e would become as silent and as still as a statue" (72).
12. A. Stubbornness (72).
13. A. Chocolate sauce (91).
14. B. Gary (108).
15. B. Strip poker (117).
16. A. Consumption (Tuberculosis) (126).
17. D. They sprayed her with cans of stink-bomb spray (135).
18. A. Pizza (140).
19. C. A week off with pay (152).
20. D. She thought she had been born on July tenth (156).
21. C. The Seafood House (250).
22. D. "Over the Rainbow" (255).
23. A. Crescent Street (351).

2. True or False

1. FALSE. He was 16 (3).
2. FALSE. They both had black hair (7).
3. TRUE (7).
4. TRUE (18).
5. FALSE. They had no phones at all (24).
6. FALSE. She cleaned it every Friday (29).
7. TRUE (34).
8. TRUE (43).
9. FALSE. He was in the 11th grade (57).
10. FALSE. The spot overlooked the James River, which actually runs to the southeast of Richmond, Virginia (73).
11. FALSE. He took up the intramural basketball team (78).
12. FALSE. He did have a red car, but it was a birthday gift from his *grandmother* (79).
13. FALSE. Reuben was older than Ormand by a little more than a year (103).
14. TRUE (115).
15. FALSE. She didn't have time to wash it so she brushed it 100 times instead (129).
16. FALSE. Wrong book. Sally Jean was buried in a cemetery just outside of Richmond, Virginia (151).
17. TRUE (153).
18. TRUE (181).
19. TRUE (238).

20. TRUE (254).
21. FALSE. She flew to the Big Apple (407).

3. Bonus Questions

1. She was told that they named her Dawn because she was born at the break of day (1).
2. Seven pounds, fourteen ounces (26).
3. In the bottom of a dresser drawer (28).
4. A turquoise blue cotton dress with three-quarter sleeves (34).
5. Three days suspension and probation (101).
6. A white and black wool sweater and a black skirt (129).
7. Grace (165).
8. Four (181).
9. They referred to Laura Sue as "little Mrs. Cutler" (190).

4. Super Bonus Questions

1. "The child would be sneaky, cowardly" (8).
2. Dark blue (37).
3. Jimmy Longchamp. When Dawn Longchamp's snooty Emerson Peabody classmates heard that her name was Dawn, one of them asked her if her brother's name was "Afternoon" (47).
4. Rebecca Clare Longstreet and Stephanie Kay Sumpter (58).
5. He was killed in a car accident (18).
6. A tan sport jacket and tan slacks (185).
7. The Cutler's Cove Sanitation Company (387).

5. The "Not What It Sounds Like" Bonus Question

He agreed to teach her to play the piano if she would take up the flute for the Emerson Peabody school orchestra (77).

6. Epistolary Bonus Questions

1. Eugenia Grace Cutler (197).
2. Ormand Longchamp (236).
3. Ormand Longchamp (401).

7. A Boring and Disgusting Bonus Question

Her period (273).

8. Who Said It?

1 E (98).
2 A (285).
3 D (331).
4 B (185).
5 C (281).

Chapter 13. SECRETS OF THE MORNING

1. Multiple Choice

1. B. The Bernhardt School for Performing Arts (1). (It should be noted that in Book 14, *Twilight's Child*, the name of the school is given as The *Sarah* Bernhardt School *of* Performing Arts.)
2. C. An unnamed perfume by Elizabeth Arden (5).
3. A. Heartburn (9).
4. C. Always tip a New York cabbie (11).
5. C. The oboe (19).
6. A. Dark brown (24).
7. A. A pirouette (24).
8. C. Bones (24).
9. B. English and vocal music (26).
10. D. Upstate New York (28).
11. B. Acting (31).
12. A. Hyperbole (34).
13. C. *The Sea Gull* (35).
14. D. A double fudge chocolate sundae (53).
15. D. Their dour personalities (63).
16. B. He committed suicide (67).
17. A. He was a maintenance man in the laundry (68).
18. C. Antonio's (87).
19. C. She was restricted to the dorm for six months (96).
20. B. Checkers (99).
21. B. April (114).

2. True or False

1. FALSE. It was on the East Side (2).
2. TRUE (14).
3. TRUE (15).
4. TRUE and FALSE. She *did* play Ophelia, but she got rave reviews, not bad ones (15).
5. FALSE. He taught English (28).
6. FALSE. It only had two diamonds, one at twelve and one at six. (29).
7. TRUE (31).
8. FALSE. He had blonde hair (35).
9. FALSE. Arthur Garwood saw her naked as she stepped out of the shower not knowing Arthur had just walked into the bathroom (38).
10. FALSE. He enlisted in the army (44).
11. TRUE (48).
12. FALSE. The school had neither (51).
13. TRUE (51).
14. TRUE (62).
15. TRUE (62).
16. FALSE. He was only 15 (76).
17. FALSE. It was known as Performance Weekend (99).
18. TRUE (101).
19. FALSE. The class was

limited to six students (124).

20. FALSE. She sang (yet again) "Over the Rainbow" (127).
21. FALSE. His favorite city was London (131).
22. TRUE (225).
23. TRUE (274).
24. FALSE. The first person was Miss Emily; the *second* person was Luther (305).
25. TRUE (395).

3. Bonus Questions
1. Rudolph Valentino (15).
2. Two blocks (27).
3. Dawn Cutler. She was the only person he ever told that he was adopted (101).

4. Super Bonus Questions
1. "When you don't look both ways crossing a one-way street." This was the joke the New York cabbie told Dawn Cutler when he picked her up upon her arrival in New York City (10).
2. Agnes Morris's grandfather clock. It was named after Douglas Fairbanks (12).
3. Light yellow (20).
4. On York and Twenty-eighth in New York City (87).
5. The first phrase of a love song Michael was famous for called "Forever, My Love" (203).

6. "Strong and manly" (225).

5. Trick Bonus Question
"Brooooklyn, New York." This is a trick question because he was from Brooklyn, but when he told the name of the borough to Dawn, he pronounced it "Brooooklyn." So the correct answer is "Brooklyn" *and* "Brooooklyn" (7).

6. Sartorial Bonus Questions
1. Pink ballerina slippers (11).
2. A black chiffon dress over black leotards and silver dancing shoes (24).
3. Light blue (34).
4. He usually wore a black shirt and black slacks (61).
5. Baby-pink blouses, pleated ivory skirts, white sneakers, and Bobby socks (122).
6. A sleeveless black taffeta dress (136).
7. Dark blue (247).
8. Faded blue overalls and a flannel shirt (259).

7. Epistolary Bonus Questions
1. "As it had never been lit before" (33).
2. Agnes Morris (59).
3. "Darkness grips the

world in an iron fist"
(104).

4. Daddy (Ormand)
   Longchamp (113).
5. Arthur Garwood (119).
6. "Every night they have
   a fight and this is what
   they say . . ." (130).
7. Jimmy Longchamp
   (180).
8. Jimmy Longchamp
   (246).
9. Trisha Kramer (255).
10. Emily Booth (284).
11. Trisha Kramer (314).
12. William B. Cutler (399).

**8. A Macabre Bonus
Question**

The love of his life,
Agnes Morris (67).

**9. The "Punch Line,
Please?" Bonus
Question**
" 'I can't get over the
hump' " (76).

**10. A Euphemistic Bonus
Question**
Charlotte Booth's word
for sex (347).

11. Who Said It?
1 E (47).
2 A (273).
3 B (38).
4 D (184).
5 C (400).

Chapter 14.   TWILIGHT'S CHILD

1. Multiple Choice
1. C. Saddle Creek (3).
2. B. Mr. Dorfman (5).
3. A. He operated a linen
   factory (6).
4. A. Violet (8).
5. C. A diamond
   engagement ring (28).
6. C. Guarding the
   Panama Canal (51).
7. A. October 26th (57).
   [See "Gaffe Alert" in
   this chapter's "Leafing
   Through" section.]
8. C. A strudel (77).
9. A. Bronson Alcott (89).
10. C. He had heart failure
    and collapsed over his
    mother's grave (99).

11. D. Humpty Dumpty
    (122).
12. C. A degenerative bone
    disease (132).
13. B. Hungarian (134).
14. A. Sherry (135).
15. D. He was an investor
    and a banker (138).
16. C. A cancer of the
    blood (141).
17. B. Bronson Alcott
    (146).
18. B. Champagne (187).
19. B. She called her
    "Don" (192).
20. D. They invited nearly
    300 people. (217).
21. C. They invited close to
    500 people. (217).

22. A. Hoagie's Diner (229).
23. C. Stanley (231).
24. B. Rose (231).
25. D. He was an investment broker on Wall Street (260).
26. C. English (270).
27. D. He said he was a jewelry salesman (355).
28. B. A kidney ailment (357).

2. True or False

1. FALSE. It was a two-story colonial (6).
2. FALSE. He was black (6).
3. FALSE. He had "carrot-red" hair (7).
4. TRUE (14).
5. TRUE (23).
6. FALSE. He bought her the ring in Amsterdam while stationed over there with the Army (28).
7. TRUE (43).
8. FALSE. He wore a tuxedo (82).
9. TRUE (85).
10. TRUE (108).
11. FALSE. It was on a high hill (130).
12. TRUE (139).
13. FALSE. He owned a bowling alley in Tampa (203).
14. TRUE (209).
15. FALSE. It was held in a church in Washington, D.C. (217).
16. TRUE (242).
17. TRUE (280).
18. He *was* threatening about it, but he only asked for $5,000 (359).
19. TRUE (409).

3. Bonus Questions

1. Millie Francis (31).
2. Bronson Alcott (45).
3. She was "barely over thirteen months" (50).
4. "Mellon" (231).
5. The Marion Lewis School (271).

4. Super Bonus Questions

1. 12 Hardy Drive (17).
2. Queen Elizabeth (77).
3. Dawn Longchamp; Jimmy Longchamp; Bronson Alcott; and Laura Sue Alcott (201).

5. Sartorial Bonus Questions

1. White (7).
2. A strapless off-white satin gown with a lace bodice lined with pearls (82).
3. An emerald, diamond, and ruby bracelet (82).
4. She wore a pearl-white satin strapless gown that was cut so low half her breasts were revealed (128).
5. A black leather miniskirt and a white silk off-shoulder blouse. Both were exceptionally revealing (202).

6. Epistolary Bonus Questions

1. Wedding-dress white (57).
2. "GOOD LUCK DAWN AND JAMES" (86).
3. "DAWN AND JAMES AT CUTLER'S COVE" (87).
4. "I'm confessing that I love you . . ." (92).
5. "The lobster you eat today, yesterday swam in Cape Cod Bay" (98).
6. "My Stepfather Raped Me, but I Had No One to Tell" (380).

7. **"Red Alert for Dawn" Bonus Question**
Betty dyed her hair blonde, at the request of Dawn's rapist brother, Philip (217).

8. **"Figure It Out" Bonus Question**
January 2nd. We're told that they were born "a day after New Year's Day" (231)

9. **Who Said It?**
1 D (9).
2 E (329).
3 A (86).
4 C (175).
5 B (344).

Chapter 15. MIDNIGHT WHISPERS

1. Multiple Choice
1. B. Princess (2).
2. A. A lion (6).
3. B. A giraffe (6).
4. C. An owl (6).
5. D. The Wicked Witch (6).
6. C. Dennis the Menace (10).
7. B. A gold watch (18).
8. D. Parcheesi (22).
9. D. *Lady Chatterley's Lover* by D. H. Lawrence (28).
10. C. Brushed back on the sides and flat on top (29).
11. A. Abraham Lincoln (29).
12. B. "Long and boring" (30).
13. D. Twirl her hair with her forefinger (32).
14. B. A "vulture of love" (37).
15. A. Arthritis (44).
16. B. "High Hopes." The second song she sang was "Over the Rainbow." See the *Leafing Through* list, "The 5 Times the Song 'Over the Rainbow' Is Mentioned in V. C. Andrews's Novels" in Book 13, *Secrets of the Morning* (50).
17. A. Steven (64).

18. D. A gold identification bracelet (64).
19. C. A boiler in the basement blew up (81).
20. B. A poodle (88).
21. A. Tie his socks together (110).
22. C. 1,000 (157).
23. A. Georgia (165).
24. C. A Chopin nocturne (191).

2. True or False
1. TRUE (3).
2. FALSE. It had a pink polka-dotted canopy (5).
3. TRUE (9).
4. TRUE (13).
5. TRUE (21).
6. TRUE (29).
7. FALSE. He liked to tease her that she had to call him "Uncle Gavin" because of their familial relationship. Gavin was her father Jimmy's half-brother, making him technically her step-uncle (33).
8. FALSE. Her uncle Philip asked her first (48).
9. FALSE. Nussbaum baked it in the shape of a piano (58).
10. TRUE (58).
11. TRUE (61).
12. FALSE. Trisha was the *first* person to leave (68).
13. TRUE (69).
14. TRUE (90).
15. FALSE. He often used the *den* as a second office (100).
16. FALSE. Fern asked if she could borrow the gold watch Dawn and Jimmy had given Christie (119).
17. TRUE (124).
18. TRUE (162).
19. FALSE. He sold his valuable baseball card collection (216).
20. FALSE. "His hot wetness spurted inside me" (227).
21. TRUE (289).
22. FALSE. His sport was tennis (334).
23. TRUE (439).
24. TRUE (440).

3. Bonus Questions
1. "Family business" (7).
2. He made labels out of adhesive tape, wrote his name on them, and then pasted them on "his" dresser drawers (132).
3. Julius the chauffeur. He stayed because the family still needed a driver (179).
4. Charlotte's parents' suite (336).

4. Super Bonus Questions
1. Brahms or Beethoven (9).
2. Tchaikovsky or Liszt (9).
3. A makeup mirror (71).
4. A stationery set (71).
5. He received Unsatisfactory marks for every behavior category and two Unsatisfactories in his school subjects (78).
6. $12. She was one of The Meadows' plantation slaves (296).
7. "She came on Emily's broom" (347).

5. Epistolary Bonus Questions

1. Trisha Kramer. ("Aunt Trisha") (1).
2. "HAPPY SWEET SIXTEEN CHRISTIE, WE LOVE YOU," in pink lettering (43).
3. A gold identification bracelet from Gavin
4. Gavin Longchamp, written by Christie Longchamp (152).
5. Gavin Longchamp (174).

6. Sartorial Bonus Questions

1. A pink silk strapless dress with a sweetheart neckline (14).
2. A dark red dress that almost reached her ankles (25).
3. A pair of old jeans and a faded sweatshirt (25).
4. A see-through skirt slit up her thigh, the bikini bottom of an exercise outfit, and a see-through blouse with no bra underneath (47).
5. A college sweatshirt, jeans, and sneakers with no socks. The sweatshirt was faded, the jeans were tight, and the sneakers were dirty (67).
6. Dark blue dungarees, a white T-shirt, and a black cotton jacket (258).
7. Jeans, sneakers, a black sweatshirt, and a black and gold high school jacket. (He was such a nostalgic guy, eh?) (429).

7. Literary Bonus Question

In Chapter 10 of D. H. Lawrence's erotic masterpiece, *Lady Chatterley's Lover,* Constance Chatterley, the restless wife of an impotent husband, has a massive simultaneous (and impregnating) orgasm during illicit sex with her husband's gamekeeper. To wit:

He too had bared the front part of his body and she felt his naked flesh against her as he came into her. For a moment he was still inside her, turgid there and quivering. Then as he began to move, in the sudden helpless orgasm, there awoke in her new strange thrills rippling inside her. Rippling, rippling, rippling, like a flapping overlapping of soft flames, soft as feathers, running to points of brilliance, exquisite, exquisite and melting her all molten inside. It was like bells rippling up and up to a culmination. She lay unconscious of the wild little cries she uttered at the last. But it was over too soon, too soon, and she could no longer force her own conclusion with her own activity. This was different, different. She could do nothing. She could no longer harden and grip for her own satisfaction upon him. She could only wait, wait and moan in spirit as she felt him withdrawing, withdrawing and contracting, coming to the terrible moment when he would slip out of her and be gone. Whilst all her womb was open and soft, and softly clamoring, like a sea-anemone under the tide, clamoring for him to come in again and make a fulfillment for her. She clung to him unconscious in passion, and he never quite slipped from her, and she felt the soft bud of him within her stirring, and strange rhythms flushing up into her with a strange rhythmic growing motion, swelling and swelling till it filled all her cleaving consciousness, and then began again the unspeakable motion that was not really motion, but pure deepening whirlpools of sensation swirling deeper and deeper through all her tissue and consciousness, till she was one perfect concentric fluid of feeling, and she lay there crying in unconscious inarticulate cries. The voice out of the uttermost night, the life! (from

Chapter 10 of *Lady Chatterley's Lover*)

Aunt Fern wanted Christie to read it because she felt that it was about time Christie "found out what it was all about." Christie is raped by Uncle Philip in Chapter 9 of *Midnight Whispers* (28).

8. Funereal Bonus Questions

1. He was hit by a car and killed. Fluffy was a Long-champ family cat (97).
2. She saw Grandmother Cutler's eyes glaring out at her from the stone monument (155).

9. Disgusting Bonus Question

Apple (139).

10. Prurient Interest Bonus Questions

1. 14. The boy was 17 (353).
2. She took off her shoes, her socks, her blouse, and her skirt. She fled the room when she was down to her bra and panties, even though she was supposed to take them off too (384).

11. Who Said It

1 C (83).
2 A (382).
3 B (383).
4 E (291).
5 D (440).

THE
V. C. ANDREWS
TRIVIA AND QUIZ
———— BOOK————

Stephen J. Spignesi

A SIGNET BOOK

CONTENTS

"ATTIC HAIKU"

(for Jennifer and Amanda)

Grim ghosts of children
Water dead paper flowers:
Screams in dusty hell.

—Stephen Spignesi
January 1993

TANKSALOT . . .

. . . recalling the thought of kindnesses done.

—Catullus, *Carmina*

Ringrazio affettuosamente to the following colleagues, cohorts, and confreres:

- **Pam,** my wife, the toppermost of the poppermost, has my love and gratitude.
- **Kristy Swanson,** vampire slayer extraordinaire, was unbelievably helpful with this book, and I owe her a huge debt of thanks. My interview with her and the pictures she let me review from her collection are the kinds of things that elevate a book from average to terrific, and she has my sincerest thanks and appreciation.
- **Gary Ink** and **Publishers Weekly** were helpful and generous in allowing me to reprint an interview with V. C. Andrews from their pages, and they have my gratitude.
- **Doug Winter,** my friend and colleague, was extremely helpful and generous in allowing me to quote from his lengthy interview with V. C.; he has my respect and thanks.
- **Elaine Koster** came up with the idea for this book and then thought well enough of me to ask if I

wanted to do it, and to her I owe more thanks than can be tallied.

- **Ed Stackler,** my editor on this and several other books, is a man who knows what he's doing. It is a good thing to have such a man a mere phone call away. As always, my sincerest thanks and appreciation to Ed and his helpful assistant, Liz.

- **John White,** my literary agent, is my friend and counselor, and it is he to whom I owe as much gratitude as I can muster. And that still ain't enough! Thanks and fond appreciation to John and his wife, Barbara.

- *USA Today* and *Hollywood Scripts* have my sincerest thanks for their helpful research assistance.

- **George Beahm,** friend and confidant, once again, has my warmest thanks and appreciation.

- **My family,** including my mother, Lee Mandato; my brothers Paul and David; my sister Janet; my sisters-in-law Sheryl, Linda, Laura, and Maureen; my brother-in-law Jerry; my stepfather Frank; my mother- and father-in-law Tony and Dolores; and my nieces and nephews Jennifer, John, Amanda, Joey, and Amy, all have my love and gratitude.

- **Bob, Sue, Bill,** and **Cathy** at Minuteman Press in East Haven are always there for me and they all have my fondest thanks.

- And finally, *al mio amico,* **Mario Coppola,** for his *joie de vivre* and his uncanny ability to translate my incoherent verbal meanderings into flawless Italian.

STEPHEN SPIGNESI
April 1993
New Haven, Connecticut

INTRODUCTION
"Life At You Like Bullets"

I like to place ordinary people—some with extraordinary talents—in bizarre circumstances. Once, when I was given an award, I was introduced as the writer who fires life at you like bullets. My characters do have life's calamities fired at them like bullets when they are helpless and can't dodge. They are wounded, but live to struggle on, and before my book is over, they have suffered perhaps, grown, become stronger undoubtedly, and have learned to cope, no matter what the circumstances.

> —V. C. Andrews, from a 1985 interview with
> Douglas E. Winter in *Faces of Fear*

The Darkness: Greed. Deception. Incest. Pain. Tragedy. Revenge. Rape. Secrets. Lies. Grief. Cruelty. Vengeance. Death.

The Light: Love. Hope. Beauty. Honesty. Innocence. Respect. Music. Tolerance. Faith. Art. Joy. Life.

Such are the wildly disparate yin and yang elements of the classic V. C. Andrews story.

The heroine in V. C.'s tales is always a teenage girl beset upon by forces and desires that can easily destroy her: Life *is* thrown at her like bullets, but inevitably, as V. C. wisely acknowledges in the epigraph to this introduction, her characters use these trials as learning tools and as experiences that help her grow and mature.

V. C.'s girls—Cathy Dollanganger, Heaven Casteel, Annie Stonewall, Leigh VanVoreen, Dawn Cutler, Christie Longchamp—are all young women who have to grow up fast. Their innocence and naiveté add enormously to their appeal and the reader ends up cheering these adolescent heroines on as they move through—and try to survive—any number of horrible "calamities."

Survival at any and all costs.

That is these young women's "call to honor."

Another unique appeal of V. C.'s stories is her unique and commanding use of place as character. All her stories take place in a modern Gothic landscape that is intimately familiar yet somehow different; like a room seen in a reflection: reversed but recognizable. Foxworth Hall, Corrine's mansion, Farthinggale Manor, Whitefern, The Meadows, The Cottage, Cutler's Cove Hotel. The places her characters move through are the places of the classic fairy tale: hulking dark mansions; charming rustic cottages; crumbling old plantations; huge labyrinthine hotels. Her places take the reader there and very effectively fulfill the promise of a story well told, which is, of course, to *take you away.*

Contemporary popularity notwithstanding, though, V. C. Andrews's stories are *not* catalogs of popular culture, as are the tales of, for instance, one of her dark fantasy colleagues, Stephen King. V. C.'s sagas are stately and poised; the cadence and rhythm of the plot and her use of language are somehow hypnotic, an effect that results in the novels virtually transcending the conventions of contemporary fiction and transmuting into modern fables. Her literary "recipes" always include certain tried-and-true ingredients, elements her readers and fans would miss if they were not there. These include innocent teenage heroines; dark family secrets; mysterious mansions; insane matriarchs; perverted lustful uncles; stalwart and heroic cousins or brothers; evil sisters and stepsisters; evil grandmothers and aunts; and, of course, charming, hopeless romantics, both male and female.

When these ingredients are all present, sparks fly, and we're taken away to the world where V. C. Andrews rules supreme.

To Be Continued . . .

Now let's talk about literary longevity.

As of this writing (January 1993), there have been sixteen V. C. Andrews novels published (*Flowers in the Attic* through *Darkest Hour*).

V. C. Andrews died in December 1986. Since then, there have been nine "V. C. Andrews" novels published. How can this be?

In *Heaven* (which was apparently the first novel to be published after her death), in a note to V. C.'s readers, Pocket Books said that V. C. Andrews had "left . . . a legacy of novels yet to be published" and revealed that "she had completed working on a number of novels prior to her passing."

The paperback editions of the next five novels (*Dark Angel* through *Web of Dreams*) included no note from the publisher. The twelfth V. C. Andrews novel, *Dawn*, included a letter to the reader from the Andrews family that revealed, among other things, that when V. C. became ill, she "began to work even harder, hoping to finish as many stories as possible" and that "just before she died we promised ourselves that we would take all of these wonderful stories and make them available to her readers." They then acknowledge that beginning with the last couple of books in the Casteel series, the family and Pocket Books had "been working closely with a carefully selected writer to organize and complete Virginia's stories and to expand upon them by creating additional novels inspired by her wonderful storytelling genius."

The name of the "carefully selected writer" chosen by the Andrews family to continue the V. C. Andrews tradition is also a carefully guarded secret. I happen to know who is writing the later Andrews novels because the name has occasionally appeared in print over the years. It has not been widely disseminated, however, and out of respect for the wishes of the Andrews family, I will not reveal it here.

Apparently, this writer worked with, first, V. C.'s completed but unpublished novels, then with her "idea notebook," and now, it seems, with new, original ideas. The most recent novel published as of this writing, *Darkest Hour* contains the letter from the Andrews family reproduced previously, but with some important changes. The line that originally read, "Just before she died we promised ourselves that we would take all of these wonderful stories and make them available to her readers" now reads, "Just before she died we promised ourselves that we would find a way of creating additional stories based on her vision." This new letter mentions "creating new novels" and stories that have been "*inspired* [emphasis added] by her wonderful storytelling talent." This seems to indicate that the writer is writing brand-new novels in the V. C. mold and publishing them with the family's authority as "A V. C. Andrews Book"—sort of like different writers doing *Star Trek* novels and publishing them as a *"Star Trek"* book. However, the last line of this most recent letter says, "Other novels, including some based on stories Virginia was able to complete before her death, will be published in the coming years and we hope they continue to mean as much to you as ever."

Admittedly, this is vague, to say the least, but I, for one, think it's all right and actually necessary that it be so.

It's obvious that this "carefully selected writer" is pulling from V. C.'s unpublished stories, idea jottings, and family ideas that V. C. may have verbally communicated before she died, plus whatever unfinished manuscripts may have been found in her personal papers, to write the new V. C. novels.

The point, I think, is that V. C. was such a unique storyteller and this new writer is so careful about being true to her vision, that the new novels could easily have been written by V. C., and her family has decided to keep the tradition alive.

Of course, I would be remiss if I did not acknowledge the financial incentive to keep a phenomenally successful series of novels active and generating income—but there's no law against making money in this country, is there? And to give the family credit, the novels published after her death, whatever conglomeration of V. C.'s work, new writing, and rewriting they may contain, would do her proud. They come as close as they can to a genuine "V. C. Andrews" novel, and for all we know, great portions of them may actually be V. C. Andrews's work.

We, as fans, will never really know who wrote what,

but as long as the stories entertain us and do justice to V. C.'s storytelling abilities, then this is an issue that shouldn't really matter.

The V. C. Andrews Trivia and Quiz Book is meant to act as a companion to V. C. Andrews's series of novels.

V. C. Andrews's stories comprise three series and one "stand-alone" novel as follows (in narrative order):

The Dollanganger Saga
>   *Garden of Shadows*
>   *Flowers in the Attic*
>   *Petals on the Wind*
>   *If There Be Thorns*
>   *Seeds of Yesterday*

The Casteel Family Series
>   *Web of Dreams*
>   *Heaven*
>   *Dark Angel*
>   *Fallen Hearts*
>   *Gates of Paradise*

The Cutler Family Series
>   *Darkest Hour*
>   *Dawn*
>   *Secrets of the Morning*
>   *Twilight's Child*
>   *Midnight Whispers*

The Stand-Alone Novel
>   *My Sweet Audrina*

The V. C. Andrews Trivia and Quiz Book contains features that will add to the enjoyment of her stories, allowing you to stay in her world for a longer time than you would by simply reading the book and putting it away.

After a brief biographical profile in Part I, Part II looks at V. C.'s books. For each of the fifteen novels covered, the following topics are included:

• **The Chapters**

   V. C. Andrews always titled her chapters, so this volume will feature a listing of the chapters in each of her books. Because there is never a table of contents in V. C.'s novels, having a handy list of chapters to refer to when reading the book (or taking one of the *Trivia and Quiz Book*'s quizzes for that matter) can help a lot. It's also interesting to see the whole story laid out in chapter titles, and to see how V. C. moved from one plot development to the next. [See "Chapter Facts" for an interesting spin on V. C.'s titling of her chapters.]

• The Story Synopsis

This is a straightforward, impartial, and objective chronicling of the events in the story. This feature will prod your memory when you take the quizzes and help you navigate through the sometimes intricate series of events that occur in the novels. By necessity, an occasional plot surprise is revealed in passing along the chapter-to-chapter events. If you prefer not to have important story developments told to you before you read the book, then skip the synopses and read the V. C. Andrews novel first. The synopsis will always be there and you can go back to it whenever you need a little help in recalling just who did what to whom, where it happened, and when it occurred.

• The Quizzes

The Quizzes comprise the first part of a massive, comprehensive two-part dissection of V. C. Andrews's novels. (The second part is the "*Leafing Through . . .*" sections.) For each book, I have included a series of multiple-choice, true or false, bonus, and "Who Said It?" questions. The questions for each novel range from ridiculously simple to mind-bogglingly difficult. As in my three previous books of popular-culture quizzes (my two *Stephen King Quiz Books* and *The Official Gone With the Wind Companion*), my intention is to send you back to the works being quizzed. For many of these questions, I do not expect readers to be able to pull the answers out of their heads. The answer information is usually too specific for that. But it is my hope that you will go seek out the answer in the original books. This is the fun part—to be able to go back to the novels, do some rereading, and track down the correct answers. The vast majority of the quizzes are in order: that is, the questions follow sequential chains of events as they occur in the novel. This acts as a kind of "hint" system, allowing you to home in on at least the right chapter where the answer can be found, if not immediately the right page. And if you are at a complete loss and simply cannot find the answer to a specific question, the "Answer" chapter not only provides the correct answer, it also supplies the page number (from the paperback editions of the novels) where the correct information can be found. At the very least, this page-number feature can serve as a terrific "browsing" guide.

- **Leafing Through ...**

The unique "*Leafing Through ...*" feature provided for each book presents loads of entertaining information and trivia in a much-loved format—the list. The number of trivia items for each novel averages out to well over 100, and lists include everything from straightforward information about furnishings and food to bizarre and salacious information about sex and violence. The information in each list is presented without editorial comment (other than my sometime admittedly tongue-in-cheek list title). It is my belief that there are times when the accurate and dispassionate presentation of information allows the data to speak for itself, making a stronger statement than the comments of critic or writer. "*Leafing Through ...*" is a "reading" feature to be turned to when you need a break from the quizzes.

Following the novels section is one "Final and Ultimate" quiz question, and, for variety, a V. C. Andrews Crossword Puzzle.

Part II concludes with "Chapter Facts," a V. C. Andrews checklist. "Chapter Facts" is a fun feature that looks at the connections, associations, and similarities that appear in dozens of V. C. Andrews chapter titles.

Part III of *The V. C. Andrews Trivia and Quiz Book* takes a detailed look at what is so far the only film adaptation of a V. C. novel, *Flowers in the Attic*. This section includes:

- **Flower Facts:** A detailed look at the *Flowers in the Attic* movie
- **V. C. Speaks:** The *Publishers Weekly* interview with V. C. Andrews on the making of *Flowers in the Attic*

- **Buffy Blooms:** An exclusive interview with *Flowers in the Attic* star, Kristy Swanson
- **A Lost Garden:** A Look at Wes Craven's shelved *Flowers in the Attic* script

The V. C. Andrews Trivia and Quiz Book concludes with a comprehensive answer section, complete with page reference numbers.

V. C. Andrews died young—she was only 62 years old. But she left behind a legacy of powerful, dramatic, and emotionally satisfying novels that have found a massive audience since the publication of *Flowers in the Attic* in 1979. *The V. C. Andrews Trivia and Quiz Book* is a tribute to her life, her work, and her memory.

In *Songs of Experience*, William Blake wrote, "Hear the voice of the Bard!/Who present, past, and future see."

V. C. Andrews had the "voice of the Bard" and we are all fortunate that we have an enduring record of the present, past, and future that she saw.

> *Absent in body, but present in spirit.*
> —1 Corinthians 5:3

PART I

V. C. Andrews, 1924–1986

A Biographical Profile

[V. C. Andrews was a very private person and details about her life are truly sketchy and difficult to find. The following brief profile was compiled from information found in Douglas E. Winter's excellent in-depth interview with V. C. Andrews that is included in his fascinating 1985 book, *Faces of Fear* (Berkley Books). Doug's interview with V. C. is the most comprehensive ever published and my sincerest thanks go out to him for his help and kindnesses].

V. C. Andrews was born in 1924 in Portsmouth, Virginia, one of three children. Her father was a career Navy man who opened a tool-and-die business when he retired. Her childhood years were spent in Portsmouth and Rochester, Virginia.

She "didn't have a terrible childhood," she told Douglas Winter in 1985. She read voraciously and also excelled in art. She won a scholarship at the age of fifteen for a literary parody she had written.

In her late teens, a fall down a flight of stairs tore a membrane and led to bone spurs. That fall, combined with botched orthopedic surgery, would lead to her ultimate dependence on a wheelchair later in life.

Andrews did commercial and portrait art for a time, before beginning what she described as "closet" writing after her father's death in the late 1960s and the family's move to Manchester, Missouri.

Winter writes, "In 1972, while living in Apache Junction, Arizona, Andrews began to devote all of her time to writing, completing her first novel, a science fantasy entitled *The Gods of the Green Mountain*."

Seven years later, after nine novels and twenty short stories, Virginia Andrews sold *Flowers in the Attic.*

Winter explains the sequence of events that led to the use of Andrews's initials rather than her name:

> It is notable that it was not Andrews's decision to use her initials instead of her first name on her books. Her experience is no different than that faced some fifty years ago by women writing for pulp horror magazines, who often found that neutering initials or pseudonyms were necessary when writing stories of horror and violence.
>
> "The publisher sent me a copy of the galley of *Flowers in the Attic,* and it read, 'Virginia Andrews.' Then, when they sent me the cover, it said, 'V. C. Andrews.' So I immediately called up and complained. And they said, 'It was a big mistake by the printers, and we can't change it—we've already printed a million copies of the cover and it's too expensive to throw them away."
>
> "Then later, I learned the truth. It was an editorial decision. Men don't like to read women writers, and they wanted men to read the book. They wanted to prove to men that women could write differently—that we don't write only about ribbons and frills and kisses and hugs, that we can really write something strong." [*Faces of Fear,* p. 175]

When Winter's interview took place, V. C. was apparently in good health. She was living with her mother in Virginia Beach, Virginia (a location familiar to V. C.'s readers) and she spoke of possibly directing a film based on one of her books. She also spoke of *The Gods of the Green Mountain,* a medieval novel, a fantasy trilogy, and a book about ESP being published sometime in the future.

V. C. noted that she did not want to write an autobiography, explaining, "My life isn't finished yet. I wouldn't have a good ending." She died in December of 1986. She was 62 years old.

PART II

The Novels

—1—

FLOWERS IN THE ATTIC
(1979)

She sleeps up in the attic there
Alone . . .

—Charlotte Mew, *The Farmer's Bride*

CHAPTER LISTING

Part One

Flowers in the Attic, V. C. Andrews's first published novel, began the terrifying and beautiful saga of the beleaguered Dollanganger children. The book was first published in November 1979 by Pocket Books; by 1992 it was in its 48th printing. The book contains a prologue, 22 chapters in two parts, and an epilogue.

Flowers in the Attic was made into a film in 1987, directed (appropriately) by Jeffrey Bloom. [See the film section.]

In a 1985 interview with Douglas E. Winter, Andrews remarked, "I like to amaze my editor and tell her that I wrote [*Flowers in the Attic*] in one night. I did. I plotted the whole thing in longhand—it was eighteen pages. And then I typed it into ninety." *Flowers in the Attic* spent 14 weeks on the *New York Times* best-seller list.

The following feature consists of quiz questions broken into "multiple choice," "true or false," "bonus," and "Who Said It?" sections, followed by *Leafing Through . . .,* which offers some interesting "petals" of information and arcana drawn from *Flowers in the Attic.*

STORY SYNOPSIS

After their father is killed in a car accident on his birthday, Chris, Cathy, Cory, and Carrie Dollanganger are forced to move with their mother into her family's ancestral home, a huge, hulking mansion ruled over by a dying, tyrannical grandfather and a cruel, sadistic, religiously obsessed grandmother. Corrine, the children's mother, has to agree that her father cannot know about the children, and so the four of them are locked into a room high up in the house and not allowed to come out. They are told it is temporary: As soon as their mother can win back the grandfather's affection (and thus be assured of inheriting the enormous estate), the children will be freed. But things don't work out that way. The grandmother takes charge and the first thing on her horrible agenda is to whip Corrine as punishment for the terrible sin that made her leave the mansion in the first place. Days, then weeks, then months go by, and still the children are held captive. Chris and Cathy, the two oldest children, begin to awaken sexually, which causes (as the daddy character [played by Robert Duvall] in the 1991 film, *Rambling Rose* put it) a "damnable commotion," and the two younger twins begin to wither away from lack of proper food, exercise, and sun. Corrine doesn't seem to notice that her children are failing: She's too busy having a grand old time traveling to Europe and spending family money. The children are subjected to beatings, starvation, and poisoning; Cathy even has her hair covered with tar. One of the twins is killed, and the book ends with the three surviving children escaping from the house and traveling south. This is where the second volume, *Petals on the Wind*, begins.

THE QUIZZES

1. Multiple Choice

1. What kind of car was the drunk driver who killed Cathy's father driving?
    A. A green Nissan
    B. A brown Honda Accord
    C. A blue Ford
    D. A red Hyundai

2. What happened if Carrie ate any kind of fruit but citrus?
    A. She broke out in hives.
    B. She fainted.
    C. She had an asthma attack.
    D. She got diarrhea.

3. What emotional, psychological affliction did the grandmother suffer from?
    A. Claustrophobia
    B. Agoraphobia

C. Paranoia
D. Photophobia

4. What was Jim Johnston's nickname for the Dollanganger kids?
    A. "The Dresden dolls"
    B. "The China Dolls"
    C. "The Little Rascals"
    D. "The Four Stooges"

5. What percentage of his yearly income did Malcolm Foxworth tithe to his church?
    A. 5 percent
    B. 10 percent
    C. 25 percent
    D. 50 percent

6. What is a French courtesan?
    A. "A woman who saves her favors for men of the aristocracy, or royalty."
    B. "An elaborately-designed marble bidet used by women of great social standing."
    C. "An appetizer made of goose liver and shiitake mushrooms."
    D. "A midwife of Spanish descent 'imported' into France to minister to the daughters of the wealthy."

7. How many rooms were there in the Dollanganger's "pre-Foxworth Hall" Pennsylvania house?
    A. 5
    B. 6
    C. 8
    D. 10

8. How many bathrooms were there in the Dollanganger's "pre-Foxworth Hall" Pennsylvania house?
    A. 1
    B. 2½
    C. 3
    D. 4

9. How tall was the children's first Foxworth Hall Christmas tree?
    A. It was two feet tall.

    B. They didn't have a Christmas tree.
    C. It was five feet tall.
    D. It was three feet tall.

10. Cory refused to use the instructions for which of the following toys?
    A. Erector Set
    B. Mr. Potato Head
    C. Lincoln Logs
    D. Tinkertoys

11. How did Cathy learn about "man-to-man talks"?
    A. From reading *Playboy* and *Reader's Digest* magazines.
    B. From watching old Andy Hardy movies.
    C. From talks with her brother.
    D. From talks with her father.

12. Where did Joel Foxworth presumably die?
    A. Switzerland
    B. Italy
    C. France
    D. North Carolina

13. How many chimneys were on the roof of Foxworth Hall?
    A. 5
    B. 10
    C. 8
    D. None

14. What was Cathy's intended stage name?
    A. "Catherine Pavlova"
    B. "Katherine Marisha"
    C. "Catherine Dahl"
    D. "Catherine Doll"

15. Which word is missing from Chris's first Foxworth Hall Thanksgiving Day grace, "Thank you, Lord, for this _____Thanksgiving Day meal. Amen."?
    A. "Belated"
    B. "Blessed"
    C. "Ice-cold"
    D. "Horrible"

16. Who was the childhood friend with whom Cathy remembered making tar babies as a child?
    A. Georgette Campano
    B. Mary Lou Baker
    C. Michelle Austin
    D. Nancy Barbieri

17. What day of the week did Chris and Cathy spend time outdoors on the roof?
    A. Sunday
    B. Thursday
    C. Tuesday
    D. Saturday

18. What was the name of Cory's snail?
    A. "Cindy Lou"
    B. "Snail"
    C. "Bob"
    D. "Steverino"

19. What was the name of Carrie's worm?
    A. "Charlie"
    B. "Snail"
    C. "Bertha"
    D. "Mia"

20. How did the children keep track of the number of days they were held prisoner in the room in Foxworth Hall?
    A. They marked red X's on the bathroom floor tiles, one tile per day.
    B. They marked off the days with red X's on wall calendars.
    C. They pulled bristles off an old broom and kept them in a cigar box.
    D. They drew little flowers on the attic stair risers.

21. What did the children use for toilet paper after the grandmother stopped bringing them supplies?
    A. The cut up a sheet into three-inch squares.
    B. They ripped pages from the oldest books in the attic.
    C. They used Cathy's scarf collection.
    D. They didn't use anything but their hands, which they then washed in the bathroom sink.

22. What Southern state did Bart Winslow come from?
    A. Georgia
    B. Tennessee
    C. South Carolina
    D. North Carolina

23. How much stolen money did Cathy and Chris have saved up by the time they first made love?
    A. $716.53
    B. $396.44
    C. $36.36
    D. $417.87

24. According to Corrine, what disease killed Cory?
    A. Hepatitis
    B. Cancer
    C. Pneumonia
    D. Tuberculosis

25. What was the name of the highway where Cathy's father was killed?
    A. Townsend Highway
    B. North Branford Throughway
    C. Greenfield Highway
    D. Route One

26. Who recited the following prayer?: "Forgive me, Lord, for all my sins. I have always done what I thought best, and if I made mistakes, please believe I thought I was doing right. May I forever find grace in thine eyes. Amen."
    A. The grandmother
    B. Corrine
    C. Cathy
    D. Malcolm Foxworth

2. True or False

1. Chris and Cathy were five years apart in age.
2. The children's father, Christopher Dollanganger, was 79 when he died.
3. The children's father, Christopher Dollanganger, was driving a 1971 white Toyota Corolla when he died.

4. Corrine's middle name was Garland.
5. Corrine's father suffered from lung cancer.
6. If Malcolm Foxworth wasn't feeling well enough to attend church in a wheelchair, he would be carried in on a stretcher.
7. Garland Christopher Foxworth 4th graduated from Yale.
8. Corrine and Christopher were married by a justice of the peace.
9. Snails have tubular intestines that end with their mouth.
10. Cory once locked himself in a trunk in the attic while playing hide-and-seek.
11. The moon was full the night Chris and Cathy temporarily escaped from Foxworth Hall and went swimming.
12. Chris knew if it was the male or female firefly that lit up.
13. One of Bart Winslow's sisters lived in New Hampshire.
14. Purple pansies kept away evil demons and monsters.
15. There were three paintings by Picasso in the children's Foxworth Hall room.
16. The Dollangangers lived in Woodstock, Georgia, before they moved to Foxworth Hall.
17. Christopher Dollanganger worked for a computer manufacturing firm.
18. Christopher Dollanganger's best friend was Edward Stackler.
19. Alicia was twenty-one when she married Corrine's grandfather.
20. Corrine's grandfather was fifty-five when he married Alicia.
21. Corrine's typing teacher was Mrs. Helena Brady.

3. Bonus Questions

1. What furniture was in the children's Foxworth Hall room?
2. How old was Adelaide in 1879?

3. How old was Jonathan in 1879?
4. How many boxes of cigars did Christopher Dollanganger give away after Chris was born?
5. Name the stuffed and mounted animals Chris saw in the Foxworth Hall trophy room the night he went "exploring."
6. What does earth represent? What does reality represent?
7. How many children did Raymond have?
8. What did Cathy write on the blackboard in the attic before she, Chris, and Carrie escaped?
9. What did Corrine leave in the lower drawer of her nightstand when she fled Foxworth Hall with Bart?
10. What items of her husband's were returned to Corrine after his death?

4. Who Said It?

1. "You are now gazing on hell, as some might see it."
2. "Are you as good as a real momma?"
3. "Shall I dress you now, Christopher?"
4. "Put the two girls in one bed, and the two boys in the other."
5. "What is it you lack besides bananas? Name it!"

   A. Cory Dollanganger
   B. The grandmother
   C. Momma
   D. Chris Dollanganger
   E. Cathy Dollanganger

LEAFING THROUGH ...
FLOWERS IN THE ATTIC

9 Facts About Books

1. Cathy once considered titling her journals, *Open the Window* and *Stand in the Sunshine*.
2. Cory's favorite storybook was *Peter Rabbit*.
3. Carrie was fond of the story, *The Three Little Pigs*.
4. When called upon by their grandmother to recite passages from the Bible, Cathy and Chris quoted Genesis (44:4), and the Book of Job (28:12; 28:28; 31:35; 32:9).
5. Cathy read *Wuthering Heights, Lorna Doone,* and *Little Men* while held prisoner in the attic.
6. Cathy loved to read plays.
7. To help the twins learn how to write while in the attic, Cathy and Chris gave Carrie and Cory an old McGuffey's first-grade primer.
8. Corrine ordered Chris a set of encyclopedias that were bound in genuine red leather.
9. Cathy once read a book by T. M. Ellis about two "star-crossed lovers named Raymond and Lily."

2 Items About Sports

1. The children's father, Christopher Dollanganger, liked tennis, golf, and swimming.
2. Bart Winslow loved tennis and skiing.

11 Facts About Food

1. The children's first complete breakfast at Foxworth Hall consisted of bacon, eggs, toast, and cereal.
2. The children's first complete lunch at Foxworth Hall consisted of sandwiches and hot soup.
3. The children's first complete dinner at Foxworth Hall consisted of fried chicken, potato salad, and string beans.

4. The children's first dessert at Foxworth Hall consisted of fruit.
5. Two turkeys were roasted at Foxworth Hall for the first Thanksgiving the children spent in the attic.
6. The children ate their first "Foxworth Hall" Thanksgiving dinner on Lenox china.
7. The twins loved bananas. The grandfather hated bananas.
8. The children had a box of crackers and a pound of cheddar cheese hidden away in the attic when the grandmother began starving them after the "Cathy-was-naked-in-front-of-Chris" incident.
9. In Cathy's gingerbread-house nightmare, the cottage was made of gingerbread and cheese, it had a roof made of Oreo cookies, a hard Christmas candy front walk, a Hershey bar front door, a picket fence made of peppermint sticks, and shrubbery made of seven flavors of ice-cream cone. Inside the house, the sofa was made of fresh bread and hot rolls with butter.
10. Before the grandmother broke the children's period of forced starvation, they were preparing to eat raw, dead mice.
11. Corrine poisoned the children by sprinkling arsenic on their doughnuts.

16 Incidents of Sex, Violence, Prurience, and Sadism

1. Corrine was 33 when she received her first whipping from her mother. She got 48 lashes (one for each year of her age and 15 for each year of her marriage to Christopher).
2. As children, Corrine and her two brothers were not allowed to swim because that meant exposing their bodies.
3. As a child, Corrine once tried to undress the miniature handsome young man doll given to her by her mother because she wanted to see what was underneath his clothes.
4. The grandmother's Eighth Rule was "if I ever

catch boys and girls using the bathroom at the same time, I will quite relentlessly, and without mercy, peel the skins from your back."

5. Cathy and Chris once saw Bart Winslow touch their mother's breast in public.

6. Chris once saw in Corrine's Foxworth Hall bedroom an ivory chaise lounge that he felt belonged at a Roman orgy.

7. The first completely naked woman Cathy ever saw was herself. She was posing in front of a mirror, checking out her new body, when she was discovered by Chris. He did not look away. In fact, he had a front *and* rear view of his sister because Cathy was standing facing him in front of a full-length mirror.

8. When the grandmother wanted to cut off Cathy's hair, Chris defended his sister by threatening to hit his grandmother in the head with a chair.

9. When Cathy refused to cut off her own hair, the grandmother sneaked into their bedroom one night, injected Cathy with some type of sedative drug, and poured hot tar all over her hair.

10. During the "Starve the Children Because Chris Saw Cathy Naked" period, Chris cut his own wrist and let the twins drink his blood for nourishment.

11. After the "Chris Saw Cathy Naked" incident, the grandmother prevented Cathy from ever again seeing the image of her own naked body by breaking every mirror in their room.

12. The grandmother once used a green willow switch to whip Cathy and Chris.

13. Cathy once caught Chris measuring the length of his penis.

14. While exploring their mother's Foxworth Hall bedroom, Cathy and Chris found a pornographic book of color photographs of people having sex. The book had a phony dust jacket with the title, *How to Create Your Own Needlework Designs.*

15. Cathy—wearing nothing but a short, transparent blue nightie and panties—once kissed Bart Winslow while he was sleeping. Bart did not wake up.

16. Cathy and Chris first made love while lying on a smelly, stained mattress in the attic.

10 Facts About Gifts and Gift Giving

1. Before he died, Cathy's father gave her a silver music box topped by a ballerina that turned to the music.
2. The grandmother once brought Cathy a pot of yellow chrysanthemums as a gift.
3. Once, when Cathy stormed downstairs from the attic in tears after realizing she might never be a ballerina, Cory and Carrie each gave her a gift to comfort her. Cory gave her a Peter Rabbit storybook and Carrie gave her red and purple crayons.
4. Corrine once gave Chris a Polaroid camera as a gift.
5. Corrine once gave Cathy a three-piece sterling silver brush, comb, and mirror set for her birthday. Corrine called them "expensive items of vanity and pride."
6. The children's Christmas gift to the grandmother was a handmade, painted, framed collage.
7. Carrie and Cory received blue robes for Christmas; Cathy, a green velvet robe; and Chris, a red flannel robe.
8. Corrine once brought the children a huge, handcrafted dollhouse that had once belonged to her mother.
9. For Christmas, Corrine gave the children a small portable TV that her father had given to her.
10. Corrine bought gifts for her children during her honeymoon in England, France, Spain, and Italy.

5 Facts About Jewelry

1. After she and the children went bankrupt after Christopher's death, Corrine was allowed to keep only her wedding band, but she hid her engagement ring and kept that as well.
2. The grandmother was always seen wearing her diamond brooch, which held seventeen diamonds.
3. Cathy's father once gave her a garnet ring. After she outgrew the ring, she wore it around her neck on a gold chain.

4. During Chris and Cathy's clandestine visit to their mother's room, Cathy tried on 17 bracelets and 26 rings.
5. Bart Winslow wore a fraternity ring on his little finger. On his right index finger, he wore a square-shaped diamond ring.

6 Movie and TV Moments

1. Cathy and Chris once staged a scene from *Gone with the Wind* for the twins.
2. After moving back to Foxworth Hall, Corrine went to the movies with her childhood friend, Elena.
3. Chris once did a Groucho Marx impression for Cathy.
4. The twins loved to watch soap operas on their black-and-white TV.
5. The TV was constantly left on in the children's room.
6. The children looked to television commercials as a "book of rules."

The Grandmother's 22 Rules (and a Conclusion) for Chris, Cathy, Cory, and Carrie

1. Always be fully dressed.
2. Don't swear. Say grace before meals.
3. Don't open the draperies.
4. Don't speak unless spoken to.
5. Make the beds every day.
6. Study five hours a day and read the Bible daily.
7. Brush your teeth twice a day.
8. Boys and girls cannot use the bathroom together.
9. Be modest.
10. Don't play with your private parts. Don't even *think* about your private parts. In fact, don't even *look at* your private parts.
11. No dirty thoughts. [See Rule #10.]

12. Boys, don't look at the girls; girls, don't look at the boys.
13. Read aloud from the Bible every day.
14. Take a bath every day and clean the tub after.
15. Learn one Bible quote a day.
16. Don't waste food.
17. Always wear a robe.
18. Stand at attention when I enter the room.
19. Don't look at me, and don't think badly of me or your grandfather.
20. Keep quiet.
21. Don't waste toilet paper.
22. Everyone must wash their own clothes in the bathtub.

Conclusion: Don't make fun of me or ever mention your father's name.

6 Colorful Moments

1. Cathy believed that the color of hope was yellow.
2. Cathy believed that black was a losing color.
3. Cathy believed that the color of patience was gray.
4. While imprisoned, the children's Saturday clothes color was red.
5. While imprisoned, the children's Sunday clothes color was yellow.
6. While imprisoned, the children's Monday clothes color was blue.

8 Details About Dress, Wardrobe, and Clothing

1. Corrine wore a periwinkle-blue dress for her first Thanksgiving dinner at Foxworth Hall.
2. Corrine wore a green gown for her first Christmas party at Foxworth Hall.
3. The Foxworth Hall servants wore black-and-red colored uniforms for Corrine's first Foxworth Hall Christmas party.

4. Cathy wore a white nightgown with blue satin ribbons on the night Christopher went "exploring."
5. Corrine brought Cathy a pink and blue nightgown and peignoir set from Europe.
6. Corrine had four full-length fur coats while living at Foxworth Hall.
7. Corrine had three fur stoles while living at Foxworth Hall.
8. The grandmother wore a wig.

5 Facts About Pets

1. Chris always wanted an owl for a pet.
2. The pet dog in Cathy's fantasy story was named Clover.
3. The pet cat in Cathy's fantasy story was named Calico.
4. Cory's pet mouse was named Mickey.
5. Cory kept his pet mouse, Mickey, in a birdcage when the mouse wasn't climbing around on him.

—2—

PETALS ON THE WIND
(1980)

And or ever the garden's last petals were shed,
In the lips that had whispered, the eyes that had light-
ened,
   Love was dead.

  —Algernon Charles Swinburne, *A Forsaken Garden*

CHAPTER LISTING

Part One

Part Two

STORY SYNOPSIS

Petals on the Wind begins with Cathy, Chris, and Carrie on the bus after their escape from Foxworth Hall. Carrie gets sick and the children are befriended by a kindly black mute woman named Henrietta Beech. She takes them to the doctor she works for, Paul Sheffield. He invites them to stay with him; when they agree, he makes the legal arrangements permitting him to become their guardian. (Coincidentally, Corrine's second husband Bart's family lives nearby.) Cathy auditions for the Rosencoff School of Ballet and gets in; Carrie goes to a private school; and Chris attends a public high school. Dr. Paul falls in love with Cathy. Julian Marquet, Cathy's ballet instructor's son, also pursues Cathy, who is now 16. The diminutive Carrie is tormented at her school because of her size, and in a thematic nod to *Flowers in the Attic,* one day her classmates bind and gag her and leave her in *another* attic. Succumbing to passion, Cathy and Paul make love. As the months pass, Cathy develops into a magnificent ballerina, dancing as a team with Julian, and she moves to New York to study ballet. Throughout all this, Cathy continues to write nasty letters to her mother. It is now obvious that "brother" Chris is in love with Cathy. Paul and Cathy get engaged, but Cathy marries Julian instead, leaving Chris quite upset. Chris begins medical school. Julian treats Cathy like a slave and won't let her attend Chris's medical school graduation. Determined to attend, Cathy sedates him and goes anyway. Carrie goes to work for Paul. During their final performance together, Julian intentionally crushes Cathy's feet by leaping on them. Shortly after this, Julian is in a car accident and breaks his neck. Bedridden, dejected, and dead from the waist down, he commits suicide in the hospital, even though Cathy is pregnant with his son. Jory is born. Out of revenge, Cathy decides to romantically pursue Bart, Corrine's second husband. She buys a house near his and purchases a local dance school as well. Carrie commits suicide. Bart rapes Cathy. Cathy visits the grandmother, whips her, and drips hot wax on her wizened body. Cathy runs into Corrine, who denies publicly ever having had children. Livid with rage, Cathy, now pregnant with Bart's child, crashes a Christmas party given by her mother and reveals to the guests that she is really Corrine's daughter. Bart pretends her dramatic revelation is a performance, but ends up believing her. In a spectacular blaze, Foxworth Hall burns down. Bart is killed with the grandmother during the fire. Corrine is taken away in a straightjacket, but she still inherits her parents' estate. Bart Jr. is born. Cathy and Chris live together as husband and wife. Ominously, Cathy puts two twin beds in the attic of their new house. The story ends with Cathy trying to assure herself that she's not like her mother.

THE QUIZZES

1. Multiple Choice

1. What month and year did Chris, Cathy, and Carrie escape from Foxworth Hall?
    A. July 1959
    B. November 1960
    C. July 1953
    D. January 1962

2. What was Henny's job in Paul's household?
    A. Receptionist
    B. Gardener
    C. Housekeeper-Cook
    D. Chauffeur

3. What was Cathy's middle name?
    A. Leigh
    B. Corrine
    C. Christine
    D. Olivia

4. How long did the Dollanganger children live in the upstairs room in Foxworth Hall?
    A. 1 year, 10 months, 11 days
    B. 3 years, 4 months, 16 days
    C. 5 years, 5 months, 29 days
    D. 6 years, 1 month, 1 day

5. What did Henny affectionately call Cathy?
    A. "Tiny Dancer"
    B. "Dollbaby"
    C. "Sugarplum"
    D. "Fairy-Child"

6. What was the name of Paul's first wife?
    A. Julia
    B. Cindy
    C. Donna
    D. LaToya

7. What was the name of Paul's dead son?
    A. David
    B. Scotty
    C. Stephen
    D. Tyrone

8. On the day Cathy first auditioned for Madame Marisha, how many other girls and boys also auditioned?
    A. 20 girls and 3 boys
    B. 10 girls and no boys
    C. No one else auditioned
    D. 30 girls and 15 boys

9. When Cathy needed a D & C after she miscarried during her dance audition, what was the name of the gynecologist who performed the procedure?
    A. Dr. Stackler
    B. Dr. Flickinger
    C. Dr. Jarvis
    D. Dr. Zmarthie

10. How much older than Cathy was Paul?
    A. 24 years, 7 months
    B. 30 years, 1 month
    C. 17 years, 6 months
    D. 35 years, 11 months

11. What was the name of the street on which Paul Sheffield lived?
    A. Woodward Avenue
    B. Colonial Lane
    C. Bellefair Drive
    D. Elizabeth Ann Drive

12. What derogatory nickname did Julian Marquet assign to Clairmont?
    A. "Sewer City"
    B. "Hicktown"
    C. "The Sticks"
    D. "Shitsville"

13. How did Julian hurt his back when he was young?
    A. He fell off a trapeze.
    B. He was injured during a bad bungee jump.

C. He was hurt during a game of naked "Twister."

D. He tried to lift an engine.

14. To which restaurant did Paul take the children for Cathy's 16th birthday?

A. Captain Nick's Seafood Restaurant

B. The Olde New England Food & Beverage Company

C. Aniello's Italian Restaurant & Pizzeria

D. The Plantation House

15. What was the wish that Cathy made when she blew out the candles on her 16th birthday cake?

A. "Let me always succeed at what I set out to do."

B. "I hope my mother gets hit by a gasoline tanker and tastes her own blood."

C. "Please let me live long enough to give Paul the happiness he deserves."

D. "I wish John Amos would give me my Peter, Paul, and Mary album back."

16. What color did Carrie loathe?

A. Blue

B. Green

C. Yellow

D. Red

17. What university did Chris attend?

A. Yale

B. Princeton

C. Duke

D. Harvard

18. What month and year did Cathy graduate from high school?

A. June 1963

B. January 1963

C. June 1964

D. May 1965

19. What was Yolanda's drug of choice?

A. Grass

B. Cocaine

C. Alcohol

D. Mescaline

20. What did Julian teasingly call Carrie?
    A. "Sugarbuns"
    B. "Dollbaby"
    C. "Sugarplum"
    D. "Tinkerbelle"

21. Where was Julian buried?
    A. In Paris.
    B. In the Foxworth family plot.
    C. Next to his father, Georges.
    D. He wasn't buried. Instead, he was cremated and his ashes scattered over Carnegie Hall.

22. In what year and at what age did Cathy give up performing professionally?
    A. 1964; 19
    B. 1968; 23
    C. 1974; 29
    D. 1972; 27

23. What month and year was Christopher Dollanganger born?
    A. November 1942
    B. July 1939
    C. January 1941
    D. December 1942

24. What month and year was Carrie buried?
    A. July 1977
    B. August 1972
    C. January 1969
    D. March 1972

25. What expression did Cathy use frequently when she was a little girl?
    A. "Holy Crow!"
    B. "Holy Shit!"
    C. "Golly-Lolly!"
    D. "Word Up!"

2. True or False

1. Chris played "Amazing Grace" on a guitar on the bus ride during which he and his siblings first met Henny.

2. The driver of the bus on which Chris and company first met Henny was a bachelor.
3. The driver of the bus on which Chris and company first met Henny loved working Sundays.
4. Paul's in-house offices consisted of two small examining rooms and an office.
5. Carrie was dangerously anemic when Paul first examined her.
6. Paul had twelve acres of garden and ten gardeners.
7. Paul's garden had a red lacquered Japanese footbridge that arched over a small stream.
8. Paul originally told Cathy that his wife was in a coma, and had been for years.
9. Corrine attended the adoption hearing at which custody of Cathy, Chris, and Carrie was awarded to Paul Sheffield.
10. Madame Marisha taught Cathy to go on *pointe*.
11. Cathy first saw Julian Marquet perform in *Sleeping Beauty*.
12. When the children took exams for school, Cathy qualified for the 10th grade, Carrie for the third, and Chris for a college-prep school.
13. Carrie's private school was forty miles outside the city.
14. Mr. and Mrs. Parkins, and their daughter, Clara, were dolls.
15. Miss Emily Dean Dewhurst was the founder of the private school that Carrie attended.
16. Paul's smoking vice of choice was Cuban cigars.
17. Paul Sheffield liked to drink three shots of tequila with a beer chaser before he went to bed.
18. Paul made rounds at three hospitals after dinner every night.
19. Cathy's first-ever date was with her brother, Christopher.
20. Cathy told Paul she hated her mother for "a thousand and one reasons."
21. Julia Sheffield was an only child.
22. Paul took to snorting cocaine after he graduated from medical school.
23. The cake Henny baked for Cathy's 16th birthday was four layers tall.

24. Julian's gift to Cathy for her sixteenth birthday was a leather tote.
25. Paul's gift to Cathy for her sixteenth birthday was a music box.
26. Carrie's private school roommate had blonde hair and hazel eyes.
27. Carrie's private school roommate was six inches taller than Carrie.
28. Carrie's "ordeal" at school began on a Thursday in May, one week after her ninth birthday.
29. In the 1961 Christmas season, the Rosencoff Ballet Company was planning to alternate performances of *Sleeping Beauty* with a new ballet version of *Romeo and Juliet*.
30. Cathy's nickname for Julian was "Jules."
31. Chris completed college and medical school in seven years.
32. Paul Sheffield was born in September 1920.
33. Carrie was born in 1952.
34. The first words Jory speaks in the story are, "Wanna hear the music, Mommy."
35. Carrie believed she would never have children because her hips were too narrow.
36. Carrie committed suicide by shooting herself in the left eye with a Raven .25 automatic pistol.
37. Carrie saw her dead brother Cory just before she died.
38. Emma and Cathy once took Jory to see Santa Claus in Thalhimers department store in Richmond.

3. Bonus Questions

1. What "mysterious disappearance" legend was part of both Cathy and Bart Winslow's ancestry?
2. What personality traits did Jory inherit from Chris, Cory, Cathy, and Julian?
3. How many attorneys did Malcolm Foxworth have besides Bart Winslow?

4. Who Said It?

1. "I don't want to be stuck away in some man's kitchen, washing his dishes and fixing his meals and having his babies! That's not for me."
2. "You have studied the daunce?"
3. *Stop! You sicken me!"*
4. "Don't tempt me too much, Catherine—for your own good."
5. "She isn't dead yet! We'll save her! We won't let her die. We'll talk to her, tell her she has to hold on!"

A. Madame Rosencoff
B. Chris Dollanganger
C. Dr. Paul Sheffield
D. Cathy Dollanganger
E. Julian Marquet

LEAFING THROUGH . . . PETALS ON THE WIND

16 Episodes of Writing

1. Henny carried multicolored sheets of notepaper.
2. The first note Henny wrote to Cathy said, "My name Henrietta Beech. Can hear, but no talk. Little girl is very, very sick and need good doctor. Your good fortune I be on your bus, and can take you to my own doctor-son, who is very best doctor."
3. When the bus driver refused to take Carrie to a hospital, Henrietta wrote him a note that said, "Okay, man in driver's seat who hates Sundays. Keep on ignoring little sick girl, and her parents will sue big shot bus owners for two million!"
4. Paul had a sign on his house to the right of double black doors that said "For Patients Only."
5. Henny wrote Cathy a note that said, "Henny got bad eyes for seeing small things like needle eyes. You have good eyes you sew on doctor-son's missing shirt buttons—yes?"

6. After receiving a red gown (size 58) as a gift, Henny wrote, "Make good church dress, Make all friends jealous."

7. After Cathy had her D & C, Madame Marisha wrote her a note that said, "Hope you recover soon. I expect to see you next Monday, three o'clock sharp. Madame Marisha." This note told Cathy that she had been accepted into the Madame's dance school.

8. After Cathy had her D & C, Julian Marquet wrote her a note that said, "I'll be seeing you when I fly down from New York again, Catherine Doll, so don't forget me."

9. Cathy signed a letter to her mother,

> Not yours anymore,
>> The doctor doll,
>>> The ballerina doll,
>>>> The praying-to-grow-taller doll,
>>>> And the dead doll.

10. Cathy sent her mother a copy of her first "rave review" with a note that said, "It won't be long now, Mrs. Winslow. Think about that every night before you fall asleep. Remember somewhere I'm still alive, and I'm thinking of you and planning."

11. Chris wrote the following note to Cathy to accompany the locket:

> To my lady Catherine,
> I give you gold with a diamond you can barely see,
> But the gem would be castle-sized if it expressed all I feel for thee.
> I give you gold because it endures, and love like the eternal sea.
> Only your brother, Christopher.

12. Chris enclosed a note with the invitation to his medical school graduation that said:
    I am embarrassed to tell you this, but I am the top grad in a class of two hundred. Don't you dare find an excuse to keep away. You have to be there to bask in the glow of my excitement,

as I bask in the radiance of your admiration. I cannot possibly accept my M.D. if you aren't there to see. And you can tell Julian this when he tries to prevent your coming.

13. The Clairmont newspaper ran a blurb that said:

The husband and wife ballet team of Julian Marquet and Catherine Dahl, our own local celebrities, seems to have parted company. For the first time Julian Marquet will partner a ballerina other than his wife in a major television production of *Giselle*. It had been rumored about that Miss Dahl is ill, and also rumored that the ballet team are about to split.

14. After Julian's death, Cathy sent her mother a letter that said:

Dear Mrs. Winslow,

Are you still running away from me? Don't you know yet you can never run fast enough or far enough? Someday I will catch up, and we will meet again. Perhaps this time you will suffer as you made me suffer, and, hopefully, thrice the amount.

My husband has just died as the result of a car accident, just as your husband died many years ago. I am expecting his baby, but I won't do anything as desperate as you did. I will find a way to support him or her, even if I have triplets—or quadruplets!

15. Bart wrote Cathy a note that said:

I love you for reasons that have no beginning and no ending. I loved you even before I knew you, so that my love is without reason or design. Tell me to go and I will. But know first, if you turn me away, I will remember all my life that love that should have been ours, and when I'm stretched out cold, I will but love you better after death.

16. As Henny lay dying, she wrote Cathy a farewell note that ended with an affirmation of her love for Cathy, and the closing, "Soon to be in heaven."

6 Sartorial Scenes

1. The first time Cathy and the children met Paul Sheffield he was wearing a pale gray suit with a white carnation in the buttonhole.
2. Carrie screamed in a department store because a salesclerk brought her baby clothes because she was so small.
3. Cathy once bought a blue velvet dress with tiny buttons down the front that made her think of her mother.
4. Cathy wore a Paris pink gown to The Plantation House restaurant for her 16th-birthday celebration.
5. Carrie's school uniform was yellow broadcloth with a white organdy pinafore.
6. For the Christmas performance of *The Nutcracker*, Cathy dressed exactly like her mother had been known to dress: green gown; musky, Oriental garden perfume; silver evening bag; and silver slippers with four-inch heels.

7 Food and Drink Facts

1. Cathy's food "stash" consisted of Oreo cookies, a loaf of bread, apples, oranges, a pound of cheddar cheese, a stick of butter, several cans of tuna fish, beans, and tomato juice. She also stashed a can opener, dishes, glasses, and silverware.
2. One of Paul's favorite dishes was a Creole jambalaya of shrimp, crabmeat, rice, green bell peppers, onions, garlic, and mushrooms. Cathy made it for Paul's 42nd birthday party.
3. The cake Cathy made for Paul's 42nd birthday party was coconut with 26 miniature green candles fitted into red roses made of icing. She used 26 instead of 42 because that was the age that he appeared to her. Across the top she wrote "Happy Birthday to Paul."
4. Henny ate what she wanted to eat, "never counting calories or cholesterol."
5. After Bart had sex with Cathy (against her will), he ordered her to prepare beef Wellington, a tossed

salad, and chocolate mousse for his dinner the following evening.

6. Instead of beef Wellington, Cathy served Bart one hot dog, a small dab of cold beans, a glass of milk, and a box of animal crackers.

7. Cathy liked a suggestive drink called A Maiden's Delight, which was freshly squeezed orange juice, a dab of lemon juice, a dash of vodka, a bit of coconut oil, and a cherry "to dive after."

2 Tidbits About Talking

1. Paul had a bit of a Southern accent.

2. Cathy's classmates thought she talked funny, "like a Yankee." They made fun of the way she said, "water, father, farther," and any word that had an *a* in it.

6 Pieces on Art and Interiors

1. Carrie and Cathy's bedroom in Paul's house had twin beds, four tall windows facing south, and two windows facing east.

2. The bedroom also had pale blue wallpaper and matching curtains. There was a blue rug, and Cathy and Carrie each had a chair with lemon-yellow cushions.

3. All the furniture in the room was antique white.

4. Paul traveled abroad every other year to search for marble statues for his garden.

5. Paul had a reproduction of Rodin's *The Kiss* in his garden.

6. Carrie and Cathy painted their cottage rooms a soft green.

9 Incidents of Gift Giving

1. Paul once gave Carrie a milk-glass vase filled with plastic violets.

2. Chris and Cathy once gave Paul a red lounging robe.

3. Chris and Cathy once gave Henny a ruby red velvet gown.

4. When Carrie was preparing to leave for private school, Paul gave her a set of red leather luggage that had a cosmetic case in it containing a gold comb, brush, and mirror, and plastic jars and bottles. He also gave her a leather stationery case.

5. Paul gave Scotty a sailboat to go with the sailor suit he was wearing for his third birthday party.

6. For his 42nd birthday, Cathy embroidered Paul "a crewel painting of his gingerbread white house with trees showing above the roof and a part of the brick wall to the sides with a little of the flowers showing."

7. Paul gave Chris a set of medical reference volumes for his graduation.

8. Cathy gave Chris a replica of a John Cuff Side Pillar Microscope and a leather-bound book titled *Antique Microscopes, 1675–1840.*

9. Bart gave Jory a toy poodle.

21 Sex Scenes

1. Paul's garden had statues of nude men and women.

2. Chris loved Cathy in white nightgowns with blue ribbons.

3. After everyone saw *The Nutcracker,* Cathy let Chris get in bed with her, French kiss her, unbutton her nightgown, and kiss her breasts. He then carried her to his room and undressed her; when he began to make love to her, she pushed him off and they both fell to the floor naked.

4. Beneath the turquoise peignoir that Paul gave her, Cathy wore an aqua nightgown. She ripped open the peignoir to show him the nightgown, all the while accusing him of undressing her with his eyes and taking her to bed with his eyes. She told him the nightgown he bought her was not for a

15-year-old, but rather the type of nightgown a bride would wear to bed on her wedding night.

5. The night Cathy accused Paul of wanting her, she ended up on his lap, her nightgown open while he played with her nipples. He fought temptation, however, and closed her gown (but not before her nipples were hard and he had asked her, "Would you undress for me, Catherine?")

6. At one point Cathy offered to let Paul use her whenever he needed her. He turned her down.

7. When Madame Zolta first met Julian, she put his hand on his crotch to feel the size of "what was underneath."

8. Cathy had two roommates in New York. One was Yolanda Lange, who was an exhibitionist. Cathy remembered that "her breasts, when I saw them, were small hard lumps, all large dark nipples, but she wasn't ashamed of their size." Yolanda liked to walk around naked.

9. When Cathy rebuffed Julian's sexual attempts during their first ride in his Cadillac, he called her a "cockteaser." He then abandoned her in Brooklyn.

10. Carrie was proud that by the age of 15 she was wearing a real bra instead of a training bra.

11. When Julian insisted that Cathy was not to attend Chris's graduation, she told him, "I'm your wife, not your slave." He then unhooked her bra while nibbling on her neck.

12. Julian liked Cathy in black nightgowns and lingerie. She hated black underwear; it reminded her of hookers.

13. The night Julian was injured in a car accident, Cathy dreamed that Bart entered her with his "powerful male shaft."

14. Cathy had a plan to steal Bart, her mother's husband: "I was no longer a sweet, innocent virgin— two men had taught me well. I would have the knowledge to hold my own when it came time to steal my mother's husband away from her."

15. When Carrie and Alex went by an X-rated theater, Alex told Carrie that anybody who had sex was evil and perverted.

16. Carrie revealed to Cathy that she and Julian had

had some kind of sex and that she had liked it. It was probably oral sex.

17. Bart Winslow seems to have had a foot fetish. When Cathy reestablished contact with Bart in Greenglenna, he stared at her tight sweater and skirt and "what he could see of [her] foot." Also, after Bart and Cathy made love, Cathy took a bath. Cathy tells us that "Julian had never kissed my feet that smelled of roses from a long perfumed bath before I put on old work clothes. Toe by toe Bart mouthed before he started working upward."

18. When Cathy had Bart over for dinner she didn't wear a bra and she leaned over in front of him so he could see down her dress. She also wore a slit skirt that she allowed to fall open, baring her thigh.

19. When Bart kissed Cathy gently, she thought to herself, "What woman wanted to be eaten alive, choked by a thrusting tongue. I wanted to be played like a violin, strummed pianissimo, in largo timing, fingered into legato, and let it grow into crescendo."

20. When Cathy sits up naked in bed with Bart and pulls on bikini panties, Bart tells her she has a lovely behind. When she asks what about her front, he tells her it isn't bad.

21. The night of *The Nutcracker* performance, Corrine wore bright red lamé. It was cut so low in back that "a hint of her buttock cleavage could be seen."

3 Money and Shopping Moments

1. Cathy wrote her mother seven blackmail letters demanding $1 million.

2. Cathy sent Bart a check for $200 when he refused to tell her how much his fee was.

3. Paul bought Cathy her first pair of high-heeled pumps, her first nylons, her first bra, and her first cosmetics.

8 Utterances of Wisdom (and 1 Philosophy of Dubious Merit)

1. Paul once told Cathy: "[N]ever breathe on a magnolia blossom, or touch one; if you do it will wither and die."
2. Paul believed that "if there's one chance we poor humans have of reaching godliness, it's in learning to forgive and forget."
3. In a very "Scarlett O'Hara-like" line of thinking, Cathy mused that "soft, passive femininity was greatly stressed in the South. Soft, whispering clothes, drifting chiffon, dulcet voices, shy, downcast eyes, weak, fluttery hands to express helplessness, and absolutely no opinions that would conflict with male ones—and never, never let a man know you had a brain that might be better than his." (This is the example of dubious thinking, in case you couldn't guess.)
4. According to Paul, "An aggressive, domineering woman is one of God's most fearsome creatures."
5. Madame Zolta once told Cathy, "A dancer without fire is no dancer at all."
6. The four Ds of the ballet world were Drive, Dedication, Desire, and Determination.
7. According to Cathy, "Everything concerning human beings comes in shades of gray."
8. Cathy once philosophized to Bart, "I like to ponder all things considered impossible or implausible. I want everything impossible to become possible, and everything implausible to reverse and become reality. Then when everything is explainable I want new mysteries to confront me so I always have something inexplicable to think about."
9. *Petals on the Wind* ends with these last self-contemplative words by Cathy: "But ... I am not like her! I may look like her, but inside I am honorable! I am stronger, more determined. The best in me will win out in the end. I know it will. It has to sometimes ... doesn't it?"

The Funniest Love Scene Award

Julian and Cathy's first date consisted of dinner, a movie, and a stop at a club where Cathy had a soft drink and Julian had a beer. They then made a visit to a lover's lane where Cathy let him get her hot. When it looked like it was going to go too far, she grabbed her pocketbook and began beating him on the face with it.

12 Instances of Illness, Violence and Abuse (Both Physical & Psychological)

1. A cousin of Julia had "done something" to her when she was four.
2. Sissy made the other girls in the private school pay a quarter to see "the living sister of Tom Thumb ... the world's smallest woman." She wanted Carrie to take her clothes off so they could see her tiny body.
3. Twelve girls fought in Carrie's room after Sissy attacked Lacy.
4. When Cathy replaced Yolanda in *Giselle,* Julian leaped in the air and came down hard on both her feet. He broke three toes on her left foot and her small toe on her right.
5. Julian committed suicide by cutting his IV tube so that an air bubble went to his heart.
6. Cathy whipped her grandmother Olivia with a willow switch. The grandmother then urinated in the bed.
7. Cathy also dripped hot wax onto her grandmother's head.
8. Julian threatened to bind Cathy to the bed and hide her passport if she insisted on attending Chris's graduation.
9. Cory died in the last week of October, 1960. Corrine said she threw his body in a ravine and covered him with leaves, sticks, and stones. (She actually hid the body in a hidden attic room in Foxworth Hall.)
10. Henny died of a massive stroke.

11. Paul had a heart attack trying to help Henny.
12. Paul eventually had three more major heart attacks and died.

The Funniest Line in the Story Award

At one point Cathy remarks about Paul's wife, Julia, "Coma? She's alive now, and still in the same coma?"

The "Wonder Woman" Award

According to Cathy, Carrie had the following attributes:

1. She had a beautiful face.
2. She had sensational hair.
3. She had a lovely complexion.
4. She had an adorable figure ("with everything where it should be").
5. She had a beautiful singing voice.
6. She had a brilliant mind.
7. She could type fast.
8. She could take shorthand.
9. She could keep books.
10. She could cook twice as well as Cathy.
11. She was a better housekeeper than Cathy.
12. She could sew beautifully.

11 Gems About Jewelry

1. Chris once gave Cathy a gold heart locket set with a diamond.
2. Cathy once bought Carrie a ruby ring.
3. Corrine once bought a $300 locket for an unnamed young girl.
4. Paul gave Cathy a platinum two-carat diamond engagement ring.
5. Cathy and Julian brought Carrie a ruby and amethyst bracelet from Europe.
6. Cathy and Julian brought Henny a solid gold bracelet from Europe.

7. Cathy once sent Madame Zolta an antique gold locket and in it put two pictures of herself and Julian in Romeo and Juliet costumes.
8. Bart had a silver cigarette case with his monogram in diamonds.
9. Bart had a silver lighter with diamonds.
10. Bart once sent Cathy a rose brooch made of diamonds. The card said, "Perhaps this kind of rose is more to your liking."
11. For Christmas of 1972, Bart gave Cathy a two-inch wide diamond bracelet and two dozen red roses.

—3—

IF THERE BE THORNS
(1981)

No thorns go as deep as a rose's,
  And love is more cruel than lust.

—Algernon Swinburne, *Dolores* (1866)

CHAPTER LISTING

Prologue

Part One

Part Two

Part Three

STORY SYNOPSIS

It is years later. *If There Be Thorns*, we're told by Cathy in the prologue, is her sons'—Jory's and Bart's—story. Some of the important events that take place in the story include the following: Corrine gets out of the mental institution and buys a house near Cathy and Chris's house in California. Bart is very attracted to the old woman who moves next door and she begins shaping him to her will, with the able assistance of her evil butler, John Amos. Cathy adopts Cindy, a friend's daughter, but Bart does not like her. Jory meets his future wife, Melodie. Bart begins to read his dead grandfather Malcolm's journal and to emulate his nasty, bitter ways. Cathy is injured dancing and can never dance again. Bart gets crazier and crazier. Cathy and Corrine are taken captive by John Amos, who reveals that the burned-down Foxworth Hall is bring rebuilt. Corrine's house burns, and Corrine and John Amos die. Jory decides to carry on the dance tradition of the family. The story ends with Bart crazier than ever, reading the blank pages of a book he calls Malcolm's journal. Malcolm's journal was burned in the fire, though, "[n]ot that it mattered." With Chris's love and support, Cathy plans to publish her memoirs.

THE QUIZZES

1. Multiple Choice

1. How often did the Sheffields visit Chris's "institutionalized mother"?
   A. Once a month
   B. Twice a year
   C. Once a year
   D. Once a millennium

2. When the story begins, how old is Cathy?
   A. 18
   B. 37
   C. 21
   D. 45

3. When was Carrie and Cory's birthday?
   A. July 16, 1953
   B. September 21, 1947
   C. August 15, 1977
   D. May 5, 1962

4. When the story begins, how old is Bart?
   A. 9
   B. 10
   C. 8
   D. 15

5. What was the name of Jory's girlfriend?
   A. Beverly Marsh
   B. Belle Watling
   C. Melodie Richarme
   D. Mary Wilke

6. What was the name of the Sheffields' dog?
   A. Honey
   B. Clover
   C. Prince
   D. Woody

7. What kind of door knocker did Corrine have on the front door of her California house?
   A. A ram's head
   B. A lion's head
   C. Morley's head
   D. A bear's head

8. What was Jory's middle name?
   A. Christopher
   B. Janus
   C. Amos
   D. Dominick

9. What kind of pet did Bart want his entire life?
   A. A pony
   B. A pig
   C. A ferret
   D. A hamster

10. Which of the following was the opening line of Malcolm Foxworth's journal?
   A. "This journal is not being begun with any real hopes for literary longevity, but rather, because there are certain things I must put down on paper."
   B. "I bleed, and therefore I must write."
   C. "I am beginning this journal with the most bitter day of my life: the day my beloved mother ran away and left me for another man."
   D. "And so it begins."

11. What was the name of the attorney who handled Cathy's adoption of Cindy?
   A. David Tolchin
   B. Paul Sheldon
   C. Simon Daughtry
   D. John Wilkes

12. What kind of fireplace was in the fancy parlor that had the grand piano in Corrine's house?

A. Brick.
B. There was no fireplace in that parlor.
C. Natural stone.
D. Marble.

13. How old was Cindy when Cathy first brought her home?
    A. 2 years to the day
    B. 2 years, 2 months, 5 days
    C. 3 years, 1 month, 29 days
    D. 5 years, 6 months

14. What was the name of the Sheffields' parakeet that died when Jory was seven?
    A. Buttercup
    B. Daisy
    C. Clover
    D. Sylvia

15. In which month was Bart born?
    A. September
    B. December
    C. July
    D. October

16. Which of Corrine's maids often gossiped with Emma?
    A. Sally
    B. Pam
    C. Inga
    D. Marta

17. What did Bart tell his family his (imagined) fortune was worth?
    A. $20,010,055,600.42.
    B. $100,000,000.00.
    C. "A trillion, zillion dollars."
    D. "A gillion dollars."

18. What was the name of Bart's first psychiatrist?
    A. Dr. Angelyn James
    B. Dr. April Knox
    C. Dr. Mary Oberman
    D. Dr. Dave Richards

19. Where in his bedroom did Bart hide Malcolm's journal?
    A. On the top shelf of his closet.
    B. In his dresser drawer beneath his copies of *Hustler.*
    C. Under his pillow.
    D. Under his mattress.

20. Who gave Cathy the Limoges porcelain ballerina figurine that Bart deliberately dropped and broke?
    A. Paul
    B. Henny
    C. Chris
    D. Julian

21. What were Cindy's favorite sandbox toys?
    A. A red pail and a red and yellow shovel
    B. A blue plastic Big Bird
    C. A green sailboat
    D. A yellow Teenage Mutant Ninja Turtle doll

22. What role did Cathy dance in *Coppelia*?
    A. Juliet
    B. Ingeborg
    C. Viviana
    D. Swanhilda

23. What did Malcolm do to himself the day that Violet Blue smiled at him?
    A. He painted his fingernails black.
    B. He drew a cross on his chest with red lipstick.
    C. He cut off all his hair.
    D. He whipped himself with his father's black leather belt.

24. What was the name of Bart's second psychiatrist?
    A. Dr. Michael Streeto
    B. Dr. Hermes
    C. Dr. Gary Dermer
    D. Dr. Clinton

25. How did Apple die?
    A. He was starved and then stabbed with a pitchfork.
    B. His heart stopped when someone put a bullet in it.

    C. He was drowned in a well.
    D. He was run over by a threshing machine.

26. How many pages of Malcolm's journal did John Amos assign Bart to read every day?
    A. 5 pages
    B. 10 pages
    C. 100 pages
    D. 1 page

27. What was Bart's favorite flavor of lollipop?
    A. Cherry
    B. Strawberry
    C. Lime
    D. Watermelon

28. What month was Cathy born?
    A. March
    B. April
    C. November
    D. September

29. What month was Chris born?
    A. March
    B. April
    C. November
    D. September

30. What type of material was Cathy's journal covered with?
    A. Blue leather
    B. Plaid contact paper
    C. Red cardboard
    D. Brown wrapping paper

31. Where did Bart hide while he watched Cathy confront Corrine over her attention to Bart?
    A. In closet
    B. In a dumbwaiter
    C. In the fireplace
    D. Under a table

32. What were Corrine's first words to Cathy in *If There Be Thorns*?
    A. "You lying bitch!"
    B. "Yes, Cathy, it is me, your beloved mother."

    C. "Don't go in there!"

    D. "How dare you speak of loyalty after you had the nerve to seduce my second husband!"

33. What gifts did Cathy and Chris give Bart for the Christmas following the fire?

    A. A CD player and the complete Beatles library

    B. A VCR and the movies, *The Ten Commandments* and *The Robe*

    C. A slap

    D. A Shetland pony and a St. Bernard puppy

2. True or False

1. Jory once watched Chris watch Cathy dance in the attic with a dust mop.

2. Cathy had three twin beds put in the attic of their California house.

3. Cathy hung pictures of flowers on the attic walls in their California house.

4. Jory moved into his junior year of high school with very low grades, while Bart went into fifth grade with honors.

5. Cindy was six when *If There Be Thorns* begins.

6. Corrine had two large eucalyptus trees on her grounds chopped down so she could watch the Sheffields' house.

7. Bart once pretended he was Rear Admiral Bartholomew Scott Winslow.

8. Corrine's butler was John Amos.

9. Corrine gave Bart his own toy-filled room in her mansion.

10. Cathy purchased a ballet school from a woman named Marie DuBois, but then changed the name of the school to the Catherine Dahl School of Ballet.

11. Chris talked Cathy into taking fertility pills after the birth of Bart.

12. Cindy had blonde hair and green eyes.

13. When Cathy first brought Cindy home, she was wearing pink pajamas with feet.

14. Corrine bought Bart a St. Bernard he named Apple.

15. Bart had a fish tank in his room in which he kept tropical fish.
16. Bart mixed hay into Apple's dog food because he so wanted him to be a horse.
17. Bart had been told that Paul was his father and that he had died of a coronary thrombosis.
18. John Amos used an ebony cane.
19. There was no real need for air conditioning in the area where Cathy and her family lived because the Pacific Ocean kept them cool.
20. John Amos lived in a hotel room in town.
21. Bart spent his tenth birthday at Disneyland.
22. The first time Jory ever hitched a ride was after Bart was hospitalized with a leg infection.
23. John Amos liked beer.
24. Bart called Apple his "puppy-pony."
25. Malcolm wouldn't sleep on anything but silk.
26. Malcolm willed his Bible to his church.
27. Bart felt that Corrine Foxworth was the best friend he ever had.
28. Chris forgot his keys every day.
29. Bart first heard of Alicia by reading Malcolm's journal.
30. Jory hated spaghetti.
31. Marisha used a color rinse in her hair.
32. Bart fed Corrine and Cathy their bread and water on a silver tray and in a silver pitcher.
33. The Sheffields had an intercom system in every room.
34. Corrine was buried in Greenglenna next to Bart Winslow.

3. Bonus Questions

1. What cowboy "equipment" and paraphernalia did Bart once ask for from Corrine?
2. Bart felt that in his whole life he had made only three friends. Who were they?
3. How did Cathy indicate in her manuscript that she had completed the writing of her book?
4. To whom did Corrine leave the Foxworth estate?

4. Who Said It?

1. "I despise poets, artists, musicians, dancers!"
2. "Don't you ever tell anybody ghosts talk to you, or they'll think you're crazy."
3. "Well, haven't I been telling you all along that's what I am—a bitch who cares only about herself?"
4. "Conceived in fire, born in heat."
5. "I warned you not to hold it too tight. Baby chicks are fragile and you have to handle them with care."

A. Jory
B. John Amos
C. Chris
D. Bart
E. Cathy

LEAFING THROUGH . . .
IF THERE BE THORNS

The 2 *If There Be Thorns* Chapters Narrated by Cathy

1. The Prologue
2. The Epilogue

The 18 *If There Be Thorns* Chapters Narrated by Jory

1. Jory (1)
2. Introductions (3)
3. Sugar and Spice (5)
4. Shadows (7)
5. Tales of Evil (9)
6. Wounds of War (11)
7. The Horns of Dilemma (13)
8. Gathering Darkness (15)
9. The Last Dance (17)
10. Another Grandmother (18)

11. Madame M (21)
12. The Terrible Truth (22)
13. Where's Momma? (25)
14. The Search (27)
15. Detective (29)
16. Waiting (31)
17. Redemption (33)
18. Jory (34)

The 17 *If There Be Thorns* Chapters Narrated by Bart

1. Bart (2)
2. Gone Hunting (4)
3. My Heart's Desire (6)
4. Changeling Child (8)
5. Lessons (10)
6. Homecoming (12)
7. The Snake (14)
8. Malcolm's Rage (16)
9. Honor Thy Mother (19)
10. Ever Since Eve (20)
11. The Gates of Hell (23)
12. Rage of the Righteous (24)
13. My Attic Souvenirs (26)
14. Whispering Voices (28)
15. The Last Supper (30)
16. Judgment Day (32)
17. Bart (35)

38 Weird, Disgusting, and Infuriating Things About Bart and His Beliefs

1. Bart had a big head (in the physical sense, that is).
2. Bart's nerve endings didn't reach the surface of his skin, thus he couldn't feel pain the way other people did.
3. Bart had broken fingers twice and fallen from trees three times; once he broke his right arm, another

time he broke his left arm, and the third time he only got bruises.

4. Bart didn't like Cindy because she didn't care who saw her naked or who saw her sit on the potty.

5. Bart believed that seven times of anything meant good luck.

6. Bart decided that Cindy was sinning because she showed her belly button. After all, "Sin was connected to bare skin."

7. Bart believed her could hear the music of sunset colors and that lemon trees sounded like harps.

8. Bart wished he were as huge as King Kong so he could step on things he hated. Teachers would come first, and schools second, but he would step over churches. He would wear stars as diamond rings, the moon for a cap, and use the Empire State Building to swat the sun right out of the universe.

9. Bart felt that Saturday was the best day of the week because his stepfather and mother were both home.

10. Bart hitched Apple to a pony cart and pretended he was after rustlers and that Indians were after him. Bart pretended he was Snapping Sam in this Western fantasy.

11. Bart often dreamt of being dead.

12. When Apple urinated on Cathy's roses, Bart took off his own pants and joined the dog in urinating on the flowers.

13. Bart once picked up Apple's shit and squished it between his fingers.

14. Jory remembered that Bart would quote the Bible, specifically passages from the Song of Solomon about a brother's love for his sister whose breasts were like . . .

15. One night after his return home from the hospital, Bart had the following dream:

Fell into ugliness. Dead bones everywhere. Blood gushing out in great rivers, taking pieces of human beings down into the oceans of fire. Dead. I was dead. Funeral flowers on the altar. People sent me flowers who didn't know me, telling me they were glad to see me dead. Heard the sea of fire play devil music, making me hate music and dancing even more than I had.

16. Bart wouldn't spread butter and strawberry jam on his toast because he felt that he had to worry about indigestion, like Malcolm.

17. Bart began to walk bent over like Malcolm and when admonished to straighten up, said, "Crooked days make crooked ways."

18. Bart once misquoted "Do unto others as you would have done unto you," as "Do unto others as they have done unto you."

19. Bart's philosophy was "A man isn't rich if he can name what he owns."

20. Bart once told Corrine, "I despise poets, artists, musicians, dancers!"

21. Bart would get tired and sleepy after one of his frequent "mean attacks" and go to bed without dinner.

22. Bart would get out of the sun because he thought he almost heard his brains frying.

23. Before Bart tried to drown Cindy he thought to himself, "Lo, said the Lord when he spied Eve in her nakedness, go forth from Eden and let the world hurl their stones." (This sounds like a biblical quotation but it is not.)

24. Bart pretended he was a boa constrictor from Brazil as he approached Cindy in the pool.

25. Dr. Oberman's diagnosis of Bart was that he "seems programmed for self-loathing . . . [and] he doesn't like himself. Therefore he believes anyone who does love him is a fool."

26. Bart felt that Emma's cooking "ain't fit for man nor beast to eat."

27. Bart pretended he rolled his own cigarettes.

28. Bart would light matches and hold them near his face so he could feel what it must feel like "to be purified and redeemed by fire."

29. Bart once revealed to Chris that he knew the truth about him and Cathy: "You think you are safe, don't you? You think a doctor can't be punished— but God has sent the black angel of his wrath to see that you and your sister are punished for the evil you have done!"

30. Bart once imagined that he was dumped into a trash can and was dying because he was the product of incest.
31. Bart believed that he and Jory were both bad "from living with parents who weren't supposed to be parents."
32. Bart believed that "drab women were smarter."
33. Bart thought that raisins in cereal looked like "little bugs on a creamy sea."
34. Bart once told Cathy, "I am the dark angel of the Lord, and I am here to deal out justice, for mankind has not yet discovered your sins."
35. Bart once dreamt that God let him grow so tall his head touched the sky, and that he then stepped in the ocean and made tidal waves wash up over cities. This dream took place on the night that "whores, harlots and strumpets" danced in Bart's head.
36. Bart thought he saw the ghost of Malcolm in the wine cellar where his mother and grandmother were imprisoned.
37. Chris and Jory once heard Bart mutter to himself: "Bad things happen to those who defy the laws of God. Bad people who don't go to church on Sundays, who don't take their children, who commit incestuous acts, will all go to hell and burn over the everlasting fires as demons torment their eternal souls. Bad people can be redeemed only by fire, saved from hell and the Devil and his pitchfork only by fire, fire."
38. Bart taught himself how to pick locks.

Bart's 7 Murders and Mutilations

1. When Bart was four, he squeezed a baby chick that Emma had given him and killed it.
2. Bart once squashed a caterpillar with his sneaker.
3. Bart once pulled off a spider's legs one by one and then squashed the arachnid between his fingers.
4. Bart once pretended he shot a wolf.
5. Jory found Clover dead and decaying in a hollow

    tree. There was a wire twisted around his neck. This was Bart's handiwork.

6. Animals in the local Marin County zoo were being crippled.

7. Bart told his psychiatrist that once, during a full moon, he killed and ate a woman with long golden hair.

1 Tribute to the King (Stephen King, That Is)

In *If There Be Thorns,* in an apparent nod to Stephen King's novel, *The Shining,* a Mexican gardener trims the shrubs on Corrine's grounds into the shapes of animals. The bushes on the grounds of The Overlook Hotel in *The Shining* were likewise clipped into the shape of animals, and this animal topiary is one of the most memorable images in the novel. *If There Be Thorns* was published four years after *The Shining.* By this time, the genius of what many consider King's best novel had been recognized, and it's likely that its influence had been felt even by V. C. Andrews.

The 12 Words on Bart and Jory's "One New Word Each Day" List

Jory and Bart learned the meaning of these words during the telling of *If There Be Thorns:*

1. Plaintively
2. Devious
3. Beguiled
4. Disoriented
5. Intimidating
6. Ultimately
7. Sensuous
8. Intricate
9. Ruthless
10. Appropriate
11. Sympathy
12. Fornicating

The 5 Intriguing Questions
Department

1. After Chris and Cathy's argument about adopting Cindy, Cathy asks Chris, "Chris, how can you keep on loving me when I'm such a bitch?"
2. Jory hears a zipper being pulled while eavesdropping on Chris and Cathy and wonders, "Did a woman ever pull down a man's fly zipper of her own free will—even a wife?"
3. After Cathy defends keeping Bart in his room, Chris asks her if she realizes who she sounds like. He's referring to their mother, Corrine. Cathy replies, "Well, haven't I been telling you all along that's what I am—a bitch who cares only about herself?"
4. Bart wondered why women liked *C* names: Catherine, Corrine, Carrie, and Cindy.
5. Bart also wondered why Corrine didn't have to burn in the electric chair for poisoning Cory.

Gaffe Department

On page 73 of *If There Be Thorns,* Bart's full name is given as "Bart Winslow Scott Sheffield." On pages 2 and 435 of *Petals on the Wind,* however, Bart's name is given as "Bart *Scott Winslow* Sheffield." The earlier reference must be considered authoritative.

10 Examples of the Dubious
"Wisdom" That John Amos Imparted
to Bart

1. "You remember it is the god-given duty of men to dominate women who are basically weak and stupid."
2. "Sin is what men and women do together when they close their bedroom door." Also, "Sin is what women use to make a man weak."
3. "[A paramour is] a derelict soul on its way to hell."

4. "Conceived in fire, born in heat." (This was said about Bart's birth month, which I won't divulge since the month is the answer to multiple choice question number 20.)
5. John Amos told Bart that women would be his destruction in the end.
6. "Beware of beauty in women, Bart. Beware of the woman who shows you her body without clothes."
7. John Amos told Bart that Malcolm made all his money by "being more clever than those who would stop him."
8. "Your mother made all the bad things happen. Every one of the bad things was her fault—that's the way of women, especially beautiful women. Evil through and through, tricky, sinful women, out to steal from men."
9. "Women were only timid, fearful imitations of men."
10. "[Men were] meant for . . . [h]eroic things like going off to war."

22 Incidents of Sex, Violence and All-Around General Nastiness [See also "The Marin County Maelstrom," Parts 1 and 2]

1. In Malcolm's journal, Bart read of Malcolm being ordered to strip naked and then being whipped after getting caught smoking.
2. Malcolm wrote in his journal that he found great pleasure in making beautiful women do obscene things and then beating them until welts rose on their skin.
3. Jory discovered that someone (whom we learn later was John Amos) had placed a dish of dog food just out of Apple's reach.
4. Bart once violently knocked Cindy off Cathy's lap.
5. Bart cut off all of Cindy's hair with a pearl-handled knife.
6. Cathy tore some ligaments during her dancing fall and had to stay in a wheelchair.
7. Corrine scarred her own face so that she would no longer look like Cathy.

8. In order to punish herself for what she did to her children, Corrine would only sit in hard wooden chairs; she would wear nothing but "the same black rags;" and she kept mirrors on the wall so she could see how old and ugly she had become.

9. Alicia once slapped Malcolm's face when he tried to kiss her.

10. John Amos often went into San Francisco to visit hookers.

11. Bart read in Malcolm's journal of the time Malcolm watched Alicia swim naked.

12. Bart secretly watched Chris completely undress Cathy (she was wearing a white tutu) in the kitchen and then carry her off to their bedroom.

13. Bart told Cathy that his new knife (supposedly given to him by Corrine but actually given to him by John Amos) was "good for cutting off legs, arms, hair . . ."

14. Bart once threw a whole glass of milk at Cathy's face.

15. Bart once tried to stab Cindy with John Amos's knife.

16. John Amos told Bart to threaten to cut out Cindy's tongue if she told about the violence in Corrine's mansion.

17. Corrine revealed to Cathy that John Amos lusted after her when she was ten.

18. John Amos spit into the teapot before he served Corrine and Cathy their "last meal." He also dropped all their stale sandwiches on the floor and then wiped them off on his pant leg.

19. John Amos planned on burning down Corrine's house with Corrine and Cathy in it by using a gasoline-soaked string as a fuse. Bart threw the string away because he didn't like the smell.

20. John Amos slammed Chris in the head with a shovel after Chris carried Cathy out of the burning house.

21. John Amos rushed back into Corrine's burning house and struggled with Corrine. He slapped her in the face repeatedly. Corrine then slammed him in the temple with a heavy Venetian glass ashtray.

22. Corrine had a fatal heart attack while on fire after trying to rescue Cathy from the burning house. (Cathy had gone back in to rescue Bart, who was trying to rescue Corrine's portrait.)

7 Notes About Music, Poetry, and Writing

1. Bart once remembered a song that went "There was somethin' about a soldier ... that is fine, fine, fine," from a movie he saw on TV about West Point.
2. Chris brought Cathy a portable typewriter, a stack of legal pads, and other writing utensils to use while she was in the hospital.
3. Chris told Cathy to write a book based on her old journals.
4. Jory made up the following rhyme about Corrine:
   There was an old woman who lived next door.
   Who wore black rags and black covered her hair.
   She was twice Mom's mother-in-law, twice hated
   and much more.
5. After Bart confronted Chris with his and Cathy's incest, Bart sang to himself,
   Momma's gone and left me.
   Left me for good this time.
   Momma's gone and left me,
   Now I don't know how to end what I've begun ...
6. At one point, Jory and Melodie dance a beautiful performance of *Romeo and Juliet*.
7. Cathy secures a literary agent who finds a publisher willing to publish her book.

7 Philosophy Lessons

1. Chris's philosophy was, "The world belongs to those who know how to speak well, and fortunes are made by those who write well."
2. Just before Bart improved from his leg infection, Jory remembered thinking, "God works in mysterious ways his wonders to perform."
3. Jory once told his mother, "[G]reat novels aren't written in a few weeks."
4. Regarding her philosophy on writing, Cathy once told Chris that "writing absorbed her every wakeful moment, and new ideas woke her up at night."
5. Marisha believed that dancers had "sky-high

egos," and that if Cathy got one rejection for her book-in-progress, she'd "come crashing down."

6. Chris once told Jory, "Be careful whom you love first, for that is the girl you will never forget."

7. Jory eventually decided, "Between the choice of love or money I'll take love. But first comes dancing." (He had decided to carry on the family tradition, which, of course, was dancing.)

11 Items of Clothing and Jewelry

1. Cathy once embroidered pink rabbits on a white blouse for Cindy.

2. Corrine wore rubies, emeralds, and diamonds on her fingers.

3. Bart once watched Cindy swim in her plastic pool. She wore a red-and-white striped bathing suit with red straps.

4. Cathy was wearing a skimpy blue bikini when she came out after the "drown Cindy/Bart and Jory fight" scene.

5. Chris wore a pale gray suit when he first visited Corrine and Bart spied on the two of them.

6. Corrine never let John Amos see her wearing anything but a black robe and a veil.

7. Upon her arrival in California, Marisha wore an old black dress and a ratty old leopard-skin bolero "that had seen better days."

8. Marisha wore black all the time because it made her feel glad and it made her feel different. It also saved money.

9. Cathy's "at-home" footwear of preference was satin mules.

10. Corrine deceitfully told Cathy that she got her rings at a pawn shop.

11. Cathy recognized the diamond and emerald ring Corrine was wearing as the same one that she threw into the snow after Foxworth Hall burned down. (Chris picked it up later because it belonged to his mother.)

The "Uh-Oh" Department

[Any of the six "uh-ohs" in this list will have more meaning if you're familiar with V. C. Andrews's entire "Dollanganger family" saga, which consists of *Flowers in the Attic, Petals on the Wind, If There Be Thorns, Seeds of Yesterday,* and *Garden of Shadows.*]

1. After Bart tried to drown Cindy, Cathy sent him up into the attic: "You go up into the attic and stay there, Bart Sheffield, until I come up and see what has to be done to set you straight!"
2. Bart's first thought upon being exiled to the attic was, "Scary in the attic."
3. Cathy's reaction to Bart's hostility was, "A few weeks in the attic might teach him a thing or two about obedience."
4. Chris made Cathy use a yellow tablecloth at least once a week so that she would learn how to forgive and forget.
5. At one point Bart thought to himself, "Stupid daughter, hiding her four children on the second floor and thinking I wouldn't find out sooner or later. Fool. She should have known John would tell me everything." These are actually Malcolm's thoughts: Bart has assumed the old man's identity.
6. Cathy ended her "story" with "I want to write that I can only be grateful that from all the thorny stems the attic flowers managed to grow and produced at least a few roses, real roses, the kind that blossom in the sun. I'd like to conclude with that. But I can't."

The V. C. Connection

This list notes the two instances in *If There Be Thorns* where V. C. Andrews implies that Cathy Dollanganger is a doppelganger for V. C. Andrews, and that *Flowers in the Attic* was actually written by Cathy.

1. One of the chapters in Cathy's autobiographical book was titled, "The Road to Riches." Chapter 3 of *Flowers in the Attic* is "The Road to Riches."

2. Another one of the chapters in Cathy's book was titled, "The Attic." Chapter 4 of *Flowers in the Attic* is "The Attic."

6 Examples of Madame Marisha's Wisdom

1. "Nobody ever does anything for anyone else unless it gives them even more."
2. "Life is cruel, Jory, very cruel. You snatch from life what you can while you are young, for if you wait for better times to come tomorrow, you wait in vain."
3. "Being a good listener is the perfect way to avoid answering questions you'd rather ignore."
4. "The young are like that; they think the old are so senile they can't put two and two together. They think the old can live to be seventy and still not know more than they do at seventeen. They think they have a monopoly on experience, because they see us not doing very much, while every moment of their lives are full, forgetting we too were young once. And we have turned all our mirrors into windows . . . and they are still behind the mirrors looking only at themselves."
5. "Life is always like that—twenty minutes of misery for every two seconds of joy."
6. "If there were no shadows, how could we see the sunlight?"

The Marin County Maelstrom

This list offers a blow-by-blow account of Cathy, Corrine, and John Amos's violent, on-the-floor fight in Corrine's mansion.

1. Cathy butts her skull against John Amos's false teeth and breaks them.
2. Cathy knees John Amos in the groin.
3. Cathy slaps Corrine across the cheek and tackles her.
4. Corrine's chair tips over and she and Cathy fall to

the floor, rolling over and over, after which Cathy ends up sitting on top of Corrine.

5. Cathy pulls off all of Corrine's rings and throws them into the fire.
6. John Amos comes after Cathy with a fireplace poker.
7. Cathy dodges him and kicks him in the butt, and he falls flat on his face.
8. Cathy pulls burning ashes onto Corrine's rug.
9. John Amos whacks Cathy in the head with the fireplace poker.
10. John Amos then whacks Corrine in the head with the same poker.

The Marin County Maelstrom, Round 2

After Corrine insists that Cathy forgive her and come back to her, Cathy screams and lunges at her, and during their fight, knocks over a candle and sets the hay and old newspaper in the wine cellar on fire.

Cathy's List of Corrine's 5 Crimes

1. She poisoned Cory.
2. She "poisoned Carrie's mind so she had to kill herself."
3. She killed Bart Winslow by sending him back into the burning Foxworth Hall to save Olivia.
4. She poisoned Bart Sheffield's mind against his own mother.
5. She escaped justice by pleading insanity.

—4—

MY SWEET AUDRINA
(1982)

Let him in whose ears the low-voiced Best is killed by
the clash of the First ...

—Thomas Hardy, *In Tenebris*

CHAPTER LISTING

Part 1

Part 2

Part 3

STORY SYNOPSIS

Audrina lives with her mother and father, her mean aunt Ellsbeth, and Ellsbeth's illegitimate daughter, Vera, who pretends to be Audrina's sister. Audrina was named for her sister, who has been dead for 16 years when the story begins. The First Audrina was raped and killed by boys in the woods. Audrina is not allowed to go to school and everyone considers her to be a vessel that will eventually be filled with the First and Best Audrina's memories. Audrina does not seem to have memories of her own. To say any more about the plot line of *My Sweet Audrina* would be to reveal secrets we don't learn until the end of the book and ruin the story for those who have not yet read it. But I will say that this is a psychologically sophisticated and complex V. C. Andrews novel that has a happy ending. It is an excellent "stand-alone" tale.

THE QUIZZES

1. Multiple Choice

1. According to Momma and Ellsbeth, what did men like discussing more than any other topic?
   A. Wars
   B. Sex
   C. Sports
   D. Women

2. Woods surrounded Whitefern on three sides. What bordered the grounds on the fourth side?
   A. Myers Lake
   B. A toxic waste dump
   C. The River Lyle
   D. The Everdark Forest

3. How many framed portraits of the First and Best Audrina did Papa have on his desk?
   A. 6
   B. 3
   C. 1
   D. 9

4. How many pictures of the Second Audrina were there on Papa's desk?
   A. None
   B. 6
   C. 3
   D. 1

5. When was "teatime"?
   A. Sundays at noon
   B. Fridays at midnight
   C. Tuesdays at four
   D. Thursdays at ten

6. What color eyes did Aunt Mercy Marie have?
   A. Hazel
   B. Green
   C. Brown
   D. Blue

7. How old was the bed in Audrina's mother's room?
   A. 100 years old
   B. 6 weeks old
   C. 500 years old
   D. 250 years old

8. What was the most favored room in Whitefern?
   A. The Greek Dining Room
   B. The Macedonian Renaissance Parlor
   C. The Roman Revival Salon
   D. The Mayan Mezzanine

9. Where did Momma hide her romance paperbacks?
    A. In a dresser drawer under her *Playgirl* maga-
       zines.
    B. In her bedroom closets.
    C. In a strongbox next to her bidet.
    D. In a shoebox under her bed.

10. What color was Damian Adare's hair?
    A. Flaxen blonde
    B. Chestnut brown
    C. Bright red
    D. Black

11. What shape was the cupola in Whitefern's attic?
    A. Octagonal
    B. Square
    C. Round
    D. Oval

12. What was Damian's nickname for Lucietta?
    A. Lucy
    B. Setty
    C. Lucky
    D. Rose

13. What did Damian call a quarter moon?
    A. A lover's moon
    B. A horned moon
    C. A devil's moon
    D. A liar's moon

14. Why did Damian believe that Audrina would make a
    good lawyer?
    A. Because she was habitually tardy.
    B. Because she signed her name with an elaborate
       flourish.
    C. Because she never gave him a straight answer.
    D. Because she loved his gold pocketwatch and
       vest chain.

15. Who wrote the line, "to sleep, perchance to dream"?
    A. Goethe
    B. Hemingway
    C. Shakespeare
    D. Swinburne

16. What color was Audrina Number 1's Bible?
    A. Red
    B. Black
    C. Pale blue
    D. White

17. What was Lucietta's middle name?
    A. Hannah
    B. Lana
    C. Georgianna
    D. Alana

18. What type of sandwich did Lucietta consider to be a gustatory delight?
    A. Cucumber and lettuce on thin slices of cheese bread.
    B. Black olives and provolone on seedless rye bread.
    C. Feta cheese and lox on a bagel.
    D. Peppers and eggs on Italian bread.

19. What liquor did Ellsbeth and Lucietta spike their tea with at teatime with Aunt Mercy Marie?
    A. Scotch
    B. Bourbon
    C. Rum
    D. Tequila

20. What was the name of Aunt Mercy Marie's husband?
    A. Geraldo
    B. Jonathan
    C. Damian
    D. Horace

21. What was Arden's middle name?
    A. Nelson
    B. Damian
    C. Whitfield
    D. Edwin

22. What was Mrs. Allismore's "sex prediction" fee?
    A. $50
    B. $25
    C. $1,000
    D. $100

23. What was the date of Audrina's birthday?
    A. July 16
    B. December 25
    C. September 9
    D. October 31

24. What was the name of Damian's imagined eponymous company?
    A. Damian Adare and Associates
    B. The Damian Adare Company
    C. Adare and Daughter, Brokers
    D. D. J. Adare and Company

25. How old was Lucietta when she first danced in her own house?
    A. 16
    B. 12
    C. 18
    D. 10

26. Who broke Damian's favorite coffee mug?
    A. Aunt Ellsbeth
    B. Vera
    C. Lucietta
    D. Audrina

27. What chronic medical condition did Lucietta Adare suffer from?
    A. Diabetes
    B. Heart disease
    C. Chronic yeast infections
    D. Colitis

28. What was the weather like on the day of Lucietta's funeral?
    A. Rain
    B. Snow
    C. Sunny
    D. Cold

29. What movie star did Audrina once compare Billie to?
    A. Barbra Streisand
    B. Elizabeth Taylor
    C. Mae West
    D. Rita Hayworth

30. What month and day was Vera born?
    A. November 12
    B. September 24
    C. August 6
    D. October 13

31. What chronic medical condition did Billie Lowe suffer from?
    A. Diabetes
    B. Heart disease
    C. Infertility
    D. Pancreatitis

32. What word did Audrina use to describe Vera's unashamed and explicit two-handed (one north, one south) masturbation performance?
    A. "Hot"
    B. "Sick"
    C. "Gross"
    D. "Sexy"

33. What color was the skirt Audrina wore for her first day of school?
    A. Scarlet red
    B. Periwinkle blue
    C. Emerald green
    D. Snow white

34. In what month did Sylvia "come home"?
    A. April
    B. May
    C. June
    D. July

35. How old was Audrina when Sylvia came home?
    A. 9 years, 9 months
    B. 11 years, 8 months
    C. 12 years, 11 months
    D. 16 years

36. When did Audrina experience "the greatest passion of her life"?
    A. Upon learning that Vera was the *real* First Audrina.
    B. While watching *Gone With the Wind* for the tenth time.

    C. When making love with Vera in the high school shower.

    D. When making love with Arden in a storm on the grave of the First Audrina.

37. What type of psychiatric "treatment" (aside from counseling) did Audrina receive after being gang-raped?

    A. A frontal lobotomy

    B. Electric shock treatment

    C. Hypnosis

    D. Aversion therapy

38. Who "arranged" for the First Audrina's gang-rape?

    A. Arden

    B. Ellsbeth

    C. Vera

    D. Damian

2. True or False

1. Aunt Mercy Marie was skinny.
2. The only rooms in Whitefern wired for electricity were the kitchen and the bathrooms.
3. The velvet lounging chaise in the Roman Revival Salon in Whitefern was emerald green.
4. Audrina's mother once won a gold medal in a music competition.
5. Audrina's family visited the grave of Audrina Number 1 every Friday night after bingo.
6. Ellsbeth believed that Damian should have been a philosopher instead of a stockbroker.
7. The table in Whitefern's dining room was rectangular.
8. The only time Ellsbeth liked Vera was when she was out of sight.
9. Whitefern was located in the Bible Belt.
10. Vera once showed Audrina a bagful of dirty pictures cut from magazines.
11. Damian had had Vera's baby shoes bronzed.
12. The wallpaper in Audrina Number 1's room was faded bluish violet.

13. Lucietta owned a pearl choker and matching diamond and pearl earrings.
14. Ellsbeth's class ring held an emerald.
15. Audrina hated chicken liver pâté.
16. When discussing the great (and presumably late) Aunt Mercy Marie, Damian told Audrina that fat women were prized in many primitive societies.
17. Ingmar Johanson was the man who woke up Lucietta Whitefern sexually.
18. According to Ellsbeth, Damian was a throbbing love machine and a sexual dynamo.
19. Audrina kept a daily journal.
20. The first Audrina was an expert ironer of shirts.
21. Damian had books on black magic in his study.
22. Aunt Ellsbeth didn't like any music that wasn't by Shostakovich.
23. Audrina and family could hear ships' foghorns from Whitefern.
24. The dining room table in Whitefern's formal dining room made a terrific dancing floor.
25. Aunt Ellsbeth was a wonderful cook.
26. Billie once made Audrina a violet dress for her birthday.
27. Lucietta died giving birth to Sylvia.
28. Lamar Rensdale was a graduate of the Juilliard School of Music.
29. Vera's right leg was one inch shorter than her left.
30. Billie used to be an Olympic gymnastics champion.
31. Damian refused to allow Audrina to wear pants to school.
32. When Vera left Whitefern, she took with her every one of Audrina's good cashmere sweaters.

3. Bonus Questions

1. What is the "V. C. Andrews" meaning for the word "antediluvian"?
2. What size box of chocolates did Damian buy for *Audrina* after Vera fell in the cupola and broke her left leg?

3. How many armoires were there in Audrina Number 1's bedroom?
4. How did Audrina know that Jesus loved her?
5. How did Damian like his toast?
6. What type of flower arrangement was at the head of Lucietta's casket during the burial ceremony at the cemetery?
7. Complete the following lyric: "I come to the garden alone . . . _____ . . ."
8. What does "a sailor's sky" signify?

4. Super Bonus Questions

1. DEPARTMENT OF METAPHORS. In the war that went on in Whitefern, what, according to Audrina, were the bodies, the bullets, and the spilled blood?
2. Complete the following "color protection" rhyme that Vera taught Audrina.
   Step on black,_____
   Step on green,_____
   Step on blue,_____.
   Step on yellow,_____
   Step on red,_____
3. Complete the following two lines of Audrina's "rocking chair" rhyme.
   Just a playroom,_____,
   Only a playroom,_____
4. When do cultured people show their feelings?
5. According to Damian, who was "the captain of all our ships"?
6. "YOU LIKE TO DO *WHAT*!?" DEPARTMENT. What unique sexual interest did both Chris Dollanganger (from Book 1, *Flowers in the Attic*) and Vera have in common?

5. Trick Questions

1. How many miles away were the Adares' nearest neighbors?

2. True or False: The First and Best Audrina was found raped and dead under a golden raintree.

3. Fill in the following expletive that Ellsbeth shouted at Aunt Mercy Marie: "Go _____ yourself!"

6. Bonus Body Part Questions

1. What specific body parts was Sylvia Adare missing when she was born?

2. Which of Lucietta's body parts could be seen by one and all at the party that Damian threw when Lucietta was six months pregnant?

3. How long were Billie's stumps?

4. What color were Aunt Ellsbeth's nipples?

5. What body part of Audrina's did Vera pinch when Audrina was in her coma?

7. Bonus Gross-Out Question

What did Vera pick off the floor and hurl at Ellsbeth after she miscarried on the Oriental rug?

8. Who Said It?

1. "Damian would never have married you if he'd even suspected you weren't a virgin. He claims to be a modern man with liberal ideas, but he's a Victorian at heart."

2. "Think of Sylvia. Though she's better, she'll never speak with confidence or fluency. She'll never be normal enough to perform any difficult mental tasks—how is she going to survive if I die?"

3. "I'm an *A* name, too, if that means anything, and I think it does."

4. "What do you know about anything? You're a babe in the woods—or are you?"

5. "Billie, I've been looking at people in the city who have no legs. So I won't be shocked if you don't always wear those long skirts."

A. Damian Adare
B. Vera
C. Audrina
D. Arden Lowe
E. Aunt Ellsbeth

LEAFING THROUGH . . .
MY SWEET AUDRINA

4 of the Different Types of Clocks in Whitefern

1. Grandfather clocks that weren't synchronized.
2. Cuckoo clocks that contradicted each other.
3. A French clock that didn't work.
4. A Chinese clock that ran backward.

Whitefern's 6-Part "Alice in Wonderland" Decorating Motif

1. Art deco lamps.
2. *Objets d'art.*
3. Tiffany lamps.
4. Crystal prisms dangling from lamp shades, wall sconces, chandeliers, and gaslamps.
5. A fireplace in every room.
6. High carved ceilings with biblical or romantic scenes that relied heavily on "[b]are bosoms of impressive proportions."

Misandry 101: The Philosophy of Aunt Ellsbeth, the Radical Feminist

"Don't judge women by what you see in paintings and statues. Judge them only by what you yourself know about the women in your life. The day any man understands any woman will be the day the world comes to an end. Men are hateful, contrary creatures who say they want goddesses to put on pedestals. Once they have them up there, they rip off the halo, tear off the gown, slice off the wings so they can't fly and then kick the pedestal away so the woman falls at his feet and he can scream out as he kicks her, tramp!—or worse."

7 of Audrina's "Chameleon Hair" Colors

1. Flaxen blonde
2. Gold
3. Auburn
4. Bright red
5. Chestnut brown
6. Copper
7. White

The 2 Names Audrina's Mom Called Damian When She Was Unhappy with Him for Spending More Money on Himself Than on Her

1. A dandy
2. A fop

5 of Damian Adare's Anal-Retentive "Aging Fears" Personality Traits

1. He checked his hairbrush daily.
2. He went to the dentist every three months.
3. He flossed obsessively.
4. He was a big fan of frequent physicals.
5. He worried about his toenails.

Audrina's Philosophy About Women's Role in Society

"It had always been my belief that women were born to be loving mothers."

10 of the Terms Used to Describe "Audrina Number 1"

1. "First"
2. "Best"
3. "Good"
4. "Perfect"
5. "Never Wrong"
6. "Most Wonderful"
7. "Most Perfect"
8. "Most Beautiful"
9. "Fairest"
10. "Dead"

Audrina's 4-Point Self-Evaluation

1. I am not wanted.
2. I am not worthy.
3. I am not pretty.
4. I am not special enough.

Damian's Theory About Males

"I'm sorry to say most boys cannot be trusted."

4 Reasons Why Things Were Better When Damian Was a Boy (According to Damian)

1. People had been nicer.
2. Houses were built better.

3. Dogs were more reliable.
4. The weather was better.

Damian's Philosophy on Normalcy

"Normal? What is normal? In my opinion normal is only ordinary, mediocre. Life belongs to the rare exceptional individual who dares to be different."

2 More Examples of the Philosophy of Aunt Ellsbeth, the Radical Feminist

1. "All men are alike—selfish, cruel, demanding."
2. "Put your trust in no man, and, most especially, discard any dreams that disturb you."

Vera the Sexpot's Techniques with Men

"I know how to handle men. A kiss, a hug, a big smile and they melt."

Déjà Vu Department

After a confrontation with Audrina in the First Audrina's bedroom, Vera hisses at Audrina, "Someday I'm going to bring down this house and everyone in it." In Book 3 of the Dollanganger Saga, *If There Be Thorns,* Madame Marisha tells Cathy, "If you do not turn Jory over to me I will do what I can to bring down your house."

The 3 "Woods" Warnings Audrina Heard in Her Head

1. "Dangerous in the woods"
2. "Unsafe in the woods"
3. "Death in the woods"

Damian's Thinking About Generational Attitudes and Growing Old

"Husbands have a way of not wanting parents around. Nobody wants old people around to clutter up their lives and create more expenses."

The Only 2 Things Aunt Ellsbeth Would Watch on Television

1. Old movies
2. Soap operas

Lucietta's Philosophy About Men

"Men stay children at heart ... No matter how old they become they manage to keep some boy inside them, always wanting what they wanted then, not realizing that when they were boys, they wanted to be manly instead of boyish."

The 5 Places Men Were King of, According to Aunt Ellsbeth

1. The mountains
2. The woods
3. The home
4. The office
5. Everywhere

Audrina's "Skeleton Crew" Dream

"I somehow managed to slip into a light dream tortured by horrible visions of bony people ambling over a frail bridge into nowhere."

The 3 Types of Beauty the "First" Audrina Possessed, According to Damian

1. "Radiant"
2. "Transcendent"
3. "Ethereal"

Vera's Gleeful Description of the Embalming Process

"[Y]our mother is lying . . . on a hard, cold slab in a huge refrigerator in the hospital morgue. And tomorrow morning early they will open the drawer and pull her out, and transfer her remains to a mortuary, where men will come and draw out all of her blood. They'll sew her lips and eyelids together so they won't open during the viewing of the deceased—and they will even stuff cotton into—" At this point, Damian screamed at Vera for telling all this to Audrina.

12 Instances of Vera's Exhibitionism

1. She once masturbated in front of Audrina.
2. She once took off her bathing suit top in front of Arden.
3. She once undressed completely in front of Audrina, enjoying showing her "what she had."
4. She once sat in a chair in a bathing suit in front of Audrina and swung her leg over the arm of the chair, "exposing so much [Audrina] had to look away."
5. She wore the tightest sweaters "she could squeeze into," so that everyone could see what she had.
6. She once played with her own nipples and caressed her thighs and arms in front of Lamar Rensdale.
7. She once pretended that she had been stung by a bee on the underside of her breast as an excuse to pull down her bra top in front of Lamar.
8. She often made sure that her halter top would come untied when practicing at the piano.

9. She would make sure that her panties could be seen beneath her tennis dress.
10. She asserted that she would "go naked all the time if Papa and [Ellsbeth] didn't have a fit."
11. Once, in order to seduce Lamar, she first pulled up her sweater to show him her naked breasts, and then pulled down her skirt and panties, leaving her completely naked, except for the pulled-up sweater. Lamar capitulated. And Audrina watched.
12. She once took off the top of her bikini while sunbathing with Arden present.

Aunt Ellsbeth's 8-Point No-Holds-Barred Evaluation of Damian Adare

1. He was self-serving.
2. He lied.
3. He cheated.
4. He deceived.
5. He was devilishly clever.
6. He was likable.
7. He was completely without honor.
8. He was completely without integrity.

8 Things Damian Taught Audrina About the Stock Market

1. How to short stocks.
2. What buying long meant.
3. What wash sales were.
4. Facts about municipal bonds.
5. Facts about tax shelters.
6. Facts about percentage rates.
7. Details on hedging.
8. Information about tax loopholes.

Billie's Philosophy About People

"None of us is all good or all bad. People come in all shades of gray. No out-and-out devils, and no true angels and saints."

Sylvia's 13 Major Problems

1. She drooled.
2. She couldn't focus her eyes.
3. She couldn't make her feet move correctly.
4. She couldn't properly grasp things.
5. She would miss her mouth when she tried to eat.
6. She bumped into chairs.
7. She knocked things over.
8. She couldn't control her bladder.
9. She couldn't control her bowels.
10. She couldn't fill her sand bucket.
11. She didn't know enough to run away from the waves.
12. She would try to eat anything, including grass.
13. She threw up often.

2 Things Arden's Mother, Billie, Did 3 Times

1. She changed boyfriends three times a week when she was a teenager.
2. She married three times.

Billie's Philosophy About Men, Sex and Marriage

"A physical relationship is not everything, but it's very important as far as men are concerned. A good sex life makes the best cornerstone for a long and happy marriage."

A Brief Musical Interlude

1. Lucietta loved Rachmaninoff.
2. "I Love You Truly" was sung at Arden and Audrina's wedding.
3. When Audrina tensed up during wedding night sex with Arden, he told her, "You're like a violin with wires tuned so tight I can almost pluck your nerve endings and hear them twang."

Audrina's 11 Sex-Delaying/Arden-Aggravating Wedding Night Preparations

1. She took an hour-long bath.
2. She shampooed her hair.
3. She rolled her hair in curlers.
4. She dried her hair.
5. She creamed her face.
6. She removed her old nail polish.
7. She painted her fingernails.
8. She painted her toenails.
9. She sprayed on cologne.
10. She put on talcum powder.
11. She put on a fancy nightgown.

Damian The Sexist's "Test of a Woman"

When Damian wanted to "test a woman's endurance," he would pinch her bottom hard, and then note, label, and file her reactions. (Nice guy, eh?)

Audrina's 3-Point Categorization of Her Father, Damian

1. Insensitive
2. Conniving
3. Abusive

Billie's 3-Point Interpretation of Audrina's Father, Damian

1. Kind
2. Understanding
3. Charming

Arden's Answer to the Question, "Would you Rather Paint a Picture, Look At a Picture, or Sell a Picture?"

Paint.

Arden's Answer to the Question, "Would You Rather Read a Book, Write a Book, or Sell a Book?"

Write.

Billie's 7 Favorite Colors to Wear

1. Crimson
2. Scarlet
3. Magenta
4. Electric blue
5. Emerald green
6. Purple
7. Bright yellow

Vera's 7 Avaricious Notations on the Whitefern Wealth

1. The mirrors had gold leaf on them and were probably worth a fortune.
2. The Tiffany and Venetian lamps were solid brass and worth a fortune.
3. The house had genuine antiques everywhere.
4. There were original oil paintings everywhere.

5. There were genuine oriental and Chinese rugs throughout the house.
6. There was porcelain and blown glass bric-a-brac throughout the house.
7. Damian received lots of checks in the mail.

Arden's Existential Musings on Death and Reincarnation

"Death is all around us, from the moment we're born we're on our way to our graves." And, "No one really ever dies. We are like the leaves of the trees; we bud out in the spring of our birth and fall off in the autumn of our lives, but we do come back. Just like the leaves of spring, we do live again."

3 V. C. Andrews Characters Whose Ancestors Were Part of Virginia's Roanoke Island "Lost Colony"

1. Cathy Dollanganger (from the Dollanganger Saga)
2. Bart Winslow (from *Petals on the Wind*)
3. Audrina Adare (from *My Sweet Audrina*)

—5—

SEEDS OF YESTERDAY
(1984)

If you can look into the seeds of time,
And say which grain will grow and which will not,
Speak then to me, who neither beg nor fear
Your favours nor your hate.

—William Shakespeare, *Macbeth*, Act I, Scene iii

CHAPTER LISTING

Book One

Book Two

STORY SYNOPSIS

Seeds of Yesterday begins fifteen years after Corrine's death. Cathy and Chris move into the newly rebuilt Foxworth Hall ostensibly only until Bart takes occupancy of the mansion. Jory and Melodie are married; Bart is a lawyer. There is tremendous animosity between the adopted Cindy and Bart; in fact, they hate each other. Miraculously, Cathy and Chris's "dead" Uncle Joel appears, a short time after which Bart arrives and portentously announces that he has changed his last name to Foxworth. In the meantime, Jory's wife, Melodie, becomes pregnant, but this doesn't mean anything to Bart, who has the hots for her. In a horrible—and suspicious—accident, Jory is injured during a dance performance. The diagnosis: He'll never walk again. Readers slowly begin to get the feeling that, as a team, Bart and Joel are trouble for everyone in the house. Bart ultimately has an affair with his Melodie, his only brother's wife. Melodie gives birth to twins, Darren and Deirdre, and then leaves, abandoning Jory and the kids. A nurse named Toni is hired to care for Jory, Bart has an affair with her. Chris buys a house for himself and Cathy, and then a tragic death occurs. Finally, Bart becomes an evangelist and reconciles with Cindy, while Uncle Joel goes back to the monastery to die. Jory and Toni eventually marry and Toni becomes pregnant. Cathy goes up into the attic of their home to "find" a lost love. She sadly succeeds, and "The Dollanganger Saga is over."

THE QUIZZES

1. Multiple Choice

1. How old was Cathy when she returned to the rebuilt Foxworth Hall?
   A. 36
   B. 49
   C. 52
   D. 21

2. How old was Chris when he returned to the rebuilt Foxworth Hall?
   A. 36
   B. 49
   C. 54
   D. 21

3. What color was wealth?
   A. Green
   B. Red
   C. Black
   D. White

4. How long before Chris and company moved back into Foxworth Hall had Bart been discharged from his psychiatrist's care?
   A. 1 year
   B. 7 years
   C. 6 months
   D. 3 days

5. What did Malcolm do with Corrine's most-loved possessions if she misbehaved?
   A. He burned them in the fireplace.
   B. He gave them to the church to which he belonged.
   C. He gave them to his maid.
   D. He threw them into one of his horse's manure

and made her retrieve them with her bare hands.

6. Which of the following injuries did Joel sustain during his skiing accident?
   A. He broke a leg.
   B. He fractured his skull.
   C. He ruptured his pancreas.
   D. He lost an eye.

7. What language did the monks teach Joel during his recuperation at the monastery?
   A. French
   B. Latin
   C. Italian
   D. Esperanto

8. What was the topic of the feature story the American journalist who visited "Joel's" monastery wanted to write?
   A. "Robes & Sandals: Europe's Retro-Religious Fashion Craze"
   B. "Male Bonding: A New Definition"
   C. "Monastery Life: A Look Behind the Walls"
   D. "What It's Like to Be a Monk in Today's Modern World"

9. What room did Chris insist that Joel stay in while the old man was at Foxworth Hall?
   A. In the servants' quarters over the garage.
   B. In a suite of rooms in the northern wing.
   C. In a room on the second floor in the western wing.
   D. In a newly built basement apartment.

10. What was Trevor Majors's middle name?
    A. Nigel
    B. Derek
    C. Mainstream
    D. Stubby

11. How old was Trevor Majors when he married?
    A. 25
    B. 26
    C. 36
    D. 18

12. How long was Trevor Majors's trial period at Foxworth Hall?
    A. One month
    B. Six months
    C. Two weeks
    D. One year

13. What was the only color car Bart would ever buy?
    A. Black
    B. White
    C. Red
    D. Yellow

14. Bart subscribed to which of the following computer services?
    A. Prodigy
    B. Intel
    C. Compuserve
    D. The Source

15. What was the one thing Bart couldn't buy?
    A. Love
    B. Dignity
    C. Honor
    D. Respect

16. According to Cathy, being in love was like:
    A. "Christmas morning"
    B. "dreaming while you're wide-awake"
    C. "turning on a light in a dark room"
    D. "New Year's Eve"

17. How many bookings did Jory cancel when Melodie got pregnant?
    A. One year of bookings
    B. Twenty-nine performances
    C. Six months of bookings
    D. Three performances

18. What term did Melodie use to describe fox hunting?
    A. "Erotic"
    B. "Barbaric"
    C. "Loads of fun"
    D. "Asinine"

19. At what age do the muscles of male dancers begin to harden and become brittle?
    A. 25
    B. 30
    C. 35
    D. 40

20. What did Bart drink in the music room after watching Melodie and Jory make love?
    A. A straight scotch
    B. A shot of brandy
    C. A double shot of vodka on ice
    D. A half bottle of burgundy wine

21. What ballet did Jory and Cindy dance at Bart's birthday party?
    A. *Romeo and Juliet*
    B. *Samson and Delilah*
    C. *The Sleeping Beauty*
    D. *Coppelia*

22. What actress did Jory tell Cindy she looked like when he saw what she originally wore for Bart's birthday party?
    A. Madonna
    B. Vivien Leigh
    C. Marilyn Monroe
    D. Zasu Pitts

23. How many times had Jory danced the role of Samson before he danced it at Bart's birthday party?
    A. Once
    B. Twice
    C. Three times
    D. Ten times

24. According to Cathy, hospital food was always
    A. "seasonless sawdust or shoe leather"
    B. "cardboard crap or putrid mush"
    C. "cold, bland, and flavorless"
    D. "tasteless garbage"

25. Which of Cindy's friends wrote her a letter telling her about the summer camp near Boston that Cindy ended up attending?
    A. Barbara White

    B. Bary Boswell
    C. Belinda Carlton
    D. Bella Shawn

26. According to Cathy's psychology books, what type of personality did Jory have?
    A. "Racehorse"
    B. "Fox"
    C. "Bear"
    D. "Turtle"

27. Which of the following pieces of sporting equipment was *not* on display in Bart's sitting room?
    A. A rowing machine
    B. An electric treadmill
    C. Fishing rods
    D. Tennis rackets

28. How long was the white leather sofa in Bart's private sitting room?
    A. 12 feet
    B. 6 feet
    C. 18 feet
    D. 10 feet

29. Who was the first woman Bart ever loved?
    A. Paul's older sister, Amanda
    B. Olivia Foxworth
    C. Jory's wife, Melodie
    D. Tori Amos

30. What nocturnal habit of Chris's particularly irritated Cathy?
    A. He snored loudly.
    B. He would awaken her for sex every night at ten past three.
    C. He was able to sleep when she couldn't.
    D. He wet the bed.

31. What color was hope?
    A. Yellow
    B. Black
    C. White
    D. Red

32. How did Jory make the sails on his model clipper ship stand full and appear to be blowing in the wind?
    A. Paraffin wax
    B. Sugar stiffening
    C. Clear glue
    D. Minwax

33. According to Corrine's trust, how much could Bart spend on his own before being required to consult with Chris?
    A. $50,000 or less
    B. $5,000 or less
    C. $25,000 or less
    D. $10,000 or less

34. Where was Lance Spalding from?
    A. Connecticut
    B. South Carolina
    C. Florida
    D. Michigan

35. How many people did it take to decorate the Foxworth Hall foyer Christmas tree?
    A. 2
    B. 5
    C. 25
    D. 10

36. Where was Bart when Cathy died?
    A. On a tour around the world.
    B. At a brothel in Charlottesville.
    C. At a gay bar in London.
    D. At a lecture on tort law in Gstaad.

2. True or False

1. Corrine's original will stated that Bart would not come into possession of his estate until he was 25.
2. Before Cathy and Chris returned to Foxworth Hall, the rebuilt house had stood empty for one year.
3. Bart was valedictorian of his class when he graduated from Yale Law School.
4. Chris and Cathy had traveled to Asia, Egypt, and India.

5. Mel and Joel never called Malcolm "Daddy."

6. Joel got to France by working as a deckhand on a freight steamer.

7. Once Joel was in France, he earned a few francs a week working as a male prostitute.

8. Joel was able to speak fluent Italian when he had his skiing accident.

9. Personal touching was something most Foxworths avoided.

10. The first morning after their arrival at the rebuilt Foxworth Hall, Chris and Cathy descended the left staircase of the house's dual staircase from their upstairs rooms.

11. Cathy believed that only fat men should be chefs.

12. Trevor Majors was 59 years old when he was hired to work at the rebuilt Foxworth Hall.

13. Trevor Majors was a widower when he applied for the job at Foxworth Hall.

14. Bart was five feet, three inches tall.

15. One of Chris's hobbies was water coloring.

16. Cathy did her ballet exercises every day of her life.

17. Bart was enraptured by the "Mona Lisa."

18. Bart once visited Washington to watch gold being minted into coins.

19. There was a racquetball court on the grounds of the rebuilt Foxworth Hall.

20. There was an old-fashioned cast-iron tub in Jory and Melodie's bathroom at Foxworth Hall.

21. Jory used a chair for a *barre* when he first practiced his dance routines at the rebuilt Foxworth Hall.

22. Jory cleared the floor by 12 feet during his *jetés*.

23. One of Cathy's favorite rooms in the new Foxworth Hall was the music room.

24. Cindy had braces on her teeth when she was 14.

25. Heat is best for an inflamed knee.

26. Cindy dressed like a hooker for Bart's birthday party.

27. There was a huge ice sculpture of Bart on the middle table at his birthday party.

28. Jory broke his neck in his *Samson and Delilah* "accident."

29. Jory was wearing a blue silk pajama top the first

time Melodie visited him after his dancing accident.

30. Melodie brought Jory orchids the first time she visited him after his dancing accident.
31. After Jory's accident, Cathy and Chris had an elevator installed in Foxworth Hall.
32. After his return home from the hospital, Bart gave Jory a kit to build a clipper ship.
33. The color scheme of Bart's private rooms was black and white with red accents.
34. Bart had a microwave oven in his private sitting room.
35. Cathy believed that the only men who should wear beards were those with weak chins.
36. Bart had a red Jaguar.
37. Bart was a tenor.
38. Joel's Bible was covered in red leather.
39. Cindy was born in January.
40. Christopher "Doll" Sheffield was buried in the Foxworth family plot.
41. Bart eventually became a world-renowned evangelist.
42. Cindy eventually became a movie star.

3. Bonus Questions

1. How many children did the Millersons have?
2. What color panties was Cindy wearing when she first returned to Foxworth Hall and how do we know this?
3. How much money did Bart receive from Corrine's estate when he turned 25?
4. What was the name of the place where Melodie and Jory used to rent a cottage and where they heard the loons?

4. Super Bonus Question

Why didn't Chris give Cathy twenty-four karat love?

5. Who Said It?

1. "It takes all kinds to make the world go round, and the Lord giveth before he taketh away."
2. "Sport? I don't call a pack of hungry hounds chasing a cute little harmless fox a true sport—it's barbaric, that's what!"
3. Oh. Momma, don't be so stodgy. Times have changed. Nudity is in, Momma, IN. And compared to some I could have chosen, this dress is modest, absolutely prudish."
4. "NOT UNDER MY ROOF! NO SINNING UNDER MY ROOF!"
5. "We're not in the movies, Chris!"

  A. Uncle Joel
  B. Bart Foxworth
  C. Cathy
  D. Cindy
  E. Melodie

LEAFING THROUGH . . . SEEDS OF YESTERDAY

15 Foxworth Facts

1. The rebuilt Foxworth Hall was constructed of pink bricks with black shutters. The house had four white Corinthian columns and a front portico. The double front doors were black and were topped by a stained-glass window. The doors were decorated with brass heraldic shield escutcheon plates.
2. Foxworth Hall's portico floor was made of mosaic tiles in three shades of red.
3. The three chandeliers in the rebuilt Foxworth Hall

were 15 feet across, made of crystal and gold, and had seven tiers of real candles.

4. The rebuilt Foxworth Hall had dual curving staircases.
5. All eight of the original Foxworth Hall's chimneys had survived the fire.
6. The banisters and rosewood railings in the original Foxworth Hall had burned in the fire and had to be replaced.
7. The rebuilt Foxworth Hall had at least one French table that was topped with a marble urn filled with dried flowers.
8. The foyer of the rebuilt Foxworth Hall had mirrors, French furniture, and a marble floor.
9. Corrine's "swan bed" room had a black marble sunken tub. The tub had mirrors overhead and surrounding it.
10. Bart hired artisans to recarve the swan bed headboard in Corrine's room after the original was destroyed in the fire.
11. There was a brass valet in Corrine's old "swan bed" bedroom.
12. The *original* Foxworth Hall had a balcony off Corrine's original suite of rooms. Bart had it rebuilt when he restored the house.
13. The draperies and carpet in Jory and Melodie's suite of rooms at Foxworth Hall were red and very masculine. Melodie was "unthrilled" with the decor. She had wanted white walls and blue carpet.
14. Bart wanted to build horse stables on the grounds of the Foxworth Hall estate so he could have fox hunts like Malcolm used to have.
15. There were dozens of birdhouses, birdbaths, and rock garden pools on the grounds of the rebuilt Foxworth Hall.

12 Weird, Repellent, or Unpleasant Things About Uncle Joel

1. His hands were gnarled and knotted.
2. He was wizened.

3. He walked around with his arms crossed over his chest as though he were still wearing a monk's robe.
4. He kissed Cindy's hand with his thin crooked lips and false teeth. This repulsed Cindy.
5. He had a thin, brittle voice.
6. "His smile was thin [and] pitiful."
7. He had a skinny frame.
8. He had thin, pale hair that stood up in peaks like horns.
9. He only chewed with his front teeth.
10. When he put his teeth in a cup by his bed, his mouth sunk in.
11. He rarely said anything that wasn't a *double entendre*.
12. He actually *enjoyed* preaching.

18 Scenes of Sex and Violence

1. One of the first things Cindy did upon her arrival at the rebuilt Foxworth Hall was to completely undress in front of the mirrors in her mother's bedroom. She admitted to herself that she was proud that her breasts didn't sag and that her body was still "slim and firm."
2. Bart admitted to his mother that he was surprised to enjoy sex, that his "body betrayed [his] will," and that he used women.
3. At one point Cathy and Bart both watch Jory and Melodie fondle each other. The two lovers had been dancing together and got all worked up.
4. When Cindy first returned to Foxworth Hall, "Bart's dark eyes lingered on her ripe, unfettered breasts that jiggled when she walked, their peaks jutting out clearly." He also noticed—and studied—her waist, her pelvic area, her legs, and her toes. Bart, you'll recall, was her foster brother.
5. Before Bart's birthday party, Chris put his hands inside Cathy's bodice and cupped her breasts.
6. Cindy wore nothing underneath the red dress she originally wore to Bart's birthday party. The neck-

line plunged almost to her waist and her nipples were quite obvious. She defended the dress by telling Cathy that nudity was "in."

7. When Cindy told Bart that she originally wore her "hooker" dress so she would live up to his expectations, he slapped her in the face. He then chased her upstairs and spanked her. After she changed, Bart punched her cheek hard enough to leave an indentation. She then kicked him in the shin with her high heel. He then slapped her again.

8. The reason the columns broke Jory's back when they fell was because someone (Joel? Bart?) had filled them with wet sand instead of dry sand.

9. While snooping around Bart's private rooms, Cathy clandestinely saw Bart come striding out of his bedroom stark naked. She then saw Jory's wife, Melodie, come out of the bedroom wearing a peignoir and nothing underneath. Melodie's pregnant belly could clearly be seen.

10. One night when she was six months pregnant, Melodie came home with hickeys on her neck. They were put there by her brother-in-law, Bart.

11. Chris once found Bart and Melodie seated together on a sofa in the back salon. Bart had Melodie's dress open and was kissing her breasts.

12. The first night Cindy had Lance stay at Foxworth Hall, she went to bed with him. Joel, Cathy, and Bart burst in on them and found "two totally naked bodies . . . entwined on Cindy's virgin bed!" Interestingly, even after Cathy knocked and threw open the door, Cindy and Lance kept at it. First, they were in the missionary position, and then, as the three of them stood there watching, Cindy rolled on top of Lance and "lustily" rode him, all the while "crying out four-letter word vulgarities in between her moans of ecstasy." Some scene, eh? Bart took charge, though, and pulled Cindy off Lance and threw her to the floor (Foxworth Interruptus?) and then proceeded to beat his fists into Lance's face. (Lance ended up with a broken nose, two black eyes, and several cuts and bruises). It should also be noted that as Cindy crawled around naked on the floor trying to retrieve her

clothes, ol' Uncle Joel just stood there "raking his eyes" over her. (This lecherous voyeurism on the part of Joel could also qualify, I suppose, for inclusion under the "Weird, Repellent, or Unpleasant Things About Uncle Joel" category.)

13. Cindy told Cathy that all the girls at her school started having sex at the ages of 11, 12, and 13.

14. Bart saw Cindy in a transparent nightgown when he went to check her room one night. She let him stare.

15. Bart liked to visit a whorehouse located about ten miles from Foxworth Hall.

16. Victor Wade undressed Cindy (and himself) in his car. As they began to do the wild thing on the backseat, Bart ripped open the car door and dragged Victor out by his ankles. He began pummeling Victor with his fists, bloodying his nose and giving him a black eye. Victor countered with a right hook to Bart's jaw, which he followed with a kick to Bart's groin. Bart then beat Victor into unconsciousness. Then it was Cindy's turn. Bart shook Cindy so hard that her dress fell off and she stood there naked as he whipped her about like a rag doll. He then slapped her in the face; first one cheek, then the other, over and over. Finally, he threw her over his shoulder "like a sack of grain" and took her home. What a brother, eh?

17. Bart kissed his mother's toes as she dangled her feet in the pool where he was swimming.

18. When Bart saw Cindy in knee-high gold boots, skin-tight gold leather pants, and a white-and-gold horizontally striped sweater, he noticed that her breasts "jiggled freely each time she moved" and he called her "our breathless little imitation Marilyn Monroe."

14 Examples of the Philosophies of Uncle Joel

1. "Those who expect to hear evil will not be disappointed."

2. "It takes all kinds to make the world go round and the Lord giveth before he taketh away."
3. "The Lord must have known what he was doing when he made each of us so different."
4. "The Lord scorns ostentatious displays of wealth and vanity."
5. "Whores and harlots hang out in bars."
6. "My father used to say the wicked always managed to stay young and healthy longer than those who had a place waiting for them in Heaven."
7. "The Lord sees and hears all and, in time, wreaks his own justice."
8. "Pride goeth before a fall."
9. "Bitter, bitter are the days of the Foxworths despite all their wealth."
10. "Pride is the never-failing vice of fools."
11. "Lord help those fools who deceive themselves."
12. "I . . . disapprove of people who drink, who cavort and act wild on a day meant for worship."
13. "Sinful modern life makes me realize how pure the world was when I was young. Nothing is the same as it used to be. People knew how to act decently in public then, no matter what they did behind closed doors. Now nobody cares who sees them do what. Women didn't bare their bosoms when I was a boy, nor pull up their skirts for every man who wanted them."
14. "[Y]ou have to roll in the gutter filth to know what it's like to be clean, and saved."

The 6 Things Cathy Suggested Jory Consider Doing After He Broke His Back & Couldn't Dance Anymore

1. Learn to play the piano.
2. Study art.
3. Learn to write.
4. Become a ballet instructor.
5. Become a CPA.
6. Study law.

The Thoughts of Two Women About Foxworth Hall

1. Cindy: "In a way, living in Foxworth Hall is like being caught up in some deep, dark, mysterious novel, only it's too frightening when you're actually living the story."
2. Melodie: "There's something weird about this house ... This house wants to use the people inside as a way to keep it living on forever. It's like a vampire, sucking our lifeblood from all of us. I wish it hadn't been restored."

The Gifts Melodie Brought Jory the First Time She Visited Him After His Dancing Accident

1. A best-selling novel (picked out by Cathy).
2. A traveling shaving kit that contained three sterling razors, a lathering brush, a round mirror, a silver mug, soap, cologne, and after-shave lotion.
3. A mahogany box of watercolors.

The "Time Flies" Award for the Remark That Has the Most Radically Changed Meaning and Most Bizarre Double Meaning

"Out there in the audience they think most of us are gay." This was said by ballet dancer Melodie to Cathy, but Melodie meant "happy" when she used the word "gay."

2 Examples of Chris's Philosophy

1. "Life is a gift, and perhaps death is another kind of gift."
2. "Once you learn to expect only good from people, then perhaps that's all you'll get."

10 Nasty Names Cindy Called Bart

1. "CREEP!"
2. "JERK!"
3. "CREEP!" again
4. "JERK!" again
5. "Brute"
6. "Maniac"
7. "A crazy"
8. "Creepy"
9. "Senile"
10. "Damned freaky hypocrite!"

6 Nasty Names Bart Called Cindy

1. "A smart-ass little bitch in heat"
2. "A tramp"
3. "A goddamned tramp"
4. "A red-hot number"
5. "A wanton, loose slut"
6. "Rubbish"

4 Toasts

1. Chris to Cathy: "To all our tomorrows together."
2. Jory to Cindy, Chris, and Cathy: "Hail to the joys of Christmas Eve! May my mother and father always look at one another as they do this night, with love and tenderness, with compassion and understanding. May I find that kind of love in the eyes of my wife again . . . soon."
3. Cindy to Bart: "My toast to you, brother Bart. For every ugly thing you've said to me, I give you back blessings of good will, good health, long life and much love."
4. Cindy to Bart: "I wish you joy, I wish you happiness, I wish you love. I would wish you success, but you don't need that."

The Number of Showers Bart Took
Each Day

Several.

The Number of Showers Cindy Took
Each Day

At least two.

4 Examples of the Philosophy of Bart

1. "Pride goeth before destruction."
2. "My great-uncle is the best friend I've ever had. He'd never do anything to hurt me."
3. "To have blind faith in anyone but God is idiotic."
4. "Mothers always seem to run and leave the sons to suffer."

Jory's Thoughts on God and
Religion

"I believe in God ... but I don't believe in religion. Religion is used to manipulate and punish. Used in a thousand ways for profit, for even in the church, money is still the *real* God."

The Voice of V. C. Andrews

"Women have more compassion then men. Most normal men think more of their own needs. It takes an exceptionally compassionate and understanding man to marry a woman who isn't physically normal."

Yet Another "Gone with the Wind"
Reference
[Also see Book 1]

"Down the stairs drifted Cindy in a crimson hooped-skirted gown ... [it] had a tight bodice, with a flounce of fluted ruffles to cover a little of her upper arms, displaying her shoulders to advantage and creating a magnificent frame for her creamy, swelling breasts ... The skirt was a masterpiece of ruffles, caught with white silk flowers rain-dropped with iridescent crystals. A few of these white silk blossoms were tucked in her upswept hair, duplicating something Scarlett O'Hara might have liked."

4 Songs Associated with Cindy

1. "Oh, Holy Night"
2. "Swing Low, Sweet Chariot"
3. "Joy to the World"
4. "Jingle Bells"

Bart's 8-Step Plan for Revenge After Being Stiffed for His Christmas Party

1. Borrow millions, buy out all the local banks, and then foreclose on the houses that belonged to all the people who didn't show up at the party.
2. Buy out all the local stores and close them down.
3. Fire his attorneys.
4. Hire new attorneys.
5. Fire his stockbrokers.
6. Hire new stockbrokers.
7. Fire his real estate agents.
8. Hire new real estate agents.

Déjà Vu Department

We're told in *Seeds of Yesterday* that the four *D*s of the ballet world were Drive, Dedication, Desire, and Determination. This had already been established in Book 2, *Petals on the Wind*.

11 Cruel Pranks Bart Played on Jory

1. He scraped the metal on Jory's parallel bars so that he'd get splinters.
2. He put insects in Jory's coffee, tea, and milk.
3. He filled Jory's sugar bowl with salt.
4. He filled Jory's salt cellar with sugar.
5. He put tacks in Jory's bed.
6. He put tacks on Jory's chair.
7. He put a nail in the toe of Jory's shoe.
8. He put rusty blades in Jory's razor.
9. He opened Jory's windows and removed his blankets when it was raining.
10. He took away Jory's buzzer.
11. He turned off the air filter and smashed the temperature control in Jory's aquarium and the fish all died.

11 Pictures Cathy Had on Her Dresser

1. Cory's baby picture
2. Carrie's baby picture
3. Darren's baby picture
4. Deirdre's baby picture
5. Paul Sheffield
6. Henrietta Beech
7. Julian Marquet
8. Madame Marisha
9. Chris Dollanganger (Sr.)
10. Cathy at ten and Chris at thirteen
11. Cathy in a nightgown in the attic

Cathy's Thoughts About Fate

"Fate didn't choose the unloved, the derelicts, the unneeded or unwanted. Fate was a bodiless form with a cruel hand that reached out randomly, carelessly, and seized up with ruthlessness."

"The Saddest Line in the Book"
Award

Trevor finds Cathy dead in the attic. She had been decorating the room with paper flowers, "including, too, a strange-looking orange snail and a purple worm." The note she wrote before she died begins with the saddest line in the book (if you're familiar with the previous three books): "There's a garden in the sky, waiting there for me." She had gone off to meet Chris, and thus the Dollanganger Saga ends.

—6—

HEAVEN
(1985)

Love rules the court, the camp, the grove,
And men below, and saints above;
For love is heaven, and heaven is love.

—Sir Walter Scott, *The Lady of the Lake*

Tantae molis erat Romanam condere gentem.
Why such great anger in those heavenly minds?

—Virgil, *The Aeneid*

CHAPTER LISTING

Part One
In the Willies

Part Two
Candlewick Life

Part Three
Return to Winnerrow

STORY SYNOPSIS

Heaven is the first book of the Casteel family series, which consists of *Heaven, Dark Angel, Fallen Hearts, Gates of Paradise,* and *Web of Dreams. Heaven* tells the story of Heaven Leigh Casteel, a poor mountain girl born into a wretched and seemingly inescapable existence. One night, Heaven's granny shows Heaven the grave of her birth mother, Leigh, who was called Angel; later, back at the cabin, she gives Heaven her mother's suitcase, containing her clothes and a portrait bride doll. Heaven lives with her father, Luke, his second wife, Sarah, her brothers Tom and Keith, and her sisters, Our Jane and Fanny. At school, Heaven meets Logan Stonewall, the son of the new pharmacist, and they hit it off. Heaven's sister Fanny is a slut, and will figure prominently in later books in the series. Events conspire against Heaven: Her stepmother Sarah gives birth to a stillborn baby with no sex parts; Granny dies; Luke gets syphilis and when Sarah throws him out and then runs away, Heaven quits school to take care of everyone. In a cold-hearted move that he says is for the children's own good, Luke actually *sells* (pretending, of course, that they are simply being adopted) Our Jane, Keith, Fanny, Tom, and Heaven. Luke sells Heaven to Cal and Kitty Dennison and she goes to live with them in a suburb of Atlanta. Kitty is cruel and crazy because she was once impregnated by Luke. Heaven eventually stands up to Kitty's vicious mistreatment and Kitty retaliates by burning the precious portrait bride doll that belonged to Heaven's real mother. Ultimately, Heaven and Cal have an affair, and because of a deep-seated hypochondriacal psychosis, Kitty becomes catatonic and is taken back to Winnerrow to live with her mother, where it is learned that she has breast cancer, and that she *wasn't* imagining her illness. Luke remarries, Kitty dies, and the story ends with Heaven on her way to Boston to visit her real mother's family. This is where *Dark Angel* begins.

THE QUIZZES

1. Multiple Choice

1. What was the name of the mountain range where the Casteels lived?
   A. The Millies
   B. The Billies
   C. The Willies
   D. The Sillies

2. What was the name of the "entertainment" establishment in Winnerrow where Luke liked to spend a lot of his time?
   A. Shirley's Place
   B. Toad's Place
   C. Stagedoor Johnny's
   D. The Gold Coast Room

3. How soon after Angel's death did Luke marry Sarah?
   A. Same day
   B. 1 year later
   C. 1 week later
   D. 2 months later

4. Where did the Casteels get the water they used for their infrequent baths?
   A. They had a well in their backyard.
   B. They lugged it home from a nearby river.
   C. They collected it in drainpipes and rain barrels.
   D. They bought it in five-gallon drums in town.

5. How many roosters did the Casteels have?
   A. 1
   B. 2
   C. 3
   D. 4

6. How many hens did the Casteels have?
   A. 1
   B. 20
   C. 30
   D. 5

7. What was Marianne Deale's hometown?
   A. Chicago
   B. Long Beach
   C. Baltimore
   D. Boston

8. What color was Marianne Deale's hair?
   A. Pale reddish-blonde
   B. Dark brown
   C. Jet black
   D. Pure white

9. Where did Luke and Angel honeymoon?
   A. Schenectady
   B. Atlanta
   C. Niagara Falls
   D. Paris

10. What color were Logan Stonewall's eyes?
    A. Black
    B. Hazel
    C. Brown
    D. Dark blue

11. In what prognosticative practice did Logan Stonewall's mother believe?
    A. Tarot cards

    B. The Ouija board
    C. Astrology
    D. Reading animal entrails

12. What punishment did Mr. Parkins threaten his study hall students with if they spoke?
    A. 15 hours detention
    B. A bare-bottomed spanking
    C. 3 weeks suspension
    D. 6 whacks with a ruler across the knuckles of each hand

13. What did Logan give Heaven for Christmas the first year they knew each other?
    A. A subscription to *Field and Stream* magazine
    B. A VCR
    C. An emerald and opal ring
    D. A gold bracelet set with a small sapphire

14. What did Heaven give Logan for Christmas the first year they knew each other?
    A. A red cap she had knitted
    B. A cord of firewood
    C. Nude Polaroids of herself
    D. A sweater she had crocheted

15. What did Logan give Heaven for her 14th birthday?
    A. A raincoat
    B. Nude Polaroids of himself
    C. A white sweater set
    D. A pair of Reebok sneakers

16. What was the name of Luke Casteel's favorite hound?
    A. Sniffer
    B. Snapper
    C. Tipper
    D. Bob

17. What was Logan Stonewall's middle name?
    A. Grant
    B. Ford
    C. Carter
    D. Lincoln

18. At what age did a girl in the hills have to marry or risk being an old maid for the rest of her life?
    A. 13
    B. 16
    C. 18
    D. 15

19. What did Logan once tell Heaven he wanted to become after college?
    A. A geologist
    B. A male dancer
    C. A scientist
    D. An astronaut

20. How many rifles were hung on the walls in the Casteel cabin?
    A. None
    B. 12
    C. 3
    D. 1

21. Which of the following sexually transmitted diseases did Luke Casteel contract sometime before the birth of his and Sarah's deformed child?
    A. AIDS
    B. Syphilis
    C. Gonorrhea
    D. Chlamydia

22. Grandpa's nearsightedness meant that he couldn't see much past _____ feet away.
    A. 2
    B. 6
    C. 10
    D. 3

23. What did the Casteels use for light when their kerosene ran low?
    A. The fireplace.
    B. The stove burners.
    C. They caught lightning bugs in a jar.
    D. Candles.

24. Who had taught Heaven and Tom how to distinguish deadly toadstools from edible mushrooms?

    A. Granny
    B. Sarah
    C. Logan
    D. Miss Deale

25. What was the Casteels' refrigerator during the winter?
    A. A wooden box on the porch.
    B. A steel tub filled with ice.
    C. A rain barrel filled with icy water.
    D. They didn't refrigerate anything; they ate everything before it perished.

26. How did Marianne Deale like her roast beef?
    A. Bloody
    B. Burnt
    C. Medium rare
    D. Medium

27. On the Christmas morning that Heaven and her siblings would never forget, what vegetable did Heaven cook that Luke had found in a woodsy ravine?
    A. Potatoes
    B. Mushrooms
    C. Carrots
    D. Truffles

28. What was the combined selling price of Keith and Our Jane?
    A. $1,000
    B. $2,000
    C. $500
    D. $100

29. What was Keith Casteel's middle name?
    A. Luke
    B. Ryan
    C. Mark
    D. Logan

30. What was Our Jane Casteel's middle name?
    A. Heaven
    B. Ellen
    C. Leigh
    D. Annie

31. What did Cal Dennison do for a living?
    A. He ran his own TV repair and sale shop.
    B. He made feed blades in a sewing machine factory.
    C. He was a hospital orderly.
    D. He managed an X-rated theater.

32. What was the first "quick-food" restaurant Heaven ever ate in?
    A. Wendy's
    B. McDonald's
    C. Burger King
    D. Pizza Hut

33. What kind of businesses did Kitty Dennison own and operate?
    A. A beauty salon and ceramics class
    B. A beauty salon and an Avon distributorship
    C. An Amway distributorship and a tattoo parlor
    D. A pedicure salon and ceramics class

34. What was the date of Heaven's birthday?
    A. December 25
    B. February 22
    C. July 4
    D. April 1

35. How old was Heaven when she got her first period?
    A. 12
    B. 13
    C. 10
    D. 11

36. Where did Heaven sleep her first night in the Dennison home?
    A. On the living room sofa
    B. In her own bed in her own room
    C. In the same bed as Kitty and Cal
    D. On a cot in the basement

37. What was the last thing Cal Dennison said before he fell asleep on the first night Heaven spent in the Dennison home?
    A. "Kitty, I swear you're gonna be the death of me."
    B. "Jesus Christ."

    C. "I love you, Heaven."

    D. "This is my way t'teach ya some self-control."

38. How many girls did Kitty have working for her in her beauty salon?

    A. None. She didn't trust anyone enough to allow them access to her cash register.

    B. 2

    C. 8

    D. 15

39. What was Kitty Dennison's true religion?

    A. Baptist

    B. Roman Catholic

    C. Jewish

    D. Islam

40. How many employees did Cal Dennison have?

    A. 6

    B. 7

    C. 25

    D. 110

2. True or False

1. The Casteels' outhouse was 200 yards away from their cabin.

2. Sarah Casteel was five feet tall without shoes.

3. The Casteels' cast-iron stove was nicknamed Mount Vesuvius because it was always erupting vile smoke into the air.

4. Luke Casteel was the youngest of the six Casteel boys born to Toby and Annie.

5. Our Jane's nickname for Heaven was "Hev-lee."

6. When she was living in the cabin in the Willies, Heaven had nightmares every Wednesday night.

7. Heaven was 18 years old when she first met Logan Stonewall.

8. Logan Stonewall was 18 years old when he first met Heaven Casteel.

9. Miss Deale tried to communicate the pleasures of reading Shakespeare's plays and sonnets to Heaven's class.

10. Heaven once vowed that she would not allow herself to fall in love until she was 21 years old.

11. The Stonewalls had two flushing toilets in their apartment.

12. Fanny once stripped completely naked in front of Logan by the riverbank and taunted him that if he caught her, he could have her.

13. The only place Heaven daydreamed was in school.

14. The issue number of Heaven's Tatterton Original Portrait Bride Doll was Number 32.

15. Winnerrow only had one main street from which all the others branched off.

16. Logan Stonewall wore contact lenses.

17. Fanny once pranced around in front of Logan wearing nothing but a pair of panties and a shawl draped over her shoulders which she let fall open so Logan could see her budding breasts.

18. Grandpa considered Granny's apple pie to be "t'best."

19. Grandpa did not like to bathe.

20. Heaven reread *Wuthering Heights* after Keith and Our Jane were sold.

21. Lester was an accountant.

22. Reverend Wayland Wise drove a Cadillac.

23. Fanny thanked Reverend Wise ten million times for buying her.

24. Tom Casteel's selling price was $1,000.

25. Kitty and Cal Dennison had been married 20 years when they "adopted" Heaven.

26. Kitty Dennison always wished she had been named Lisa.

27. Kitty Dennison's Candlewick living room was larger than the entire Casteel cabin.

28. The wallpaper in Kitty Dennison's master bathroom was shiny black with gold designs.

29. You couldn't buy a house in Candlewick unless you earned more than $30,000 a year.

30. Cal used pink towels and Kitty used black velvet towels.

31. Kitty Dennison claimed that she could smell the scent of the Casteel outhouse on Heaven's skin.

32. Kitty Dennison had a pink washer and dryer set.

33. Kitty Dennison never went higher than the fifth grade in school.
34. Kitty Dennison's tranquilizer/sleeping pill of choice was Valium.

3. Bonus Questions

1. What's a "hockeypot"?
2. What did Granny secretly show Heaven one night that "changed the course of [Heaven's] life"?
3. According to Heaven, where did "the best kind of milk" come from?
4. Who were Miss Deale's two best students in the Winnerrow school?
5. Complete the following lyrics:
   "Rock of Ages, _____,
   Let me hide ____ ____ ..."
6. Complete the following line from one of Reverend Wise's sermons: "Give and ye shall be delivered from _____."
7. Who was the wealthiest man in Winnerrow?
8. What was the name of the restaurant where Cal took Heaven to eat after their furniture shopping spree and movie?
9. What was Kitty Dennison's favorite morning meal?

4. Super Bonus Questions

1. What specific traits did Logan Stonewall and Tom Casteel share that compelled Heaven to be attracted to Logan?
2. What did the Casteels use for a lock on their cabin door?
3. According to Tom Casteel, girls, when describing males, frequently used a certain word in front of the word "handsome" that rendered the complimentary adjective less meaningful. What was that word?
4. What three musical instruments were played at the

"party" that followed the burial of Annie Brandy-
wine and Child Casteel?

5. What color was Buck Henry's pickup truck?
6. What was the first line of the hymn on page 147 of
the hymnbook Reverend Wise used during his services?
7. What coiffurial quality did all the girls who
worked for Kitty Dennison share?
8. What was Kitty and Cal Dennison's street address?

5. Grammatical Bonus Question

Heaven did not like the way Tom often unconsciously re-
verted to speaking like a hill person. "Hillspeak" dictated
that ____ = "your," and ____ = "you."

6. Epistolary Bonus Questions

1. Who wrote the following letter, and to whom was
it "sent"?: "Can't stay no longer with a man who
just don't care enough about anything. Going
where it's better. Good luck and good-bye./Much
as I loved ya, hate ya now."
2. Who wrote Heaven the letter that began, "You just
can't know how much I've worried about you"?
3. Who wrote Heaven the letter that began, "I hope
you don't mind my familiarity"?
4. Who wrote Heaven the letter that began, "Boy, I
sure do hope you get this letter"?
5. Who wrote Heaven the letter that began, "Sometimes a man does what he feels is necessary and
lives to find out his problems could have been
solved in better ways"?

7. Disgusting Bonus Question

What did Our Jane once do to Marianne Deale in a restaurant that resulted in Miss Deale having to visit her
friendly neighborhood dry cleaners?

8. The Abortion Question

According to Granny, enough of what type of oil could cause an abortion?

9. "Easy As It Seems?" Bonus Question

According to Luke, what should Heaven have been named instead of "Heaven."

10. Trick Question

What was the first movie Heaven ever saw?

11. Who Said It?

1. "Pa treats ya like yer invisible, so naturally ya kin't know how good it feels t'like boys and men, and if ya keep on pesterin me not t'do this an not t'do that, I'm gonna let em do *anythin* they want—an I won't give a damn if ya tell Pa."
2. "Shoes ya wear tell people what yer made of—an I'm made of t'right stuff, *steel.* Kin take t'pain, t'sufferin—*an ya kin't.*"
3. "Heaven Leigh, are you daydreaming *again?*"
4. "Ya had t'play around, when I were here all t'time, jus yearnin fer ya t'need me. I HATE YA, LUKE CASTEEL!"
5. "Tom, PLEASE! I need you!"

A. Marianne Deale
B. Fanny Casteel
C. Heaven Leigh Casteel
D. Sarah Casteel
E. Kitty Dennison

LEAFING THROUGH . . . HEAVEN

10 Unpleasant Things About the Casteel Cabin in the Willies

1. No plumbing or bathrooms.
2. No electricity.
3. The walls were made of old wood with knotholes that let in the cold and heat.
4. The cabin had never been painted.
5. The tin roof was rusted.
6. The cabin had a smoke-belching cast-iron stove.
7. The inside of the cabin had no walls, just a curtain for privacy.
8. Pigs lived under the house.
9. The yard was dirt.
10. Everyone in the cabin, including the children, had to listen to Luke and Sarah have sex because there were no walls to keep out the sounds.

4 of the Names the Casteels Were Called by the Townfolk

1. Hill scum
2. Hill filth
3. Scumbags
4. Hillbillies

How Fanny Described Her Family

"Stinking rotten poor."

8 Things Sarah Taught Heaven

1. How to diaper babies.
2. How to feed babies.
3. How to bathe babies in a washtub.
4. How to make biscuits.
5. How to melt lard for gravy.
6. How to clean windows.

7. How to scrub floors.
8. How to wash clothes with a washboard.

Tom Casteel's 2 Childhood Love Interests

1. Heaven
2. Miss Marianne Deale

Some of the Books Miss Deale Allowed Heaven and Tom to Take Home from the School Library

1. *Alice's Adventures in Wonderland*
2. *Through the Looking Glass*
3. *Moby Dick*
4. *A Tale of Two Cities*
5. 3 Jane Austen novels
6. 7 Hardy Boys books
7. A volume of Shakespeare
8. Historical novels
9. A novel about George Washington
10. Books by Victor Hugo
11. Books by Alexander Dumas.

The 3 Things Heaven Told Miss Deale She'd Like to Do with Her Father

1. "[C]hisel him into a fine museum piece."
2. "Put him in a cave with a club in his hand, and a red-haired woman at his feet."
3. "Put him in the Smithsonian."

The Ice Cream Flavors Favored by the Casteel Children

1. Tom: Vanilla
2. Heaven: Chocolate
3. Fanny: Strawberry, chocolate, and vanilla
4. Keith: Whatever Our Jane had
5. Our Jane: Couldn't make up her mind; ended up with vanilla

3 of the Things Fanny Hated About Heaven

1. Her hair
2. Her silly name
3. Her "everythin"

8 of the Vegetables the Casteels Grew in Their Backyard Garden

1. Cabbages
2. Potatoes
3. Cucumbers
4. Carrots
5. Collards
6. Turnip greens
7. Tomatoes
8. Spinach

The 3 Things That Made "Mountain Living" Very Close to "Mountain Dying"

1. Death
2. Killings
3. Secret burials

The 3 Things That Were Wrong with Sarah's Stillborn Baby

1. It had no sex parts.
2. The top of its head was missing.
3. It was "icky with running sores."

The Visiting Psychiatrist's 3 Kinds of People

A psychiatrist that visited Heaven's class told them that there were three kinds of people in the world:
1. "[T]hose who serve others."
2. "[T]hose who give to the world by producing those who serve others."
3. "[T]hose who can't be satisfied unless they achieve on their own, not by serving others but by their own merits and talents, producing, and not through their children, either."

1 Example of Miss Deale's Philosophy (As Related by Tom Casteel)

"The best often comes out of t'worst."

Fanny's Tribute to Scarlett O'Hara

"There's gonna come a day when I'm neva gonna be hongry or cold agin . . . ya wait an see!" (This seems to be V. C. Andrews's nod to the scene in Chapter 25 of *Gone with the Wind,* the scene just before the intermission in the film) during which Scarlett says, "As God is my witness, as God is my witness, the Yankees aren't going to lick me. I'm going to live through this, and when it's over, I'm never going to be hungry again. No, nor any of my folks. If I have to steal or kill—as God is my witness, I'm never going to be hungry again."

3 of the Bugs That Lived in the Casteel Cabin

1. Fleas
2. Roaches
3. Spiders

4 of the Ways Pa Described Heaven to Reverend Wise

1. A "troublemaker"
2. "[Q]uick to answer back"
3. "[S]tubborn"
4. "[H]ardheaded"

6 of the Ways Pa Described Fanny to Reverend Wise

1. "[E]asygoin"
2. "[B]eautiful"
3. "[S]weet"
4. His "dove"
5. His "doe"
6. His "lovely, lovin Fanny"

23 of Kitty Dennison's "Mind-Boggling Array" of Ceramic Animals

1. Green frogs
2. Fish
3. Blue geese
4. White and yellow ducks
5. Purple and pink polka-dotted hens
6. Brown and tan rabbits
7. Pink squirrels
8. Hot-pink pigs
9. Fat cats
10. Skinny cats

11. Slithering cats
12. Dogs sitting
13. Dogs standing
14. Dogs sleeping
15. Elephants
16. Tigers
17. Lions
18. Leopards
19. Peacocks
20. Pheasants
21. Parakeets
22. Owls
23. Carousel horses

5 of the Appellations Heaven Was Not to Use When Addressing Kitty Dennison

1. Momma
2. Mommy
3. Mom
4. Motha
5. Ma

1 Example of Granny's Wisdom

"Ya takes what ya get an makes t'most of it . . ."

2 Examples of Kitty Dennison's Attitude Toward Modesty

1. The first night Heaven spent in the Dennison home, Kitty forced Heaven to sleep in the same bed with her and Cal, and Kitty wore a black see-through nightgown to bed.
2. The first morning after Heaven's arrival at the Dennisons', Kitty burst without knocking into the bathroom Heaven was using, pulled off her own

black nightgown, and sat down naked on the toilet in front of Heaven.

Kitty's 14-Item "Do's" Chore List for Heaven

1. "Every day, after every meal, wipe up the countertops, scrub the sinks.
2. After every meal, use another sponge to wipe off the refrigerator door, and keep everything inside neat and tidy, and check the meat and vegetable compartments to see nothing is rotten, or needing to be thrown out.
3. Use the dishwasher.
4. Grind up the soft garbage in the disposal, and never forget to turn on the cold water when it's running.
5. Washed dishes are to be removed immediately, put in cupboards in exact placement. Never stack cups one inside the other.
6. Silverware is to be neatly arranged in trays for forks, knives, spoons, not tossed in the drawer in a heap.
7. Clothes have to be sorted before washing. All whites with whites. Darks with darks. My lingerie goes in a mesh bag—use gentle cycle. My *washable* clothes, use cold water, and cold water soap. Wash Cal's socks by themselves. Wash sheets, pillowcases, and towels by themselves. Your clothes wash last, by themselves.
8. Dry clothes as instructed in the dryer I showed you how to use.
9. Hang clothes in closets. Mine in mine, Cal's in his. Yours in the broom closet. Fold underwear and put in correct drawers. Fold sheets and cases like what you find in the linen closet. Keep everything neat.
10. Every day wipe up kitchen and baths with warm water containing disinfectant.
11. Once a week, scrub kitchen floor with liquid cleanser I showed you, and once a month remove buildup of wax, then reapply wax. Once a week,

scrub bathroom floors, clean grout in shower stall. Scrub out tub after every bath you take, I take, and Cal takes.

12. Every other day run the vacuum over all the carpets in the house. Move the furniture aside once a week and sweep under everything. Check under chairs and tables for spiders and webs.
13. Dust everything, every day. Pick things up.
14. First thing after Cal and me are gone, clean up the kitchen. Make the bed with clean linens, change towels in bathrooms."

Heaven Casteel's Favorite Sandwich

Ham, lettuce, and tomato.

Tom and Keith Casteel's Favorite Sandwich

Tuna fish.

Kitty Dennison's 2 Good Types of China

1. Royal Dalton [sic]
2. Lenox

2 Examples of Kitty Dennison's Philosophy About Men and Sex

1. "All men are [weak and tenderhearted]. Babies more than they're lil boys. Ya kin' tell em that, makes em mad, but that's t'truth. Scared of women, all of em are, every last man in this old mean world, terrified of mommy, of wifey, of daughta, of sista, of auntie, of granny, of lovey-dovey girlfriends. Got pride, they have. Too much of it. Feared of rejection, like we don't get it all t'time."

2. "All want one thing, an bein a hill gal, ya know what it is. All is dyin t'slam their bangers inta yer whammer, an afta they done it, if ya start a baby, they won't want it."

7 Things Kitty Dennison Was Afraid Of

1. Dim places
2. The dark
3. Worms
4. Dirt
5. Dust
6. Germs
7. Diseases

3 Books Heaven Read

1. *Jane Eyre*
2. *Wuthering Heights*
3. A biography of the Brontë sisters.

—7—

DARK ANGEL
(1986)

Lost Angel of a ruin'd Paradise!
She knew not 'twas her own; as with no stain
She faded, like a cloud which has outswept its rain.

—Percy Bysshe Shelley, *Adonais* (1821)

CHAPTER LISTING

Part One

Part Two

STORY SYNOPSIS

Dark Angel is the second Casteel novel and takes up where *Heaven* ends. *Dark Angel* begins with Heaven being taken to Farthinggale Manor, the home of her mother's parents, Tony and Jillian Tatterton, who do not know she is there to stay. While exploring the grounds, Heaven gets lost in a huge hedge maze, finds a charming and mysterious cottage, and meets Tony's brother, Troy Tatterton. Back at the house, Heaven tells Tony the truth about her hill family and he offers her a deal: complete care and an expensive education in exchange for total obedience and a final and absolute relinquishment of her past. Heaven reluctantly accepts and starts classes at the Winterhaven School, where she is made to feel like an outsider. One day, Heaven sneaks off to Boston to see Logan, who inexplicably snubs her. Heaven confides in Troy about her dismay over Logan. At Winterhaven, Heaven's malicious classmates put laxative in her punch because she won't get one of them a date with Troy. Later, Heaven meets Logan again and once again he rebuffs her. Troy shows Heaven the secret tunnel beneath the Farthinggale estate grounds. Shortly after Heaven turns eighteen, her wild sister Fanny has a daughter. Succumbing to their undeniable attraction to each other, Troy and Heaven make love and decide to marry, but Troy gets pneumonia. Because of a deep-seated need to see her siblings, Heaven unwisely goes to see Our Jane and Keith in their new "adoptive" home, but they're terrified of her and reject her. Heaven then visits her other brother Tom and their father Luke and tours the circus where they both work. Later, Heaven visits Fanny, who threatens to blackmail Heaven about her past unless Heaven buys back Fanny's daughter from the Wises. Heaven also sees Cal

Dennison in Winnerrow, who tries to rape her. Heaven's car breaks down on the way to her old cabin and Logan rescues her. Heaven becomes gravely ill and an apologetic and now-loving Logan nurses her back to health. Back at Farthy, Heaven learns the secret about Tony Tatterton and her mother, as well as the truth about who is her *real* father. In a flurry of drama, Troy leaves, Jillian has a breakdown, and Our Jane and Keith are reunited with Heaven. Heaven graduates from college and learns of Troy's tragic fate. With vengeance in mind, Heaven does something nasty that brings disaster on her brother Tom. Heaven then experiences another tragic loss and the story ends with her deciding to marry Logan Stonewall.

THE QUIZZES

1. Multiple Choice

1. How many suitcases did Heaven have with her when she first arrived in Boston?
    A. 10
    B. 2
    C. 4
    D. 1

2. What was the nickname some of Tony Tatterton's friends called him to irritate him?
    A. "Tattler"
    B. "The Townster"
    C. "Townie"
    D. "Butthead"

3. What was the one word Heaven was not allowed to use when addressing Jillian?
    A. "Granny"
    B. "Grams"
    C. "Grandmother"
    D. "Grandma"

4. According to Luke Casteel, what was the cause of Leigh Casteel's death?
    A. Cancer
    B. Suicide

C. Automobile accident
D. Murder

5. What was the name of Jillian Tatterton's first horse?
    A. Knute Lobell
    B. Scuttles
    C. Ranger
    D. Stallion

6. Who built Farthinggale Manor?
    A. Tony Tatterton's grandfather
    B. Tony Tatterton's great-grandfather
    C. Tony Tatterton's great-great-grandfather
    D. Tony Tatterton's great-great-great-grandfather

7. How old was Troy Tatterton when he graduated from college?
    A. 18
    B. 19
    C. 16
    D. 21

8. How old was Tony Tatterton when Troy Tatterton was born?
    A. 2
    B. 17
    C. 21
    D. 6

9. What was Jillian Tatterton's favorite card game?
    A. Bridge
    B. Gin rummy
    C. Pinochle
    D. Strip poker

10. How much did the new cashmere coat Heaven wore her first day at Winterhaven cost?
    A. $100
    B. $395
    C. $500
    D. $1,000

11. How much money did Tony Tatterton give to Heaven for "pin money" when he left her at Winterhaven?
    A. $1,000
    B. $200

    C. $20
    D. $100

12. What was the name of the Boston restaurant where Faith Morgantile's birthday party was held?
    A. The Brick
    B. The Red Lobster
    C. Aniello's Italian Restaurant and Pizzeria
    D. The Red Feather

13. How many guests attended Jillian's "Off to California" Party?
    A. 6
    B. 10
    C. 25
    D. 100

14. What kind of car did Troy Tatterton drive?
    A. A Bentley
    B. A Rolls-Royce
    C. A Porsche
    D. An Acura

15. Even though he was studying to be a pharmacologist, what did Logan *really* want to be?
    A. An architect
    B. A biochemist
    C. A writer
    D. A forensic pathologist

16. What did Pru Carraway want from Heaven in exchange for allowing Heaven into one of the school's cliquish "private clubs"?
    A. She wanted Heaven to arrange for one of the club members to have a date with Troy Tatterton.
    B. She wanted to watch Heaven take a shower.
    C. She wanted $1,000 in cash.
    D. She wanted Heaven to give every member of the club a manicure and pedicure.

17. How many of Heaven's sweaters did the Winterhaven girls ruin after Heaven challenged them and their authority?
    A. 1
    B. 10

    C. 5
    D. 6

18. What day did Jillian normally have her hair done?
    A. Monday
    B. Thursday
    C. Saturday
    D. Friday

19. In what city was the law firm Troy Tatterton used located?
    A. New York, New York
    B. Cleveland, Tennessee
    C. Chicago, Illinois
    D. Mission Viejo, California

20. What composer's music did Heaven hear Troy playing on the concert grand piano in Farthinggale Manor one June evening before Jillian and Tony returned from London?
    A. Chopin
    B. Debussy
    C. Bach
    D. Beethoven

21. What was the name of the British nanny who cared for Troy Tatterton when he had rheumatic fever as a child?
    A. Bunny Foo-Foo
    B. Louanne
    C. Bertie
    D. Billie

2. True or False

1. The first time Heaven ever saw Jillian Tatterton, Jillian was wearing a black fur coat.
2. Jillian's first husband was Troy Tatterton.
3. Jillian Tatterton pretended that Heaven was her daughter.
4. The scent base of Jillian Tatterton's signature perfume was jasmine.
5. Farthinggale Manor's nickname was "Fart City."

6. Jillian Tatterton was once a very famous children's book illustrator.
7. The hill folks called a valley a "holler."
8. Rye Whiskey was a skinny marink.
9. Farthinggale Manor had an indoor pool.
10. Winterhaven was a hospital before it became a school.
11. Jillian enjoyed watching movies that showed naked people making love.
12. Troy Tatterton and Heaven were eleven years apart in age.
13. The Winterhaven girls often had dances with the boys from Broadmire Hall.
14. The Winterhaven girls all wore the same dowdy flannel head-to-toe nightgowns to bed.
15. The Boar's Head Café was one of the haunts of male students at Princeton.
16. The first time Heaven ever drank brandy was in Troy Tatterton's cottage.
17. The Christmas season color scheme of the Tatterton Toy Company employees' uniforms was red, green, and white with silver embellishments.
18. Tony Tatterton taught Heaven the difference between English and Western horse riding styles.
19. Troy Tatterton taught Heaven that strawberry jam enhanced the flavor of a fried egg and bacon sandwich.
20. Troy Tatterton loved the winter.
21. Troy Tatterton once spent a winter in Naples, Italy.
22. Troy Tatterton was a Harvard graduate.
23. Troy Tatterton's birthday was September 21.
24. Rita and Lester Rawlings were Jewish.
25. Tom Casteel died in a car accident.

3. Bonus Questions

1. What was the name of Cleave VanVoreen's business?
2. What British school did Tony Tatterton attend when he was seven years old?
3. When Heaven first moved into Farthinggale

Manor, how long was the Tatterton Toy Company's production backlog for toy stone castles built to scale?

4. How many bathrooms were on the first floor of Farthinggale Manor?

5. What time was breakfast served at the Winterhaven School?

6. What time was dinner served at the Winterhaven School?

7. The second week of Heaven's attendance at Winterhaven, Pru mistakenly described one of Heaven's dresses as pink. What was the actual color of the dress?

8. Why did all the blinds in the Winterhaven dorm rooms have to be opened to the same exact height?

9. How much larger proportionately than the Casteel cabin in the Willies was Troy Tatterton's cottage?

4. Super Bonus Questions

1. What were the colors of the doors to the *sealed* tunnels under Farthinggale Manor?

2. What was Heaven's position in the line of Winterhaven graduates during the processional entrance march?

3. How old was Jesse Shackleton when he married Lettie Joyner?

4. What was Heaven's grade on her first Winterhaven social studies theme paper?

5. What was the theme of Heaven's first social studies paper at Winterhaven?

6. What kind of trees were in the urns beside Farthinggale Manor's front doors?

5. Superstition Bonus Question

What protection was afforded by turning around three times when one entered a house?

6. Trick Questions

1. What was the name of the Winterhaven building where Heaven studied English?
2. What time was lunch served at the Winterhaven School?
3. What was the amount of Heaven's cab fare back to Farthinggale Manor after her disastrous trip to Boston during which she saw Logan with another girl?

7. Prurient Interest Bonus Questions

1. Who gave Heaven the first orgasm of her life?
2. Which of Jillian's body part(s) first attracted Tony Tatterton to her?
3. How many condoms did Fanny Casteel carry in her small red plastic purse?
4. How old was Fanny Casteel when she was seduced by Reverend Wayland Wise?
5. How old was Leigh VanVoreen when she was raped by Tony Tatterton?

8. Epistolary Bonus Questions

1. To whom was Heaven's letter that began, "At last I am living with my mother's family as I always hoped to do," addressed?
2. Who wrote Heaven the letter that began, "I don't understand all your fears"?
3. Who wrote Heaven the letter that began, "You found me in the wind last night, just sitting, just trying to figure out what my life is all about"?
4. Who wrote Heaven the letter that began, "Your

selfishness forced me to marry with my rich old man, Mallory"?

9. Gluttony/Conspicuous Consumption Bonus Questions

1. How much weight did Reverend Wayland Wise gain each year?
2. What was the size of Heaven's engagement ring from Troy?
3. What did Tony Tatterton give to Jillian for her 61st birthday?
4. What did Tony Tatterton buy Heaven as a gift for her college graduation?

10. Who Said It?

1. "Please, you are wasting my time. Go away now and let me finish what I'm doing. These are private quarters, *my* quarters. Off limits to the servants of Farthinggale Manor. Now scat!"
2. "It's all right. I'm not going to do anything to disturb your lives. I just wanted to see you both again."
3. "I'll leave unsatisfied some of your desires. No one should realize every dream all at once. We live on dreams, you know, and when there are none, we soon die."
4. "There's a sign above that chute. All wet washable clothes are to be put into the smaller chute."
5. "Leigh, say hello to Cleave for me when you see him next! Tell him sometimes I am almost sorry I left him for Tony."

A. Heaven
B. Jillian Tatterton
C. Mrs. Mallory
D. Troy Tatterton
E. Tony Tatterton

LEAFING THROUGH . . .
DARK ANGEL

7 Things Heaven Remembered About Granny Brandywine Casteel

1. Her long, thin white hair
2. Her stooped shoulders
3. Her dowager's hump
4. Her arthritic fingers
5. Her arthritic legs
6. Her "pitifully few" garments
7. Her worn-out shoes

Jillian's 6-Point "Review" of Her Husband, Tony

1. Jill told Heaven that she would find Tony "ten times more interesting" than herself.
2. He never needed to nap.
3. He had "boundless" energy.
4. He had no health regimen.
5. He had no beauty regimen.
6. He dressed in a flash.

The 11 Components of a "Built to Scale" Tatterton Toy Stone Castle

1. Moats
2. Drawbridges
3. A bailiwick
4. Cook houses
5. Stables
6. Quarters for the knights and squires
7. Sheds for cattle, sheep, pigs, and chickens
8. Servants
9. Peasants
10. Lords
11. Ladies

The 9-Part Menu Troy Tatterton Planned for His First Meal with Heaven

1. 6 ham, cheese, lettuce, tomato, and butter sandwiches
2. Parsley garnish
3. Radishes made to look like roses
4. Deviled eggs
5. Wedges of cheese
6. Crackers
7. Apples
8. White wine
9. Red wine

The 6 Decisions Tony Tatterton Planned to Make for Heaven

1. He would select the high school she attended.
2. He would select the college she would attend.
3. He would select her clothes.
4. He would oversee the books she read.
5. He would oversee the movies she saw.
6. He would have final approval over the boys she dated.

Tony Tatterton's Philosophy About Honesty

"Honesty is always the best gamble when you don't know whether or not a lie will serve you better. At least you get to state your case, and if you fail, you can keep your 'integrity.'"

Tony Tatterton's 5-Point Obedience Program for Heaven

1. "[Y]ou will never tell your grandmother anything that would cause her grief."
2. "[Y]ou will not see Troy in secret."

3. "[Y]ou will never again mention your father, either by name or reference."
4. "[Y]ou will do your best to forget your background and concentrate only on improving yourself."
5. "[Y]ou will give to me the right to make all important decisions in your life."

Tony Tatterton's Philosophy About Dreams

"No one should realize every dream all at once. We live on dreams . . . and when there are none, we soon die."

The 5 Shoe Colors Tony Tatterton Determined Were Adequate for Heaven Until She Needed Summer White

1. Black
2. Brown
3. Bone
4. Blue
5. Gray-and-red

Jillian Tatterton's Philosophy About Hairstylists

"Never go to a woman stylist; men are so much more appreciative of a woman's beauty and seem to know just what to do to enhance it."

Tony Tatterton's Philosophy About Fear

"We all have dragons to slay throughout most of our lives; most of them we create in our imaginations."

7 Things Winterhaven Students Were Forbidden to Do

1. Hoard food in their rooms
2. Hold secret midnight parties
3. Own a television set
4. Possess liquor (including beer)
5. Possess "printed filth"
6. Gamble
7. Leave lights on past 10:00 P.M.

The 4 Reasons Why Heaven Considered Herself Socially Inexperienced at Her First Real Party

1. She had no political opinions.
2. She had no opinions on the state of the nation's economy.
3. She hadn't read any of the recent Hollywood tell-all bestsellers.
4. She hadn't been to a current movie.

3 of the Porno Novels Prudence Carraway Had Hidden in Her Closet

1. *Fraught with Passion*
2. *The Priest and His Undoing*
3. *The Virgin and the Sinner*

The Colors of the 4 Dresses Tony Tatterton Chose for Heaven for Her First Winterhaven Dance

1. Bright blue
2. Bright crimson
3. White
4. Floral print

3 Meanings for the Color Red

1. Red was "the color medieval aristocracy had assigned to the street harlots."
2. Red was "still the color associated most with women of loose virtue."
3. Red was "the color of passion and lust and violence and blood."

The 5 Pieces of Jewelry Worn by Jillian's Mother, Jana, to Thanksgiving Dinner at Farthinggale Manor

1. A ruby and diamond ring
2. An emerald and diamond ring
3. A sapphire and diamond ring
4. A diamond ring
5. A sapphire choker necklace

The 11 Types of Women Heaven Imagined As Having Previously "Filled" Troy Tatterton's Arms

1. Rich women
2. Wild women
3. Beautiful women
4. Sophisticated women
5. Women of charm
6. Women with brains

7. Women of culture
8. Bejeweled women
9. Fashionable women
10. Witty women
11. Self-assured women

The 3 Gifts Jillian and Tony Tatterton Brought Heaven from London

1. "Clothes, clothes, and more clothes."
2. "Extravagant" costume jewelry.
3. An antique Victorian era dresser set (which included a silver hand mirror, a hair brush, a comb, two crystal powder boxes, and two perfume bottles).

The Worst Moment of Heaven Casteel's Life

The worst moment of Heaven's life occurred when she went to visit the now-adopted Our Jane and Keith and they screamed at her in terror and rejected her.

The 5 Items on the Menu Stacie Casteel Served Heaven When Heaven First Visited Her and Luke's Home

1. Tuna salad on a bed of lettuce
2. Cubes of cheese
3. Hot rolls
4. Iced tea
5. Chocolate pudding

14 of the Acts Featured in Luke Casteel's Circus

1. A half-man/half-woman
2. Dancing girls
3. The world's fattest woman
4. The world's tallest man
5. The world's smallest husband and wife
6. A snake that was half-alligator and half-boa constrictor
7. Lions
8. Leopards
9. Tigers
10. Acrobats
11. Dwarfs
12. Lady Godiva (complete with "moving" hair!) and her horse
13. Elephants
14. Clowns

Heaven's List of 6 Abuses She Endured During Her Early Life

1. She was deprived.
2. She was starved.
3. She was beaten.
4. She was burned.
5. She was humiliated.
6. She was shamed.

Heaven's "Toy Train/Life" Metaphor

"Didn't the whole human race ride trains throughout life, reaching highs, sinking to lows, riding the plateau between extremities more often than they soared or fell."

——8——

GARDEN OF SHADOWS
(1987)

If we shadows have offended,
Think but this, and all is mended,
That you have but slumber'd here
While these visions did appear.

—William Shakespeare, *A Midsummer Night's Dream*,
Act II, Scene v

CHAPTER LISTING

Prologue

14. Corrine
15. The Blackest Day

Part III

16. Shadows and Light
17. Christopher Garland Foxworth
18. The Wages of Sin
19. The End of the Line
20. Eyes That See

STORY SYNOPSIS

Garden of Shadows takes us back in time to what happened before the events in *Flowers in the Attic* took place. It is the Grandmother's story, which we learn from the opening of an addendum to her will many years after her death. The Grandmother, Olivia Winfield, is 24 years old when she meets her future husband, wealthy businessman Malcolm Foxworth. They wed quickly and she is moved to Foxworth Hall, where they sleep in separate rooms on their wedding night. We learn that Malcolm's mother was a slut who abandoned him when he was five. Portentously, Malcolm makes love to Olivia on his mother's bed. Later, Olivia explores the mansion's attic and learns that cousins of the family had once been cloistered there. (This is obviously where Olivia got the idea of what to do with Corrine's children.) In a moment of sudden dark clarity, Olivia realizes that Malcolm married her to be *a breeder.* (She got the hint when he came to her one night, naked and with an erection and said, "I want a son." A real smoothie, wasn't he?) From Olivia and Malcolm's infrequent couplings, their sons Mal and Joel are born. After his death, Olivia inherits her father's wealth. Malcolm's father, Garland, arrives from Europe with his young bride, Alicia, who is pregnant. Alicia gives birth to Christopher Garland Foxworth, who is Malcolm's stepbrother, Olivia's future daughter Corrine's future husband, and Cathy, Christopher, Carrie, and

Cory's future father. (Got that? Remember, there will be a quiz later.) Olivia starts listening to and, later, watching Garland and Alicia do the wild thing. Malcolm starts making moves on Alicia, as Garland begins to age and fail. One night, Malcolm tries to rape Alicia, and he and Garland have a fight, during which Garland has a heart attack and dies. Alicia withdraws and becomes a hollow parody of her former vibrant self. In a major betrayal of his wife *and* his father, Malcolm makes Alicia pregnant. Olivia decides Alicia must live in the attic until she has the baby. While up there alone for months, she begins to lose her mind. In a flurry of events, Corrine (whom Malcolm favors) is born, Alicia and Christopher disappear, Mal is killed, John Amos is hired, Joel leaves for Switzerland, and is disinherited by Malcolm. The family hears that Joel has been lost in an avalanche and they presume him dead. Alicia dies of breast cancer. Malcolm and Olivia take in Christopher. He arrives at Foxworth Hall and meets Corrine. Olivia and John Amos catch Christopher and Corrine having sex. Malcolm throws out Corrine, and Christopher and has a heart attack and a stroke at the same time. Olivia takes over. Malcolm hires a detective to find Corrine and Christopher. *Garden of Shadows* and *Flowers in the Attic* now begin to overlap. The detective learns they're living under the name Dollanganger, that they have a two-year-old son, and that Corrine is pregnant again. Christopher Dollanganger Sr. is killed in an automobile accident. Corrine writes to her mother and asks if she and her children can come and live at Foxworth Hall. In the dark of night, Corrine and her children arrive at Foxworth Hall, and the story of the flowers in the attic begins.

Concluding thought: "Will the circle be unbroken?"

THE QUIZZES

1. Multiple Choice

1. How long after her death was the addendum to Olivia Foxworth's will to be opened?
    A. 1 year
    B. 20 years

    C. 50 years

    D. 6 months

2. What was Olivia Foxworth's maiden name?

    A. Winfield

    B. Dollanganger

    C. Sheffield

    D. Dahl

3. What was the table made of on which Olivia kept her handcrafted dollhouse?

    A. Pine

    B. Marble

    C. Glass

    D. Oak

4. What were the two dominant odors in Olivia's father's den?

    A. Stale beer and peanuts

    B. Cigar smoke and whiskey

    C. Old Spice and bourbon

    D. Garlic and motor oil

5. What was Olivia's height?

    A. 6 feet

    B. 5 feet, 10 inches

    C. 5 feet, 1 inch

    D. 6 feet, 6 inches

6. In what month did Olivia first meet Malcolm Foxworth?

    A. January

    B. July

    C. April

    D. November

7. How many times did Olivia brush her hair after shampooing?

    A. 20 times.

    B. 50 times.

    C. 100 times.

    D. She never brushed her hair after shampooing.

8. What piece of jewelry did Olivia believe made her neck look slimmer?

    A. Her mother's blue sapphire pendant

B. Her grandmother's strand of pearls
C. Her diamond pendant
D. Her coal beads

9. How old was Malcolm when he first met Olivia?
   A. 75
   B. 55
   C. 90
   D. 36

10. What did Mr. Winfield order prepared for Malcolm Foxworth's first dinner at the Winfield home?
    A. Lasagna
    B. Chicken Chow Mein
    C. Beef Wellington
    D. Lamb chops

11. What type of church did Olivia and Malcolm get married in?
    A. A Congregational church
    B. A synagogue
    C. A Roman Catholic church
    D. A Baptist church

12. How old was Foxworth Hall when Olivia first moved in?
    A. 500 years old
    B. 100 years old
    C. Over 150 years old
    D. 1,000 years old

13. Who said that fish and guests tend to smell after three days?
    A. Thomas Jefferson
    B. Benjamin Franklin
    C. Roger Sherman
    D. George Washington

14. What was usually served for dinner at Foxworth Hall on Wednesdays?
    A. Beef stew and green beans
    B. Chicken and dumplings
    C. Lamb
    D. Tuna sandwiches and potato chips

15. What was Joel Foxworth's middle name?

    A. Malcolm
    B. Joseph
    C. Bartholomew
    D. Christopher

16. What was the date of Olivia's father's funeral?
    A. April 7
    B. April 8
    C. April 9
    D. April 10

17. What color were Alicia's eyes?
    A. Green
    B. Blue
    C. Hazel
    D. Brown

18. What was Olivia's hometown?
    A. Hartford, Connecticut
    B. Bridgeport, Connecticut
    C. New London, Connecticut
    D. New Haven, Connecticut

19. What was Alicia's hometown?
    A. Richmond, Virginia
    B. Goochland, Virginia
    C. Arlington, Virginia
    D. Newport News, Virginia

20. How old was Alicia when Garland first kissed her?
    A. 19
    B. 14
    C. 12
    D. 21

21. How much was Alicia's share of Garland's estate?
    A. $10 million in cash
    B. Foxworth Hall and $1.00
    C. $3 million in stocks
    D. Everything

22. How much was Christopher's share of Garland's estate?
    A. $2 million in stocks
    B. Foxworth Hall and $1.00
    C. $3 million in cash
    D. Everything

23. What was the name of Mal and Joel's first tutor?
    A. Lance Fauntleroy
    B. Simon Chillingworth
    C. Ahmed Rahija
    D. Sebastian Rapuano

24. Who were the only two people to whom Malcolm's study was not off limits?
    A. Malcolm and the maid who cleaned it once a week
    B. Malcolm and Olivia
    C. Malcolm and John Amos
    D. Malcolm and Joel

25. What was the severance pay Olivia insisted that Malcolm provide the servants when he let them go after Alicia's staged departure from Foxworth Hall?
    A. Two months salary
    B. Two years salary
    C. $50,000
    D. Two weeks salary

26. Who was the only Foxworth Hall servant saved from being fired after Alicia's staged departure?
    A. Mary Stuart
    B. Mrs. Steiner
    C. Olsen
    D. Mrs. Wilson

27. How much money did Olivia insist that Malcolm transfer into individual trusts for each of their two sons?
    A. $2 million each
    B. $1 million each
    C. $500,000 each
    D. $1.00 each in cash, but $10 million in stocks to be split equally between the brothers

28. What type of music did Alicia listen to "endlessly"?
    A. Jazz
    B. Classical
    C. Rock
    D. Blues

29. Where was Mal and Joel's boarding school located?
    A. Charleston

B. New Orleans
C. Richmond
D. Atlanta

30. What type of food did Alicia dream about on the night before Thanksgiving Day?
    A. Pickles and pizza
    B. Steak, ice cream, and cookies
    C. Chocolate, olives, and watermelon
    D. Lemon meringue pie and hamburgers

31. How long was Olivia's "phony" labor?
    A. 12 hours
    B. 3 days
    C. 10 hours
    D. 26 hours

32. How many people were invited to the Christmas party Malcolm gave following the birth of Corrine?
    A. Over 1,000
    B. 25
    C. Close to 500
    D. 250

33. How many crystal champagne fountains did Malcolm have spewing bubbly at the Christmas party he gave following the birth of Corrine?
    A. 10
    B. 4
    C. 2
    D. 100

34. What size orchestra did Malcolm hire for the Christmas party he gave following the birth of Corrine?
    A. A 10-piece orchestra.
    B. A 60-piece symphony orchestra.
    C. 2 guitar players and a harpist.
    D. He didn't hire an orchestra; he only had a piano player.

35. How old were Corrine and Olivia, respectively, when they first got their periods?
    A. 13 and 15
    B. 14 and 16
    C. 10 and 12
    D. 12 and 14

36. Who was the most heartbroken about Mal's death?
    A. Olivia
    B. Corrine
    C. Joel
    D. Malcolm

37. How many companions did Joel have with him when he was purportedly lost in an avalanche?
    A. 10
    B. 5
    C. None. He was alone.
    D. 2

38. What was the name of the detective John Amos and Olivia hired to find Corrine and Christopher after Malcolm's stroke?
    A. Dithers
    B. Cruthers
    C. Mathers
    D. Macintosh

2. True or False

1. Olivia had a small bosom.
2. Olivia was a feminist.
3. Malcolm Neal Foxworth graduated from Harvard.
4. Malcolm Foxworth was sixteen when his mother died.
5. The first time Olivia went horseback riding alone with a man was when she went on a fox hunt with her father.
6. On Olivia's wedding day it rained.
7. Malcolm Foxworth had six phones on his desk in Foxworth Hall.
8. The chaise lounge in Malcolm's mother's bedroom was upholstered in light gray satin.
9. Mal was born exactly nine months and two weeks after Malcolm and Olivia's wedding reception.
10. Corrine "thought the stock market was a place to buy and sell stockings."
11. Alicia's father died two days before Garland proposed to Alicia.
12. Alicia was a good crocheter.

13. Even though Malcolm had seen his stepmother, Alicia, buck naked through the hole in his trophy room wall, Alicia had never seen Malcolm completely nude.
14. According to Malcolm, Alicia liked her sex rough.
15. Joel suffered from allergies as a child.
16. Malcolm cut off Alicia's hair after he learned she was pregnant with his child.
17. Olivia found her "three-month size" pregnancy pillow in Malcolm's trophy room.
18. John Amos asserted that Malcolm became Judas after the "death" of Joel.
19. Alicia was suffering from rapidly spreading breast cancer when she wrote to Malcolm asking for financial help for Christopher.
20. Alicia lost all her money in the Great Depression.
21. Christopher believed that railroads were the transportation of the future.
22. Christopher was the champion rower on his scull team at Yale.
23. Christopher was valedictorian of his class at Yale.
24. Corrine and Christopher decided on the name Dollanganger when they saw it on the side of a dairy truck in Omaha.

3. Bonus Questions

1. What was a "pneumonia blouse"?
2. Who owned and operated the biggest lumber mill in Charlottesville?
3. Culinarily, what does "Alfresco" mean?
4. What were the only colors Alicia would initially wear after Garland's death?
5. What was Olivia's only "donation to warmth and beauty" in the room in the north wing where Alicia had to remain in hiding?
6. What was the name of the teacher who gave Corrine her first menstrual "necessary"?

4. Super Bonus Question

1. What is the "connection" between director Martin Scorsese and Olivia?
2. From your answer to the Super Bonus Question, determine what year Olivia first met Malcolm.

5. Trick Question

Who wrote the book *Tales of Garland Foxworth*?

6. Who Said It?

1. "I won't insult your intelligence and tell you that you're beautiful; but you are extremely attractive and it's quite apparent that you have an extraordinary mind. How is it no man has captured you yet?"
2. "When it was over and he had spent himself, he knew exactly where he was and who I was. That was when he told me never to speak about it or he would harm Christopher."
3. "There are sins and there are sins. Even your generous contributions to the church can't undo the evil significance of what you have done."
4. "My son might be many things, but one thing he is for sure and that is a financial genius."
5. "Those children are the devil's spawn, born of an unholy union abominable in the eyes of God."

A. Alicia Foxworth
B. John Amos
C. Garland Foxworth
D. Malcolm Foxworth
E. Olivia Foxworth

LEAFING THROUGH . . .
GARDEN OF SHADOWS

5 of Malcolm Foxworth's Priceless Thoughts About Women and Marriage

1. "I find most so-called beautiful women vapid and rather silly. It's as if their good looks are enough to see them through life. I prefer intelligent women who know how to think for themselves, women who can be real assets to their husbands."
2. "I find most women today tedious with their effort to be beguiling. A man who is serious about his life, who is determined to build something significant of himself and his family, must, it seems to me, avoid this type."
3. "Marriage is more than the logical result of a romance; it's a contractual union, teamwork. A man has to know that his wife is part of the effort, someone on whom he can depend. Contrary to what some men think, my father included, a man must have a woman who has strength."
4. "[E]ver since Eve, women have betrayed me. Especially women with beautiful bodies and seductive bodies."
5. Malcolm believed that a woman should be "a good wife, a good mistress of her husband's house . . . and, of course, a good breeder."

1 of Malcolm Foxworth's Priceless Thoughts About Money and Business

"Good business sense takes training, practice . . . Only the so-called nouveau riche are wasteful. You can spot them anywhere. They are obscene."

The Malcolm/Bart Connection

Malcolm had "always been known for hosting the finest, most extravagant parties." This was an inclination that Malcolm's grandson, Bart, zealously emulated. (See Book 5.)

V.C. Andrews's Use of an Image Used by Stephen King (and Later by Me)

"Everything of value had been draped with sheets . . . The shapes beneath the sheets looked like sleeping ghosts." Stephen King used the image "the shape under the sheet" in his 1981 nonfiction book on the horror genre called *Danse Macabre,* and I later used the image as the title of my own 1991 book about King, *The Shape Under the Sheet: The Complete Stephen King Encyclopedia.*

Malcolm Foxworth's Romantic "Style"

"Sometime before morning I heard the door creak open, and when I opened my eyes, I saw Malcolm Neal Foxworth, naked in the moonlight, his manliness looming over me. 'I want a son,' he said . . . When I felt his seed emerging . . . I could almost hear him willing it to find its destination . . . 'I hope, Olivia,' he said, 'that you are as fertile as I expected.' "

Malcolm Foxworth's Thought on Why He Wouldn't Let His Sons Sit with Him at the Dinner Table

"Because . . . what they do is not pleasing to the appetite."

Alicia's 3 Dinner Etiquette "Offenses" (According to Olivia)

1. She talked with food in her mouth.
2. She fidgeted in her seat.
3. She drank wine like water.

The 8 "I Always Feel Like/ Somebody's Watching Me" Awards (with Thanks to Michael Jackson)

1. Olivia enjoyed listening to Garland and Alicia make love. She would eavesdrop on them by putting her ear on the wall near the dressing table in her room.

2. Olivia once watched Garland and Alicia make love by the lake near Foxworth Hall.

3. Malcolm enjoyed watching his father and Alicia make love. He spied on them through a hole hidden behind a framed photograph on the wall of his trophy room.

4. Olivia had once spied on Alicia and Garland skinny-dipping in the lake.

5. After Garland's death, Olivia would listen through the wall to Alicia sobbing in her bedroom.

6. Unbeknownst to Corrine, Olivia once watched her strip and try on one of her real grandmother Corrine's nightgowns. Olivia would watch through the hole in the wall in Malcolm's trophy room.

7. John Amos once watched Corrine and Christopher swim in their underwear. "Obscene" and "lewd" was the way he described what he saw.

8. Olivia once spied on Corrine and Christopher when they were half-naked and entwined on the swan bed. Christopher was kissing Corrine's naked breasts. Olivia was not pleased with this development. As Olivia pondered what to do (for what was apparently long enough for Chris and Corrine to get completely undressed and begin what Olivia called "the union that should exist only in marriage), John Amos pushed open the door and began screaming at them. "Sinners!" and "Fornicators!" were two of the epithets he hurled.

6 of the "Trophies" in Garland's Trophy Room

1. A tiger head
2. An elephant head
3. A grizzly bear
4. An antelope
5. A mountain lion
6. A brown bear

2 of Malcolm's Ideas About Musicians

1. "[M]usicians were weak, effeminate men who made little money."
2. [Musicians were] "a bunch of spineless ... effeminate ... artsy types."

3 Examples of Olivia's Wisdom

1. "Life makes you strong. If you don't let it make you strong, it will kill you."
2. "Everything had a reason, a purpose, and would be explained in the hereafter."
3. "Womanhood brings pain along with its joys, and every month you'll be reminded of this."

3 Visits to the "Oedipus Wrecks" Department

1. After Garland's death, Malcolm went often to his stepmother Alicia's room for sex. When he stroked her body and kissed her breasts, though, he would call out Corrine, which was his own mother's name.
2. The first time Malcolm made love to Olivia, he also called out "Corrine," which was his own mother's name.
3. The third time Malcolm made love to Alicia after Garland's death, he made her dress in one of his

mother's nightgowns and come out of the bathroom as though she had just gotten ready for bed.

The 5 Things Olivia Denied Enjoying When Alicia Moved into Hiding in the North Wing of Foxworth Hall

1. She did not enjoy having to pretend that Alicia's baby was her own.
2. She did not enjoy the knowledge that her husband had been untrue to her.
3. She did not enjoy having to fire her servants.
4. She did not enjoy lying to her own sons.
5. She did not enjoy lying to Alicia's son.

Olivia's Art Gallery

When "decorating" Alicia's room in the north wing, Olivia hung two paintings she had found in the attic. One was of "grotesque demons chasing naked people in underground caverns." The other was of "unearthly monsters devouring pitiful souls in hell." We learned in Book 1 that the paintings were by Goya.

The 6 Places Alicia Fantasized Visiting After Going Crazy in the North Wing Room

1. The back of a car
2. A restaurant
3. A park
4. An ice cream parlor
5. A ferry
6. A puppet show in the attic

The 4 Things Corrine Told Olivia She Wanted After She First Got Her Period

1. Marriage.
2. Love.
3. She wanted to go dancing every night.
4. She wanted to go on "cruises to exotic lands where the women don't wear blouses and the men beat drums."

The 5 Things Malcolm Was Surrounded by in His Office on the Day of Joel's Funeral

1. His possessions
2. His hunting trophies
3. His business ledgers
4. His *objets d'art*
5. The ghosts of all the women he had ravished in his office

Malcolm's Prediction as to the Type of Children Corrine and Christopher Would Have

According to Malcolm, Christopher and Corrine's children would have horns, humped backs, forked tails, and hoofed feet. He believed that they would be generally what you might call "deformed creatures."

—9—

FALLEN HEARTS
(1988)

Mein Herz ich will dich fragen:
Was ist denn Liebe? Sag'!—
'Zwei Seelen und ein Gedanke,
'Zwei Herzen und ein Schlag!'

What love is, if thou wouldst be taught,
    Thy heart must teach alone—
Two souls with but a single thought,
    Two hearts that beat as one.

—Friedrich Halm, *Der Sohn der Wildnis* (1842) Act II

CHAPTER LISTING

STORY SYNOPSIS

Fallen Hearts is the third book in the Casteel series and it begins two years after *Dark Angel* ends. Heaven is now a teacher in Winnerrow and is planning to marry Logan. Luke Casteel declines to give her away, but her sister Fanny is her maid of honor. Tony Tatterton does not attend the wedding, but invites Heaven and Logan back to Farthinggale Manor to spend a few days before they begin their honeymoon. By now, Tony's wife Jillian is insane and only talks about Leigh's "seduction" of her husband. At Farthy, Heaven and Logan make love in her old bedroom. Tony offers Logan a job, which he eagerly accepts, and Heaven reluctantly agrees to live at Farthy. Tony gives them a wedding reception, after which Heaven and Logan travel back to Winnerrow to tell Logan's parents about his new job and to pick a site for the new Tatterton Toy factory to be built in Winnerrow. While Heaven and Logan are visiting Winnerrow, Fanny tries to seduce Logan. When Heaven and Logan return to Farthinggale Manor, a maid tells Heaven that she heard mysterious piano music in the house at night. Heaven once again gets lost in the maze, and then learns an amazing secret about the dead Troy Tatterton, which has an overwhelming emotional impact on her life and her future. Tragedy befalls Jillian, and Fanny tells Heaven that she's pregnant with Logan's baby. Fanny blackmails Heaven into agreeing to pay child support. Heaven and Logan buy a house in Winnerrow, and Heaven learns that she is pregnant and that it might not be Logan's child. Tragedy strikes Luke and his wife Stacie, and Heaven and Logan take Luke and Stacie's son, Drake, to live with them. Fanny decides that *she* wants Drake, and a bitter custody battle ensues. In a devastating act of betrayal, Tony Tatterton tries to rape Heaven. Fanny steals Drake, but the custody battle is settled out of court when Heaven resorts to repeating the "sins of the father." Fanny gives birth to Luke; Heaven gives birth to Annie. The story ends when Heaven mysteriously receives a gift—an intricately detailed model of Troy Tatterton's cottage.

THE QUIZZES

1. Multiple Choice

1. When Logan presented Heaven with a "rainbow castle" made of (among other sweet things) ice cream, cherries, and whipped cream, how much weight did Heaven say she'd gain in an hour if she ate it?
   A. 1,000 pounds
   B. 300 pounds
   C. 25 pounds
   D. 1,000,000 pounds

2. What was the name of the newspaper that announced Heaven and Logan's engagement?
   A. *The Winnerrow Journal*
   B. *The Willies Gazette*
   C. *The Winnerrow Reporter*
   D. *The Winnerrow Register*

3. What month did Heaven and Logan marry?
   A. February
   B. June
   C. July
   D. September

4. What did Heaven's Willies students give her and Logan as a wedding present?
   A. A SaladShooter and a case of lettuce grown on The Coons family farm.
   B. A case of moonshine and "store-bought" pillowcases.
   C. A Bible with all their names written in it.
   D. A needlepoint of Heaven's Willies cabin with "Home Sweet Home, from your class" stitched on it.

5. What newspaper was Tony Tatterton carrying when Heaven and Logan first arrived at Farthy after their wedding?

    A. *The New York Times*
    B. *The Wall Street Journal*
    C. *USA Today*
    D. *The Washington Post*

6. What kind of drink did Logan request upon his arrival at Farthy following his and Heaven's wedding?
    A. A highball
    B. A white wine
    C. A beer
    D. A Captain Morgan rum and Coke

7. What was the position Tony Tatterton offered Logan Stonewall with Tatterton Toys right after Logan and Heaven were married?
    A. Vice-president in charge of marketing
    B. Production manager
    C. President of the company
    D. Chief comptroller

8. What kind of furniture did Tony Tatterton buy to furnish Heaven and Logan's Farthinggale Manor suite?
    A. Early American
    B. Oriental
    C. French Provincial
    D. Contemporary

9. What colors were the servants' uniforms at Heaven and Logan's wedding reception at Farthinggale Manor?
    A. Red and white
    B. Black and white
    C. Green and white
    D. Yellow and mauve

10. Approximately how many people attended Heaven and Logan's wedding reception at Farthinggale Manor?
    A. 100
    B. 400
    C. 1,000
    D. 650

11. What song did the orchestra play for Heaven and Tony Tatterton's dance at the wedding reception for Heaven and Logan at Farthinggale Manor?

    A. "Daddy's Little Girl"
    B. "Sunrise, Sunset"
    C. "Baby, You're a Rich Man"
    D. "You Are the Sunshine of My Life"

12. Who was given the authority to decide on a suitable location for the new Tatterton Toy Company factory in Winnerrow?
    A. Heaven
    B. Logan
    C. Fanny
    D. Our Jane

13. How much money did Logan add "to sweeten the deal" to the purchase price of the land he bought as the site for the Tatterton Toy factory in Winnerrow?
    A. $1,000,000
    B. $5,000
    C. $25,000
    D. $1,000

14. According to Paul Grant, what material did he feel should be used to construct the Tatterton Toy factory in Winnerrow?
    A. Brick
    B. Wood
    C. Steel
    D. Concrete

15. According to Heaven, what was "the cruelest season of all"?
    A. April
    B. Unrequited love
    C. Life
    D. Loneliness

16. What did Fanny originally intend to name her and Logan's baby if it was a boy?
    A. Wayland
    B. Logan
    C. Tom
    D. Luke

17. What did Fanny originally intend to name her and Logan's baby if it was a girl?
    A. Darcy

    B. Heaven
    C. Annie
    D. Sarah

18. How many and what kind of dogs did Fanny own?
    A. Two Great Danes
    B. Three pit bulls
    C. One German shepherd
    D. Six poodles

19. How much did Heaven agree to pay Fanny during the months Fanny was pregnant with Logan's child?
    A. $600 a week
    B. $5,000 a month
    C. $2,500 a month
    D. $1,000 a week

20. What was Anthony Hasbrouck's nickname?
    A. "Tony"
    B. "Sonny"
    C. "Sally Piles"
    D. "Tony the Nose"

21. How did Stacie and Luke Casteel die?
    A. They were killed in a head-on auto accident.
    B. They died of asphyxiation during kinky sex with masks.
    C. They died during a mutual suicide pact.
    D. They drowned when their cruise ship sank in the Atlantic.

22. How much did Luke Casteel pay Tony Tatterton for the circus?
    A. $1,000
    B. $500
    C. $100
    D. $1.00

23. Who dyed Heaven Stonewall's hair back to its natural black color?
    A. Maisie Setterton
    B. Kitty Dennison
    C. Jillian Tatterton
    D. Fanny Casteel

24. How much did Heaven pay Fanny for custody of Drake Casteel?
    A. $1,000
    B. $10,000
    C. $100,000
    D. $1,000,000

2. True or False

1. Logan Stonewall proposed marriage to Heaven in his father's pharmacy.
2. Heaven refused to invite her students to her wedding.
3. Heaven's wedding invitation to Fanny was the last one she mailed.
4. Randall Wilcox had black hair.
5. Heaven wore a wrist corsage for her wedding.
6. Fanny made modifications in the dress she wore for Heaven's wedding so that the top of her breasts were exposed.
7. Heaven's wedding band was gold.
8. Martha Goodman tricked Jillian Tatterton into taking her tranquilizers by telling her they were vitamins.
9. Rye Whiskey was a superstitious man.
10. By the time Heaven and Logan were married, Keith Casteel had begun smoking a pipe.
11. Keith Casteel was a member of his college rowing team.
12. Tony Tatterton loved rock and roll and was a huge fan of The Rolling Stones.
13. Heaven and Logan's wedding cake at the reception at Farthinggale Manor was three tiers high.
14. When Logan and Heaven began negotiations for the land purchase for the new Winnerrow Tatterton Toy factory, Tony Tatterton wired a large sum of money to the Winnerrow National Bank.
15. Jillian Tatterton committed suicide by running a garden hose from the exhaust of Tony's Rolls-Royce up into her bedroom, starting the car, and then lying in bed with the hose next to her.

16. Jana Jankins was senile by the time her daughter Jillian committed suicide.
17. Jillian Tatterton's two sisters and brother did not arrive at Farthinggale Manor until the morning of Jillian's funeral.
18. At the time of Jillian Tatterton's suicide, Amy Luckett was married.
19. When Heaven saw her after Jillian's suicide, Amy Luckett had lost a tremendous amount of weight since the time she and Heaven were classmates at the Winterhaven School for Girls.
20. The Hasbrouck House was a colonial-style house.
21. Logan took everyone out to dinner at the Cape Cod House to celebrate Heaven's incipient pregnancy.
22. Mrs. Cotton was a very thin woman.
23. J. Arthur Stein carried a pocket watch.
24. Luke Casteel saved a newspaper clipping from the *New York Times* that announced Heaven and Logan's marriage.
25. Tony Tatterton always read *The Wall Street Journal* at breakfast.
26. Fanny Casteel and Randall Wilcox got married in Hadleyville.
27. Heaven's toy cottage played a Beethoven sonata.

3. Bonus Questions

1. In what medium was the picture of the Willies cabin scene that hung over Heaven and Logan's Farthinggale Manor bed painted?
2. To whom did Ole Mallory leave his estate?
3. What was Anthony Hasbrouck wearing the first time Heaven and Logan visited him about buying his house?
4. On what floor was J. Arthur Stein's law office located?
5. What was the name of the camel in Luke Casteel's circus?

4. Super Bonus Questions

1. What was the name of Tony Tatterton's great-great-grandfather?
2. What was the name of Tony Tatterton's great-grandfather?
3. What was the name of the funeral parlor that handled the funerals of Stacie and Luke Casteel?
4. What was the name of the church where Stacie and Luke Casteel's funeral was held?
5. What was the phase of the moon the night Drake Casteel was kidnapped?
6. What kind of flower did Logan Stonewall wear in his tuxedo lapel at his wedding reception at Farthinggale Manor?

5. Epistolary Bonus Questions

1. Who wrote Heaven the letter that began, "Unfortunately, business activities involving the circus will make it impossible for me to attend your wedding"?
2. Who wrote Heaven the letter that began, "Now, more than ever, last night seems like a dream"?

6. Conspicuous Consumption Bonus Question

What was Tony Tatterton's wedding gift to Heaven and Logan (in addition to the lavish reception at Farthinggale Manor)?

7. The "Can It Be What I Think?" Bonus Question

What specific personal "masculine ritual" did Heaven always dream of watching her future husband perform?

8. The "You Can't Get There from Here," Ultimate Bonus Question

What line follows the line, "Nor certitude, nor peace, nor help for pain" in Matthew Arnold's poem, "Dover Beach"?

9. Who Said It?

1. "Don't talk about the dead and gone, Miss Heaven. If you dig up their troubled past, you'll disturb their sleep and they'll haunt ya. I got enough hauntin' me these days."
2. "For me, Death had become a doorway to a new world, an escape from the misery of living without you."
3. "I told you time and time again, Leigh, not to come to my bedroom half dressed. You're not a child anymore. You can't parade around like that, especially in front of Tony."
4. "In my own way I am doing a great deal for the people in Winnerrow. It was my dream to do something significant there, to continue to do something significant there."
5. "Don't be angry with me, Heaven, for caring about you and wanting you to be happy."

A. Jillian Tatterton
B. Tony Tatterton
C. Rye Whiskey
D. Heaven Stonewall
E. Troy Tatterton

LEAFING THROUGH . . .
FALLEN HEARTS

The 3 Ways Heaven Showed the People of Winnerrow That She Was No Longer a "Scum-of-the-Hills" Casteel

1. She drove an expensive automobile.
2. She wore fine clothing.
3. She carried herself as "a cultured and sophisticated woman."

Reverend Wayland Wise's Interpretation of Heaven Casteel

"You are the most dangerous kind of female the world can ever know. A great man will love you for your beautiful face, for your seductive body; but you will fail them all, because you will believe they all fail you first. You are an idealist of the most devastatingly tragic kind—the romantic idealist. Born to destroy and to self-destruct."

5 Examples of Fanny's Sexual Misconduct with Logan Stonewall

1. At Heaven and Logan's wedding reception, she threw her arms around his neck and pressed her breasts into his chest.
2. She then grabbed his buttocks with both hands.
3. She then stuck her tongue almost down his throat when she "kissed the groom."
4. She appeared at Logan and Heaven's house in the Willies claiming her plumbing broke, and when Logan allowed her to use the shower, she came out wrapped only in a towel that she made sure fell open.
5. She once visited Logan on a hot night and allowed her dress to fall down to her waist. She wasn't

wearing anything underneath the dress. She then "raped" Logan.

Logan Stonewall's Take on New England

"New England looks a lot like the Willies, only without the mountains and the shacks."

8 Indications of Jillian Tatterton's Slow Descent into Madness

1. The first time Heaven saw her after she and Logan were married, she felt that Jillian looked "like a circus clown."
2. "Her hair was dyed a bright yellow and stuck up in thin, stiff strands."
3. "Her face looked like cracked porcelain, her cheeks blotched with bright red rouge."
4. "Eyeliner was slashed across her lids, the line drooping at the crinkly corners of her eyes."
5. "Her lipstick was thick, vibrant, caked at the corners of her mouth."
6. Jillian was staring into a blank oval space on the wall where a mirror had been.
7. Her room was in complete disarray, looking "as though it had been ransacked by a madwoman."
8. Jillian thought Heaven was Heaven's mother, Leigh.

4 of the Fashion Designers Whose Clothing Was Worn by Guests at Heaven and Logan's Wedding Reception at Farthinggale Manor

1. Saint Laurent
2. Chanel
3. Pierre Cardin
4. Adolfo

Heaven's Fantasy About the Guests Who Attended Her and Logan's Wedding Reception at Farthinggale Manor

"After my second glass of champagne, I giggled at the idea that a small army of mannequins had become animated and escaped from the windows of the most elegant Boston shops."

Heaven's Philosophy About Ghosts

"Ghosts and spirits don't exist, they're merely the creations of uneducated superstitious minds ... There's nothing out there, nothing but reality, hard and true."

Heaven's Philosophy About Guilt

"Guilt is one of the most difficult weights for the mind to endure."

3 Instances of People Being Described as "Gay" When the Word Is Used to Mean "Merry" and "Ebullient" Rather Than Its More Contemporary Connotation

1. "Tony was such a serious man ... It was rare to see this light, gay side of him."
2. "I remembered how gay and active he and Jillian had been when I first arrived at Farthy."
3. "We were all still in a gay and celebrating mood as we entered Farthinggale Manor."

The 6 Faces Heaven "Saw" as She Walked Through the Underground Farthy Tunnels on Her Way to an Illicit Rendezvous with Troy

1. Granny
2. Luke
3. Tom
4. Fanny
5. Jillian
6. Tony

12 Dramatic Changes That Came over Tony Tatterton After Jillian Tatterton's Suicide

1. He seemed older.
2. His hair appeared grayer.
3. His eyes seemed darker.
4. The wrinkles in his forehead appeared to be deeper.
5. He moved more slowly.
6. He didn't dress as impeccably as he had in the past.
7. He didn't brush his hair.
8. He didn't shave.
9. He became obsessed with old photographs and other memorabilia.
10. He "cloistered" himself in his office for hours on end.
11. He couldn't bear being interrupted.
12. He became very short with Heaven and Logan.

Heaven's Philosophy About Men

"Men ... [h]ow false they could be. They never stopped being little boys, selfish little boys."

Heaven's Charming Metaphorical Description of Her Sister Fanny

"You're like a flower planted in manure."

Granny's Philosophy About Life

"Life is jist like the seasons, chile. It's got its springs and its summas and ya got ta cherish every moment of the spring when it comes ta ya, cuz nothin' stays fresh and young and pretty foreva, chile, nothin'. The frost gets inta people, jist like it gets inta the ground."

9 of the Circus Employees Who Attended Stacie and Luke Casteel's Funeral

1. Giants
2. Midgets
3. A bearded lady
4. Animal trainers
5. Acrobatic groups
6. Magicians' assistants
7. The ringmaster's assistant
8. Management types (in suits)
9. Clowns

The 6 People (and 1 Incident) for Whom (and for Which) Heaven Cried After Tony Tatterton Tried to Rape Her

1. The mother she had never seen or known (Angel)
2. Tom
3. Troy

4. Luke
5. Stacie
6. Herself

Incident Epilogue: Heaven also cried because Logan had had sex with her sister Fanny and made her pregnant.

Heaven's Philosophy About Ego and Pride

"[W]hen ego and pride are at stake, cowards and beggars could become heroes and kings."

Logan Stonewall's Less-Than-Flattering "Review" of Fanny Casteel's Attorney Wendell Burton

"He's an ambulance chaser of the worst sort, a parasitic, wormy type. Whenever someone dies in an accident, he's at the funeral parlor, handing out his card, hoping they'll hire him to sue someone."

The 6 Witnesses Who Testified at the Custody Hearing over Drake Casteel

1. Peter Meeks
2. Reverend Wayland Wise
3. Peggy Sue Martin
4. Fanny Casteel
5. Logan Stonewall
6. Randall Wilcox

—10—

GATES OF PARADISE

(1989)

Mutual Forgiveness of each vice,
Such are the Gates of Paradise.

—William Blake, *The Gates of Paradise,* prologue

Prologue

Part 3

STORY SYNOPSIS

Gates of Paradise is the fourth book in the Casteel series and begins approximately seventeen years after *Fallen Hearts* ends. Annie, Heaven and Troy's daughter, is a painter, and she is very close to Fanny and Logan's son, Luke, Jr. Drake is Luke, Sr.'s and Stacie's son. They are all obsessed with Farthinggale Manor and the family's dark secrets and history, but Heaven does not want Annie fantasizing about Farthy. Luke and Annie turn eighteen, Drake visits Farthy, and Annie wants to know why Heaven left Farthy and Tony Tatterton. Fanny gives herself a birthday party and embarrasses everyone in the family with her behavior. On the way home, there is an accident and tragedy befalls Heaven and Logan. Annie is paralyzed in the accident and ends up at Farthy where she is to recuperate under the watchful eye of Tony Tatterton, who is now weirder than ever. Annie is reluctant to stay there but has nowhere else to go. Annie is given Heaven's room and Tony begins thinking of Annie as Heaven. One day, Annie sees a man crying by her parents' graves. Ominously, Leigh, Annie, and Heaven begin to flow into one person in Tony's mind. Tony convinces Annie to dye her hair blonde, like Heaven's. Annie begins to paint. Tony bathes and dresses Annie and begins to act even *weirder.* Annie meets Troy, who helps her to take her first post-paralysis step. Tony completely disconnects, causing Annie to make the decision to leave the mansion. Tony tries to rape Annie and reveals to her that he's really her grandfather and that he was Heaven's father. Luke and Fanny come and take her away from Farthy, and shortly thereafter, Tony dies. Troy reveals that he's really Annie's father and that there is therefore no blood relationship between her and Luke, which means that they can marry. Happy ending. The End.

THE QUIZZES

1. Multiple Choice

1. Who was the only person Annie Casteel felt she could share her deepest secrets with?
   A. Fanny Casteel
   B. Luke Casteel, Jr.
   C. Tony Tatterton
   D. Rye Whiskey

2. What type of higher education degree did Luke Casteel, Jr. study for at Harvard?
   A. An M.B.A.
   B. A Ph.D.
   C. A B.A.
   D. An A.S.

3. What was the name of Luke, Jr. and Annie's English teacher?
   A. Miss Koster
   B. Miss Stackler
   C. Miss Marbleton
   D. Miss Korb

4. What song did the jewelry box Aunt Fanny bought Annie for her eighteenth birthday play?
   A. "Memories" from *Cats*
   B. "What I Did for Love" from *A Chorus Line*
   C. "Over the Rainbow" from *The Wizard of Oz*
   D. "More" from *Mondo Cane*

5. What did Fanny give her son Luke, Jr. for his eighteenth birthday?
   A. Subscriptions to *Penthouse* and *Hustler* magazines. (*Playboy* was "way too tame for ma boy," according to Fanny.)

    B. A boxed Rolling Stones CD set.
    C. His own color TV.
    D. A black Jaguar.

6. What did Annie give Luke, Jr. for his eighteenth birthday?
    A. Polaroids of herself in her underwear.
    B. A solid gold, black onyx pinky ring.
    C. A leather coat.
    D. A complete set of James Michener's novels, signed by Michener to Luke.

7. What was Luke Casteel, Jr.'s middle name?
    A. Drake
    B. Toby
    C. Townsend
    D. Anthony

8. Whose bust was in the front yard of the Winnerrow School?
    A. Robert E. Lee
    B. Martin Luther King
    C. Abraham Lincoln
    D. Jefferson Davis

9. How long was Annie Stonewall in a coma following the car accident that killed her parents?
    A. 2 days
    B. 10 weeks
    C. 1 year
    D. 4 months

10. What was the cause of Annie Stonewall's post-accident paralysis?
    A. Inflammation caused by the trauma around her spine
    B. Bone fragments pressing on a series of nerves
    C. Psychosomatic hysteria
    D. Internal bleeding

11. What magazine was Mrs. Broadfield reading in Annie's hospital room the first time Aunt Fanny visited Annie after the car accident?
    A. *Glamour*
    B. *People*

C. *Newsweek*
D. *Playgirl*

12. What was the first item of Jillian's jewelry that Tony Tatterton gave to Annie?
    A. An opal pendant
    B. A pearl ring
    C. Diamond earrings
    D. A cameo brooch

13. Who signed Annie Stonewall's release from Boston Memorial Hospital?
    A. Dr. Carson
    B. Dr. Ruth
    C. Dr. Biondi
    D. Dr. Malisoff

14. What year was Farthinggale Manor built?
    A. 1850
    B. 1750
    C. 1900
    D. 1899

15. What English school did Tony Tatterton attend when he was seven years old?
    A. Oxford
    B. Eton
    C. Cheshire Academy
    D. Rimmington Hall

16. Instead of sheep, what did Annie Stonewall fall asleep counting her first night in Farthinggale Manor?
    A. Nude male dancers
    B. Questions
    C. Possibilities
    D. Toasters

17. What was Millie Thomas's hometown?
    A. Kansas City
    B. New York
    C. Boston
    D. Indianapolis

18. Which of the following body parts was the first "post-coma" extremity that Annie found she could move?
    A. The little toe on her left foot

B. The little toe on her right foot
C. The big toe on her left foot
D. The big toe on her right foot

19. What was Annie Stonewall's derogatory nickname for her nurse, Mrs. Broadfield?
    A. "Florence Farthinggale"
    B. "Flab Lady"
    C. "The Nurse From Hell"
    D. "Tubby Tits"

20. What side effects did Annie experience when she took sleeping pills?
    A. She got extremely horny.
    B. She threw up.
    C. She had nightmares.
    D. She began to enjoy Neil Diamond.

21. What was Troy Tatterton's alias?
    A. Brother Timothy
    B. Allen Konigsberg
    C. Reverend Douglas E. Winters
    D. Timothy Brothers

22. What melody did Troy Tatterton's toy cottage play when the roof was removed?
    A. Samuel Barber's "Adagio in A Minor"
    B. A Chopin nocturne
    C. Mozart's "Turkish Rondo"
    D. "Lady Madonna"

23. How did Tony Tatterton die?
    A. A massive coronary.
    B. He committed suicide by hanging himself from a Farthy chandelier.
    C. A stroke.
    D. Lung cancer.

24. Who delivered the eulogy at Tony Tatterton's funeral?
    A. Annie Stonewall
    B. Fanny Casteel
    C. Rye Whiskey
    D. Troy Tatterton

2. True or False

1. Luke Casteel, Jr. had green eyes.
2. Annie Stonewall's license plate read "FOXYLADY."
3. Aunt Fanny had a hangover on the morning of Annie's eighteenth birthday.
4. Heaven and Logan's bedroom at Hasbrouck House had red satin drapes.
5. Luke gave Annie an oil painting of Farthinggale Manor for her eighteenth birthday.
6. Luke, Jr. received a full-tuition scholarship to Harvard.
7. Roland Star was an eminent meteorological prognosticator.
8. Annie Stonewall received blows to her spine and head in the car accident that killed her parents.
9. The first time Drake Casteel visited Annie at Farthinggale Manor, Annie told him he looked like a lawyer.
10. Tony Tatterton once sent up to Annie a novel by William Dean Howells.
11. Tony Tatterton bought Annie a red beret to wear while painting.
12. Prior to Tony Tatterton, the only people who had seen Annie Stonewall completely naked were her parents, her doctors, the nurses, and the coaches and first string of the Winnerrow High School football team.
13. Troy Tatterton's cottage had six rooms.
14. Annie Stonewall took her very first post-paralysis step in Troy Tatterton's cottage.
15. Doc Williams was tall and thin.
16. One of Annie's favorite meals was roasted Cornish hen with mint jelly.
17. Before he died, Tony Tatterton had Drake Casteel cut out of his will.

3. Bonus Questions

1. How tall was Drake Casteel?
2. How many weeks severance pay did Tony Tatterton give Millie Thomas when he fired her?

3. How many steps led up to the platform of the gazebo at Hasbrouck House?
4. What color was the leather skirt Aunt Fanny wore to Hasbrouck House the morning of Annie's eighteenth birthday?
5. How did Fanny react to Luke, Jr.'s good news from Harvard?
6. "How many times does twenty go into forty?"
7. To whom did Luke Casteel, Jr. dedicate the day of his valedictorian commencement address?
8. What department store did Millie Thomas work at before coming to work at Farthinggale Manor?
9. Who assembled Annie's artist's easel?
10. What did the writing on Annie's "welcome back to Hasbrouck House" cake say?

4. Super Bonus Questions

1. What kind of wood was the headboard of Heaven and Logan's bed made of?
2. What were Logan Stonewall's last words?
3. What was Tony Tatterton's initial "Annie" visitation schedule immediately after her paralyzing car accident?
4. Was the name of Annie Stonewall's personal maid at Farthinggale Manor, Linda Fantarella, Abigail Freemantle, Millie Thomas, or Tori Amos?
5. What color sweater was Annie wearing when she took her very first step following her accident?
6. What five services did Annie receive at Dorothy Wilson's Winnerrow beauty shop after she returned to Hasbrouck House?
7. What was the complete name of the Winnerrow hospital?

5. Epistolary Bonus Questions

1. Who wrote Annie the letter that began, "The years may come and go, and time, like the magical maze we've dreamt about, might separate us."?

2. Who wrote Annie the letter that began, "I have news that I know will excite you"?
3. To whom did Heaven write the letter that began, "I know you have spoken to Tony since graduation, and I was happy to hear about the reception you received for your speech"?
4. To whom did Annie write the letter that began, "It seems one confusing thing after another has happened to keep you from paying me a visit here at Farthy"?

6. Conspicuous Consumption Bonus Question

What did Logan and Heaven give Annie for her eighteenth birthday?

7. Trick Question

Did Luke, Jr. receive a standing ovation after his valedictorian commencement address?

8. Boo-Boo Bonus Question

We are told that Logan once bought Annie a gold locket on "a twenty-four-carat gold chain." What, as they say, is wrong with this picture?

Who Said It?

1. "Young man, I don't have all day to spend explaining medical procedures to you. It's time for Annie's therapy session, anyway, and she can't have visitors during that time."
2. "LUKE! LUKE! DON'T GO. LUKE, COME UP AND GET ME."
3. "Just like ya all not ta wait for me."
4. "I love you, Annie. I can't help it. I'll live with it and suffer with it until the day I die."
5. "Annie, haven't I asked you not to torment yourself and me by talking about Farthinggale?"

A. Annie Stonewall
B. Heaven Stonewall
C. Aunt Fanny
D. Tony Tatterton
E. Luke Casteel, Jr.

LEAFING THROUGH . . .
GATES OF PARADISE

4 of the Dolls Tony Tatterton Sent Annie Casteel over the Years

1. Chinese dolls
2. Dolls from Holland
3. Dolls from Norway
4. Dolls from Ireland

5 of the Sarcastic Nicknames Drake Called Luke, Jr.

1. The great Buddha
2. Plato
3. Einstein
4. Sherlock Holmes
5. Twinkle Toes

Heaven's Philosophy About Wealth

1. "Never think you're better than anyone because you've grown up privileged . . . The rich are often driven by the same base motives as are the very dirty and very poor. Maybe even more than the poor . . . because they have more idle time to drift into their private madness."
2. "Rich girls can be very cruel because their money and wealth protects them like a cocoon."

Luke Casteel, Jr.'s Motto

"Tall mountains may be harder to climb . . . but the view from the top is always worth it. Go for the tall ones."

Heaven's (Actually Troy's) Philosophy About Love

"Love is . . . [a]s fragile as one of our tiniest, most intricate, most delicately crafted toys. Hold on to it too tightly, and it will crumble in your fingers, but hold on to it too loosely, and the wind might blow it away and shatter it on the cold ground."

5 Instances of Lewd and Crude Behavior by Fanny Casteel at Her 40th Birthday Party

1. She stuck her tongue in Logan's mouth when he gave her a birthday kiss.
2. She pressed one of her breasts into his arm as he was kissing her.
3. She danced lasciviously.
4. She showed off her breasts while standing on top of an overturned garbage can.
5. She playfully rebuffed a young man when he suggestively asked her "How many times does twenty go into forty?"

The "Déjà Vu" Department

Cathy Dollanganger (from *Flowers in the Attic*): "Somewhere near the front door, my brother and I would be hiding, and after he'd called out his greeting, we'd dash out from behind a chair or the sofa to crash us into his wide open arms, which seized us up at once and held us close, and he warmed our lips with kisses."

Annie Stonewall (from *Gates of Paradise*): "When I was little, I would hide behind the high-back blue chintz chair in the living room and press my tiny fist against my lips to suppress a giggle as he pretended to look everywhere for me . . . 'Here I am, Daddy,' I would sing out, and he would scoop me up and cover my face with kisses."

3 of the "Simplest Things" That Made Annie Stonewall Sad After Her Automobile Accident

1. A "lone bird on a willow-tree branch"
2. The "sound of a car horn in the distance"
3. The "laughter of little children"

Yet Another "Gone with the Wind/ Scarlett O'Hara" Reference

"I'll wear a tuxedo and you'll come floating down the long stairway, looking like Scarlett O'Hara in *Gone With the Wind* with your dress trailing behind you . . . 'Annie, you're looking more beautiful than ever,' he recited, imitating Clark Gable in the movie. 'But I must keep my wits about me. I know the way you manipulate men with your dazzling beauty.' "

"Like Mother, Like Daughter" Department

From *Fallen Hearts:* (Heaven Casteel is speaking):

1. "My heart felt like a brick in my chest."
2. "I . . . awakened with . . . my heart like a stone in my chest."

From *Gates of Paradise:* (Heaven's daughter, Annie, is speaking):
   "The tears and the agony made my heart feel like a brick in my chest."

27 of the "Tony Tatterton" Warning Signs That Annie Should Have Heeded

1. "He kissed me, his lips lingering longer than I expected."
2. The day before Annie left Boston Memorial Hospital, Tony brought her her mother's dress to wear to "return to Farthy."
3. As indicated in the above item, Tony fantasized that Annie was returning to Farthy, even though she had never been there before in her life.
4. "He stared so long [at me] without saying a word that I began to feel uncomfortable."
5. When Tony helped load Annie into the car for her trip to Farthy, "his lips grazed [her] cheek and he held [her] snugly against him." Annie was surprised at how tightly he held her.
6. When Tony carried Annie into Farthy to begin her recuperation, she could not help but feel that he was treating her like a new bride being carried over the threshold.
7. Immediately upon her arrival at Farthy, Tony kissed her earlobe.
8. Upon her arrival at Farthy, Tony Tatterton installed Annie in the room that had first been Leigh's and then Heaven's.
9. Tony gave Annie clothes to wear that had originally belonged to Leigh and Heaven.
10. Tony said he would have the pool filled because he knew Annie liked to swim. The pool was dilapidated and no one had ever told Tony that Annie liked to swim.
11. He thought Scuttles, Jillian's first horse, was still alive.
12. He whispered Heaven's name when he kissed Annie.
13. He felt her up when she was paralyzed.
14. He decided he would tell her what to read and what TV shows to watch.
15. He addressed her as "Heaven."
16. He subjected her to lengthy good-night kisses.
17. Tony once told her that it was "wonderful" to have

Annie at Farthy and to "be able to take you back in time with me."

18. Tony once told Annie that she, Heaven, and Leigh sometimes ran together as one person in his mind.

19. Tony once told Annie that the past was more important to him than the future.

20. Tony talked Annie into dying her hair silvery blonde, the color of Leigh and Heaven's hair.

21. He referred to her as moving through the halls of Farthinggale Manor "again."

22. He told her that one of Heaven's nightgown's was one of *her* favorites.

23. He began to rave about her "feminine shoulders that can tease and torment the strongest men."

24. He told her he didn't want any of her "hillbilly relatives" showing up at Farthy. (He had originally made that admonition to Heaven.)

25. He came into her bedroom completely naked and started calling her Leigh and telling her he loved her.

26. The morning after his naked parade into Annie's room, he asked her if she wanted him to rub some body oils on her.

27. When Aunt Fanny came to Farthy to take Annie away, Tony told her she couldn't take Annie because she was his.

Granny Casteel's Philosophy About Hard Times

"Hard times ages ya like bad weather ages the bark on a tree. If yer smart, that's the tree ya'll lean on."

Rye Whiskey's Philosophy About "Spirits" and How They Felt About Young People

"Spirits hate young people roamin' 'bout. Makes 'em jittery 'cause the young folks got so much energy and brightness 'bout them."

Overreaction 101: 19 of the Things Annie Said Good-Bye to at the Memorial Service for Heaven and Logan Stonewall

1. Mommy and Daddy
2. Herself as a little girl
3. Family get-togethers
4. Family encouragement
5. Her mother's embrace
6. Her father's laughter
7. Sunday dinners
8. Holidays
9. The reasons for the holidays
10. Thanksgiving dinners
11. Singing around the piano
12. Playing charades
13. Looking for Easter eggs
14. Eating chocolate rabbits
15. Sunday walks
16. Vacations at the shore
17. Staying up on New Year's Eve
18. Presents
19. Everything "that made life delightful"

Overreaction 202: 18 of the Things Annie Missed After a Short While Spent at Farthinggale Manor

1. Her own room
2. The scent of her own linens
3. The feel of her own quilts
4. Her own dresses
5. Her own shoes
6. Giggling on the phone with her girlfriends
7. Listening to music
8. Parties
9. Dancing
10. Laughing with people her own age
11. Simple things
12. Complicated things

13. Seeing flowers in her front yard
14. Watching her mother crochet
15. Her father reading the newspaper
16. Luke
17. Watching him walk down the street
18. Talking on the phone with him

Mrs. Broadfield's Philosophy About Rich Kids

"[R]ich young girls ... don't know what it is to sacrifice and struggle, to do without, to live through pain and hardship ... [R]ich, pampered spoiled people are weak and they don't have the strength to fight adversity when it strikes, so they remain crippled ... they're invalids, trapped by their own wealth and luxury, stupid blobs."

The 4-Course "Revenge" Meal Mrs. Broadfield Had Rye Whiskey Prepare for Annie

1. Fried chicken
2. Whipped potatoes
3. Steamed vegetables
4. Laxative powder to taste

The 3 Ways Annie Described Mrs. Broadfield

1. Sadistic
2. Vengeful
3. Hateful

—11—

WEB OF DREAMS
(1990)

'Tis true, there's magic in the web of it . . .

—William Shakespeare, *Othello*

We should show life neither as it is nor as it ought to be, but as we see it in our dreams.

—Anton Chekhov, *The Seagull*

CHAPTER LISTING

Prologue

STORY SYNOPSIS

Web of Dreams is the final book in the Casteel series, but does not continue Luke and Annie's story from *Gates of Paradise*. *Web of Dreams* is a "prequel" to the Casteel Saga; it tells the story of Leigh VanVoreen, Heaven's mother. The story begins with Luke and Annie arriving at Farthinggale Manor for Troy Tatterton's funeral. Annie finds her grandmother Leigh's diary, and the rest of *Web of Dreams* is Leigh's story. It begins on Leigh's 12th birthday. Her mother Jillian is taking her to Farthinggale Manor to meet Tony Tatterton, for whom she's doing some artwork. Troy Tatterton is four when Leigh first meets him. Jillian suddenly divorces Leigh's cruise line-owner father, Cleave, and announces her forthcoming marriage to Tony Tatterton. Tony catches Leigh unzipped before the wedding rehearsal and does her the "favor" of zipping her up. (The "Uh-Oh Alert" should be sounding right about now.) Later, Tony considerately undresses Leigh for her bath after she's caught outside in a snowstorm. In a dramatic series of events, Leigh learns that Cleave is not her real father, Jillian and Tony marry, and young Troy ends up in the hospital. Jillian decides that she wants Leigh to spend more time with Tony and "tire him out" so that he won't bother *her* for sex. Leigh begins attending the Winterhaven School, and Tony conceives the Tatterton Portrait Doll. After much coaxing and duplicitous reassuring, Leigh reluctantly agrees to pose naked for the first doll. Tony feels her all over while he's painting her portrait. (Sound the "Uh-Oh Alert" again.) Much to Leigh's dismay, Cleave remarries, and later, she is stunned to learn that Tony has painted *himself* naked into the painting he did for the doll he made of her. Eventually, Tony rapes Leigh, his own stepdaughter, but Jillian doesn't believe Leigh when she confides in her.

Leigh learns she is pregnant (with Heaven, of course), and she flees Farthy to go live with her Grandma Jankins in Texas. On the way, she meets Luke Casteel in Atlanta. Immediately trusting Luke, Leigh tells him everything. He proposes marriage, she accepts, and they are quickly wed. Luke and Leigh travel to the Willies to live with Luke's Ma and Pa. Leigh dies giving birth to Annie's mother, Heaven. Annie finishes reading the diary and *Web of Dreams* ends with her closing the diary and the doors of Farthinggale Manor and going to attend her father's funeral.

THE QUIZZES

1. Multiple Choice

1. What was the "title" of Leigh VanVoreen's diary?
   A. *The VanVoreen Chronicles*
   B. *My Life & Times*
   C. *My Story*
   D. *Leigh's Book*

2. How tall was the Christmas tree that was put in Leigh's playroom when she was five?
   A. 4 feet
   B. 25 feet
   C. 6 feet
   D. 2 feet

3. What was the cover of Leigh VanVoreen's diary made of?
   A. Black vinyl
   B. Pink cloth
   C. Rose-colored leather
   D. Brown paper

4. What did Leigh's Grandpa Jankins do for a living?
   A. He was a foreman at an oil field.
   B. He was a bookie.
   C. He was an electrical engineer.
   D. He was a judge.

5. How many times a night did Jillian VanVoreen brush her hair?

   A. 200
   B. 1,000
   C. 100
   D. None. She never brushed her hair. She believed
      brushing weakened the roots.

6. What tune did Cleave VanVoreen's pocket watch play
   when the cover was opened?
   A. "My Way"
   B. "Greensleeves"
   C. "As Times Goes By"
   D. "The Lady Is a Tramp"

7. What was in the birthday package for Leigh that
   Jillian referred to as "girl business"?
   A. A bra
   B. Crotchless panties
   C. A diaphragm
   D. A case of feminine hygiene spray

8. According to Leigh, what profession did some of her
   girlfriends at school aspire to?
   A. Prostitute
   B. Court stenographer
   C. Airline stewardess
   D. Brain surgeon

9. What historical figure did Leigh think of the first
   time she saw Tony Tatterton's Farthinggale Manor
   butler, Curtis?
   A. George Washington
   B. Genghis Khan
   C. Abraham Lincoln
   D. Charlie Chaplin

10. What was Tony Tatterton wearing the first time Leigh
    met him?
    A. A red velour bathrobe with white silk pajamas.
    B. A burgundy velvet smoking jacket and dark
       slacks.
    C. A black double-breasted suit with a black shirt
       and red tie.
    D. Nothing. The first time Leigh met Tony was
       when she accidentally walked in on him as he
       was stepping out of the shower.

11. What room in Farthinggale Manor did Leigh consider the most "impressive"?
    A. The dining room
    B. Tony Tatterton's bedroom
    C. The billiard room
    D. The upstairs bathroom

12. What piece of jewelry did Tony Tatterton give Leigh VanVoreen for her twelfth birthday?
    A. A gold and diamond ocean liner pendant
    B. A diamond initial "L" pendant
    C. A ruby and diamond ring
    D. An opal and emerald bracelet

13. What did Tony Tatterton's mother die from?
    A. Pancreatic cancer
    B. Suicide
    C. A rare blood disease
    D. Heart disease

14. What did Tony Tatterton's father die from?
    A. Prostatic cancer
    B. Testicular cancer
    C. A heart attack
    D. Suicide

15. At the time of their marriage, what did Tony Tatterton believe Jillian VanVoreen's age was?
    A. 21
    B. 25
    C. 32
    D. 28

16. What was the name of the clothing store where Leigh and Jillian VanVoreen bought their Thanksgiving outfits for Leigh's first Thanksgiving dinner at Farthinggale Manor?
    A. Françoise Limited
    B. Gary Dermer Limited
    C. Andre's Boutique
    D. Joseph Francis

17. What was the culinary specialty of the French chef Jillian hired to cater her and Tony's wedding?
    A. The "most darling" spinach crepes
    B. Lobster bisque

    C. Clams casino
    D. Peasant bread

18. What color was the bridesmaid gown Leigh wore in Jillian's wedding?
    A. Pink
    B. White
    C. Green
    D. Aqua

19. Where in Farthinggale Manor was Jillian and Tony Tatterton's wedding ceremony held?
    A. The dining room
    B. Tony's downstairs office
    C. The trophy room
    D. The great entry hall

20. Which of Leigh's body parts did Tony Tatterton offer to wash after he got her naked and into a hot bath after Leigh's ordeal in the maze during a snowstorm?
    A. Her feet
    B. Her back
    C. Her breasts
    D. Her inner thighs

21. What did Jillian give Tony Tatterton for their first Christmas together as man and wife?
    A. A Porsche.
    B. An original Matisse print.
    C. A pair of Levi button-fly jeans.
    D. A solid gold tie clip with diamonds, engraved "Love, Jillian" on the back.

22. What did Leigh give Troy Tatterton for Christmas the first Christmas after Jillian and Tony Tatterton's wedding?
    A. A chemistry set
    B. A toy train set
    C. An erector set
    D. A fully functioning, professional jukebox

23. Who was the "first Tatterton model"?
    A. Jillian Tatterton
    B. Leigh VanVoreen
    C. Mildred Pierce
    D. Lillian Rumford

24. How old was Tony Tatterton when he began drawing and painting nude people?
    A. 16
    B. 9
    C. 11
    D. 25

25. What sexual practice did Leigh learn about from Marie Johnson?
    A. French kissing
    B. Fellatio
    C. Cunnilingus
    D. Sexual intercourse with the woman on top

26. What was Mildred Pierce's profession?
    A. Lawyer
    B. Surgeon
    C. Secretary
    D. Accountant

27. In what state did Mildred Pierce's children live?
    A. Connecticut
    B. Maine
    C. Arkansas
    D. Montana

28. What was engraved on the gold locket that Troy Tatterton gave to Leigh for her birthday?
    A. "With love forever, Troy"
    B. "Oodles of cooties from Troy"
    C. "For my sister, Leigh"
    D. "Love, Troy"

29. What did Mildred and Cleave give Leigh for her thirteenth birthday?
    A. A music box that played some of *The Nutcracker Suite*.
    B. A mink jacket.
    C. A cruise ship.
    D. They named a cruise ship after her.

30. What word did Tony Tatterton use to describe Jillian and Leigh's beauty?
    A. "Bitchin' "
    B. "Erotic"

C. "Mesmerizing"

D. "Sumptuous"

31. How much money did Leigh have in her wallet when she decided to run away from Farthinggale Manor and head for Texas?

   A. More than $50

   B. $6.99

   C. $129.76

   D. Barely $20

32. How much money did Leigh steal from Tony Tatterton when she decided to run away from Farthinggale Manor and head for Texas?

   A. Nearly $200

   B. Barely $100

   C. $1,000

   D. Close to $50

33. Where did Grandma Jankins live?

   A. Goldthwaite, Texas

   B. Fullerton, Texas

   C. Clarendon, Texas

   D. Nacogdoches, Texas

34. What magic trick did Luke Casteel perform for Leigh VanVoreen the first time he met her?

   A. He changed a one-dollar bill into a five-dollar bill.

   B. He pulled a quarter out of her nose.

   C. He made her handkerchief disappear.

   D. He took her bra off without taking off her blouse.

35. What was the name of the restaurant Luke Casteel took Leigh VanVoreen to before he proposed to her?

   A. Spike's Joint

   B. Winner's Row

   C. Ma's Place

   D. The Willies Diner

2. True or False

1. When Annie and Logan returned to Farthinggale Manor for Troy Tatterton's funeral, the house was boarded up and deserted.

2. In her "hair falling out" dream, Leigh VanVoreen was wearing a silk sweater.

3. Leigh's mother usually took care of buying Leigh's clothes, things for the house, and all needed gifts.

4. Troy Tatterton was 18 years old when Leigh first met him.

5. Curly had curly red hair.

6. Michelle Almstead had a swimming pool.

7. *The Jillian* had four swimming pools.

8. The Spensers once took Leigh VanVoreen to an Italian restaurant called Rick's Place.

9. Ray Fulton's family had a seaside home on Cape Cod.

10. Troy Tatterton was the first man to see Leigh naked after Leigh passed the age of 10.

11. Cleave VanVoreen gave Leigh a gold heart locket for Christmas the first Christmas after his divorce from Jillian.

12. Troy Tatterton awoke with a bad cold on the New Year's Day following his brother Tony's marriage to Jillian.

13. Tony Tatterton took Leigh to an Italian restaurant called Giuseppe's while waiting for news about his recently hospitalized brother, Troy.

14. Jennifer Longstone was taller than Leigh VanVoreen.

15. Tony Tatterton began drawing Leigh for her Tatterton portrait doll from the bottom up, starting with her bare feet.

16. Jillian Tatterton loved to travel.

17. Joshua John Bennington lived just outside of Boston.

18. Joshua John Bennington's family had a home in West Palm Beach, Florida, and a beach house on Cape Cod.

19. A 10-piece band performed at the birthday party Jillian gave for Leigh prior to her being raped by Tony.

20. At her "pre-rape" birthday party, Leigh went off with Joshua Bennington and "directed" him to touch her breasts.

21. Troy Tatterton was the man who took Leigh VanVoreen's virginity.

22. The reason Cleave VanVoreen sent Chester Goodman to tell Leigh he could not make their date was because a VanVoreen ocean liner had broken down in the Atlantic.

23. Luke Casteel described his beat-up old pickup truck as his "Rolls-Royce."

3. Bonus Questions

1. What was the "most precious gift" Leigh VanVoreen received on her 12th birthday?

2. How old was Troy Tatterton when he first started swimming?

3. What was engraved on the back of the charm that Tony Tatterton gave Leigh VanVoreen for her 12th birthday?

4. What was the color of Mrs. Wilson's eyes?

5. What was the first "name" Leigh ever heard her mother call her father to his face?

6. What was the price range of clothing at Andre's Boutique?

7. What was Mildred Pierce wearing the first time Leigh met her?

8. What was the memento Jillian had designed to give to the guests at the birthday party for Leigh that took place prior to her being raped by Tony?

9. What outfit did Tony Tatterton wear to breakfast the morning after he raped Leigh?

10. What was the "name" of Luke Casteel's beat-up old pickup truck?

11. What were the names of Luke Casteel's two dogs?

4. Super Bonus Questions

1. At what age did Leigh VanVoreen see a Punch and Judy puppet show at a museum?

2. Who were the guests and what was the seating arrangement at the very first meal Leigh VanVoreen ever ate at Farthinggale Manor?

3. What was the name of Cleave VanVoreen's second-biggest luxury liner?
4. How did Jillian VanVoreen learn to speak French and Italian?
5. What specific type of diamond hair accessory did Lillian Rumford wear to Leigh's first Thanksgiving dinner at Farthinggale Manor?
6. What were the two French phrases that Marie Johnson said to Jennifer and Leigh upon her arrival at Winterhaven after a vacation in Europe?
7. What did Tony Tatterton consider his "greatest artistic achievement"?

5. The Kinky Bonus Question

What did Leigh's mother say Leigh's father's skin tasted like?

6. The Prurient Interest Bonus Questions

1. Other than her father, who was the first man that Leigh VanVoreen ever kissed?
2. What was Leigh VanVoreen's favorite book of all the titles in Tony Tatterton's "enormous" library?

7. The Prurient Interest "Which Twin Has the Toni?" Bonus Question

Did Leigh have a tiny birthmark under her right breast or under her left breast?

8. The Epistolary Bonus Questions

1. Who wrote Leigh VanVoreen a letter that was signed, "Fondly, Raymond"?
2. Who wrote Leigh the letter that began, "I hope this letter finds you safe and well"?
3. To whom did Leigh VanVoreen write the letter that

began, "I am sorry that I had to run away, but you wouldn't listen to me"?

4. To whom did L. Stanford Banning write the letter that began, "As you know, I did locate your step-daughter in the hills of West Virginia"?

9. The Unkind and Heartless Bonus Question

Who was the homeliest bridesmaid in Jillian and Tony Tatterton's wedding party?

10. The Arcane Reference Bonus Question

What Greek goddess did Leigh feel her mother looked like as she danced with her new husband, Tony Tatterton, at their Farthinggale Manor wedding reception?

11. The "Who Could Possibly Know This?!" Bonus Question

On what page and in what paragraph of Jillian VanVoreen and Tony Tatterton's prenuptial agreement did it state that in the event of a divorce (for *any* reason), Jillian would get half of what Tony was worth?

12. Who Said It?

1. "Is everyone known by what their father does?"
2. "I wish you would treat her more like what she is and not like some tomboy."
3. "I am opening an office in Europe to try to capture the growing European market for travelers who want to come not only to America, but also travel to the vacation spots I have been establishing with my travel experts."
4. "I want to take care of you from now on, protect you, love you. Never again will anyone, even someone rich and powerful, hurt you."

5. "I just want to put this back. Somehow, I feel it belongs here among all the other memories."

A. Jillian VanVoreen
B. Luke Casteel
C. Annie Stonewall
D. Leigh VanVoreen
E. Cleave VanVoreen

LEAFING THROUGH . . .
WEB OF DREAMS

12 of Leigh VanVoreen's 12th Birthday Gifts

1. A dozen cashmere sweaters
2. A dozen skirts
3. Silk blouses
4. Gold hoop earrings
5. A diamond bracelet from Tiffany's
6. Chanel perfume
7. Scented soaps
8. A pearl comb and brush set
9. Lipstick
10. A leather-bound diary
11. A cashmere skiing outfit
12. A bra

15 of Jillian VanVoreen's Timely Tips About Men, Women, and Intercourse Between the Sexes

1. "Men, especially men of position and wealth, like to be seen with women who are stunning."
2. "Never let a man know exactly what you're thinking."
3. "Always remember . . . women can *never* be as promiscuous as men. Never . . . It's all right for

men to be that way. It's expected. They want to prove their manhood, but if a woman is that way, she will lose everything important. Nice girls don't go all the way. Not until they're married."

4. "Don't marry a man who is more in love with his business than he is with you."

5. "It's good to practice keeping a man waiting for you."

6. "Always wear high heels, they are much more flattering to one's legs."

7. "[M]en never stop being little boys. They like to be babies and pampered, and they are always so stubborn."

8. "Never let a man take you for granted."

9. "[N]ever marry anyone who is a slave to his business, no matter how rich he might be or handsome."

10. "It's all right to fish for compliments . . . A woman should sound a little insecure, no matter how sure of herself she might be."

11. "Men appreciate women who are not talkative and gossipy around the dinner table. Men like to dominate the conversations with their talk of politics and business."

12. "Men can be so insistent, so annoying with their male drives and needs. They'll pester you to death until you give in to their lust."

13. "A woman has to guard her beauty like a precious jewel, keep it encased, protected, permit men to look upon her, gaze at her longingly, but rarely touch because every touch absorbs, takes away, diminishes."

14. "[M]en like it when beautiful women pretend to be modest."

15. "GOOD GIRLS DON'T GO ALL THE WAY!"

Still Another "Gone with the Wind" Reference (as Uttered by Leigh VanVoreen)

"I had never dreamed about living on an estate or going to parties with aristocratic people whose homes were so old and famous they had their own names like Tara in *Gone with the Wind*."

4 of the Things Jillian Jankins VanVoreen Had Wanted to Do When She Was Young

1. She wanted to live in a garret.
2. She wanted to be the lover of a poor poet in Paris.
3. She wanted to be a starving artist.
4. She wanted to display her works along the River Seine.

Jana Jankins's Thoughts About Feminist Ideology

"A woman had only one purpose in life—to be a wife and a mother."

Tony Tatterton's Philosophy About Rich People

"Rich people tend to get bored faster."

Rye Whiskey's 4-Course Menu for the First Meal Leigh VanVoreen Ever Ate at Farthinggale Manor

1. Fruit cup
2. Salad
3. Cajun shrimp on wild rice
4. Peach melba

Cleave VanVoreen's Philosophy About Love

"Love can be like that, you know, like a blast of sunlight reflecting off the water. You can't look directly into it; you've got to shade your eyes or close them altogether, and when you do that, you see only what you want to see."

Cleave VanVoreen's Philosophy About Men

"When a man is settled in his ways, it's difficult, if not impossible, for him to change."

4 of the "Familiar Scents" Leigh Remembered About Her Father

1. His after-shave
2. His cologne
3. His pipe tobacco
4. The smell of the sea

Jillian VanVoreen's Philosophy About Pity

"Pity is the most degrading emotion. Even if you are upset, don't give anyone the satisfaction of knowing it. It makes them feel superior."

The 3 Times Tony Eagerly Suggested That Leigh Get Naked and into a Hot Tub After She Got Lost in the Maze During a Snowstorm (After Which He Undressed Her and Offered to Wash Her Back)

1. "Jillian . . . you should get Leigh into a warm bath . . ."
2. "Jillian, you should get her into a warm bath . . ."
3. "Jillian, get her into a warm bath . . ."

Jillian Tatterton's Philosophy About Temperament and Beauty

"People with quiet, happy dispositions age far more slowly than people who are always annoyed and upset."

The Best Line of Bullshit Tony Tatterton Ever Came up with as an Excuse to Feel Leigh's Nude Body as She Posed for Her Tatterton Portrait Doll

"Sometimes, an artist has to make contact with his subject so he truly absorbs the lines and curves in his consciousness."

10 Things Leigh Found Wrong with Her Father, Cleave's, Second Wife, Mildred Pierce

1. She was tall.
2. She was thin.
3. Her nose was long.
4. Her nose was bony.
5. She had a poor complexion.
6. She had pockmarks on her forehead.
7. Her hair looked like she rarely washed it.

8. Her hair was dull.
9. Her hair had a lot of gray streaks.
10. She had no figure.

4 of the "Cloud" Questions Troy Tatterton Asked Leigh VanVoreen

1. "What makes the clouds move?"
2. "Why doesn't the wind blow right through them?"
3. "If I were up there, would the wind push me, too?"
4. "[W]ould it break me into pieces like a cloud?"

16 of the Attractions at the Circus Where Luke Casteel Worked

1. One-eyed giants
2. A snake lady
3. The smallest man in the world
4. The bearded lady
5. Boris the lion tamer
6. The "greatest acrobatic team in the air"
7. Siamese twins
8. The fattest man in the world
9. Midgets
10. The tallest man in the world
11. The strongest man in the world
12. Jugglers
13. Fire eaters
14. A knife throwing act
15. The magician, the Amazing Mandello
16. Gittle the Hungarian fortune-teller

—12—

DAWN
(1990)

Ah, sad and strange as in dark summer dawns
The earliest pipe of half-awaken'd birds ...

—Alfred, Lord Tennyson; *The Princess*

CHAPTER LISTING

STORY SYNOPSIS

Dawn is the first book of the Cutler family series. The series consists of *Dawn; Secrets of the Morning; Twilight's Child; Midnight Whispers;* and *Darkest Hour.* Dawn Longchamp lives with her brother, Jimmy, her mother, Sally Jean, and her father Ormand. The story begins with the family moving to Richmond, Virginia. Sally Jean learns she is once again pregnant, and later, Dawn's sister, Fern, is born. Ormand gets a job at the Emerson Peabody School and Jimmy and Dawn go there for free. Dawn is tormented at school. One of her classmates, Clara Cutler, inexplicably hates her. Dawn meets Clara's brother, Philip, to whom she is attracted. Dawn's mother, Sally Jean, gets sick. Dawn goes parking with Philip and lets him feel her breasts. She likes it. Jimmy runs away and is brought back, and when Dawn kisses him, he doesn't pull away when her breast touches his arm. Dawn sings at a school concert; afterward she once again goes parking with Philip and this time he bares and plays with her breasts before a car comes. Tragedy strikes Sally Jean, and in a major development, Ormand is arrested at the hospital for allegedly kidnapping Dawn at birth. Dawn learns a horrifying secret about her true identity, and who her real parents and siblings are. She is sent to Cutler's Cove Hotel where she meets her true parents and her mean grandmother and is given a job as a chambermaid. Her mother, Laura Sue, is a nervous wreck; her father, Randolph, is strange; her brother tries to make it with her. One day, Jimmy visits the hotel. Dawn and Jimmy have sex in a hidden room and are caught by Clara Sue, who then blackmails Dawn. Philip commits the ultimate crime against Dawn. Clara Sue calls the police on Jimmy and he is taken away. Dawn learns that Randolph is not her father; her real father is a famous singer. Dawn confronts her mother, who confirms the story, and the novel ends with Dawn being sent away to New York to study singing.

THE QUIZZES

1. Multiple Choice

1. How old was Dawn when the Longchamps moved away from Granville?
   A. 14
   B. 12
   C. 19
   D. 23

2. What color hair did Daddy (Ormand) Longchamp have?
   A. Shining white
   B. Dark brown
   C. Radiant blonde
   D. Fiery blonde

3. Where in Virginia did the Longchamps move to after they left Granville?
   A. Fairfax
   B. Boykins
   C. Richmond
   D. Weyers Cave

4. What was the name of the Granville bar Ormand Longchamp was known to frequent?
   A. Frankie's Bar and Grill
   B. The Brick
   C. Cheers
   D. The Kingsland Pub

5. What was the only thing of real value that the Longchamp family possessed?
   A. A first edition of *Lolita*
   B. An antique diamond ring
   C. An original Picasso sketch
   D. A strand of cultured pearls

6. What did Mr. Wengrow tap on his homeroom desk if he wanted to get a student's attention?
   A. A baseball bat
   B. A pencil
   C. A yardstick
   D. A cricket bat

7. What was Dawn Longchamp's first class her very first day at Emerson Peabody?
   - A. English
   - B. Chemistry
   - C. Physics
   - D. Phys ed

8. What was the students' derogatory nickname for their principal, Mrs. Turnbell?
   - A. Mrs. Turncoat
   - B. Mrs. Turkey Balls
   - C. Mrs. Turnkey
   - D. Mrs. Turn-Your-Stomach

9. What was the name of Dawn Longchamp's Emerson Peabody music teacher?
   - A. Mr. Cutler
   - B. Mr. Moore
   - C. Ms. Swanson
   - D. Mr. Bloom

10. What musical instrument was Dawn teaching herself to play at the time she began attending Emerson Peabody?
    - A. Guitar
    - B. Piano
    - C. Flute
    - D. Violin

11. What did Jimmy do whenever he was worried or frightened about his mother?
    - A. He would sit at the kitchen table and eat Oreos until he threw up.
    - B. He would go into the bathroom and masturbate for an hour.
    - C. He wouldn't talk and he wouldn't move.
    - D. He would go outside and kick the parking meter in front of the house two hundred times.

12. What trait ran in Sally Jean's family?
    - A. Stubbornness
    - B. Promiscuity
    - C. Drunkenness
    - D. Selfishness

13. Complete the following vow made by Philip Cutler:

"Cross my heart and hope to fall in a well full of
_____ _____."
  A. Chocolate sauce
  B. Cow dung
  C. Strawberry Jell-O
  D. Motor oil

14. What was Jimmy Longchamp's middle name?
  A. Stephen
  B. Gary
  C. Dominick
  D. Paul

15. What sex game did Philip Cutler tell Dawn he'd like
    to play with her someday?
  A. Strip checkers
  B. Strip poker
  C. Strip chess
  D. A game of his own invention called "Who
     Came First?"

16. What disease killed Sally Jean Longchamp?
  A. Consumption (Tuberculosis)
  B. Liver cancer
  C. AIDS
  D. Polio

17. What cruel trick did Dawn's Emerson Peabody
    "friends" play on her the night of her first school re-
    cital?
  A. They put itching powder in her panties and bra.
  B. They put Spanish Fly in her soda.
  C. They put a live worm in each of her shoes.
  D. They sprayed her with cans of stink-bomb
     spray.

18. What kind of food did Philip Cutler take Dawn out
    for after her first Emerson Peabody music recital?
  A. Pizza
  B. Chinese food
  C. Tacos
  D. Hamburgers and fries

19. What did Emerson Peabody give to Ormand
    Longchamp after Sally Jean's death?
  A. Two weeks off with pay

B. A frozen turkey and a fruit basket
C. A week off with pay
D. $100

20. What did Dawn believe was the date of her birthday?
    A. July 16
    B. December 14
    C. May 1
    D. July 10

21. What was the name of the seafood restaurant where Randolph Cutler planned to hold the first Cutler "family outing" that included Dawn?
    A. The Guppy Grotto
    B. The Fishing Hole
    C. The Seafood House
    D. Seafood and More

22. What was Dawn's favorite song?
    A. "Yesterday"
    B. "We Will Rock You"
    C. "The Way You Look Tonight"
    D. "Over the Rainbow"

23. What Cutler Cove street did Mrs. Dalton live on?
    A. Crescent Street
    B. Circle Drive
    C. Arc Lane
    D. Roundabout Drive

2. True or False

1. Jimmy Longchamp was ten years old when he and his family moved away from Granville.
2. Sally Jean and Jimmy Longchamp both had red hair.
3. Jimmy Longchamp was born on a farm.
4. Dawn was only 14 years old when she first set foot in a bar.
5. The Longchamps had two phones in their Richmond apartment.
6. Sally Jean Longchamp cleaned Mrs. Anderson's house every Sunday.
7. Jimmy Longchamp originally wanted to wear dun-

garees and a polo shirt for his first day of classes at Emerson Peabody.

 8. Louise Williams had a red ponytail.
 9. Philip Cutler was in the tenth grade when Dawn first met him.
10. Philip Cutler liked to take girls parking at a spot on a hill that overlooked the Anna River.
11. The first extracurricular school activity Jimmy Longchamp took up at Emerson Peabody was the intramural football team.
12. Philip Cutler had a red car that was given to him by his father.
13. Ormand Longchamp was older than Reuben Longchamp.
14. Philip Cutler was a starting pitcher on the Emerson Peabody varsity baseball team.
15. Dawn Longchamp washed her hair twice the night of her first Emerson Peabody recital.
16. Sally Jean Longchamp was buried in a family plot behind their cabin in the Willies.
17. Ormand Longchamp was arrested and charged with the kidnapping of Eugenia "Dawn Longchamp" Cutler.
18. The Cutler family lived in the old section of the Cutler Cove Hotel.
19. Randolph Cutler wore a ruby pinky ring.
20. Philip Cutler once bought Grandmother Cutler as a birthday gift perfume that cost $100 a bottle.
21. After leaving Cutler Cove, Dawn took a train to New York.

3. Bonus Questions

 1. What was the "first of a thousand lies" told to Dawn by her "Momma" and "Daddy"?
 2. What did Fern Longchamp weigh at birth?
 3. Where did Sally Jean hide her pearls?
 4. What did Dawn wear for her first day of classes at Emerson Peabody?
 5. What was Jimmy Longchamp's punishment for be-

ing "convicted" of starting the Emerson Peabody cafeteria fight?

6. What was the Emerson Peabody school uniform?
7. What was Eugenia Cutler's middle name?
8. How many chandeliers hung in the lobby of the Cutler Cove Hotel?
9. How did the Cutler Cove Hotel staff differentiate between Grandmother Cutler and Laura Sue Cutler, both of whom had to be addressed as "Mrs. Cutler"?

4. Super Bonus Questions

1. What would supposedly happen to the child if a rat or mouse was in the house when the mother was pregnant?
2. What color jacket was Mrs. Turnbell wearing the first time Dawn and Jimmy met her?
3. Who was Afternoon?
4. Name the two snobby Emerson Peabody students whose fathers were teachers at the school.
5. How did the husband of the waitress who befriended Jimmy Longchamp when he ran away from Richmond die?
6. What was Randolph Cutler wearing the first time Dawn ever set eyes on him?
7. What was the name of the company that Mrs. Dalton's son-in-law worked for?

5. The "Not What It Sounds Like" Bonus Question

What was the deal Mr. Moore offered Dawn in exchange for piano lessons?

6. Epistolary Bonus Questions

1. On whose grave marker was written, "Gone But Not Forgotten"?
2. To whom did Dawn write the letter that began, "As

you know by now, I have been returned to my rightful home and real family, the Cutlers"?
3. To whom did Dawn write the letter that began, "No matter what had happened, I realize I will always call you Daddy"?

7. A Boring and Disgusting Bonus Question

What did Laura Sue Cutler consider the most boring and disgusting thing in her life?

8. Who Said It?

1. "When a brother and sister have the same bad habits, it is not hard to determine that they have them because they come from the same background."
2. "Never, never in the long and prestigious history of this hotel, has a guest had anything stolen out of his or her room."
3. "Philip, what are you doing? I'm taking a shower!"
4. "Mrs. Cutler runs a very tight ship. No excess, no waste. Whoever don't pull his load goes."
5. "I have a full figure, a mature woman's figure. Everyone says so."

A. Grandmother Cutler
B. Mrs. Boston
C. Clara Sue Cutler
D. Dawn Cutler
E. Mrs. Turnbell

LEAFING THROUGH . . . DAWN

"Déjà Vu" Department, Part 1

From *Heaven:* "In what we called our bedroom was one big brass bed with a saggy old stained mattress over coiled springs that squeaked and squealed whenever there was activity on that bed. Sometimes what went on in there was embarrassingly close and loud; the curtain did little to muffle sound." From *Dawn:* "I stopped because we heard Momma moan. Then we heard what sounded like Daddy laughing. A moment later there was the distinct sound of the bedsprings. Jimmy and I knew what that meant. In our close quarters we had grown used to the sounds people often make whenever they make love."

"Déjà Vu" Department, Part 2

1. Leigh Casteel (in the Casteel family series, Books 6, 7, 9, 10, and 11) had a small birthmark beneath her right breast.
2. Dawn Longchamp had a small birthmark just below her left shoulder.

Ormand Longchamp's Philosophy About Luck

"When your luck turns bad, there's nothing to do but change it. A branch that don't bend breaks."

10 of the Emerson Peabody Student Rules

1. "You will address your teachers as either sir or ma'am."
2. "You will come to school dressed neatly and be clean."
3. "Never challenge a command."
4. No bad language.
5. No fighting.
6. No disrespect "in any form or manner."
7. Students are expected to treat each other with respect.
8. No tardiness.
9. No loitering.
10. No vandalism.

4 of the Rotten Things Dawn Longchamp's Emerson Peabody Classmates Did to Her Clothes on Her First Day of School

1. First they broke into her locker and stole her clothes.
2. Then they stuffed them all in the toilet.
3. They then jammed toilet paper into the bowl as well.
4. And finally, someone urinated on everything.

Sally Jean Longchamp's Philosophy About People Whose Eyes Were Too Close Together

Sally Jean once told Dawn "never to trust anyone whose eyes were too close together. She said their mommas, just before giving birth, must have been surprised by snakes."

Philip Cutler's 9-Step Sexual "Seduction of Dawn Longchamp" Agenda the Night of Dawn's First Emerson Peabody Music Recital

1. He and Dawn French kissed.
2. He felt her breast over her sweater.
3. He put his hand under her sweater and on her bra.
4. He took off her bra.
5. He kissed and tongued her bare breast.
6. He put his hand under her skirt.
7. He played with her panties.
8. He tongued her bare nipple.
9. He put his hand inside her panties.

Grandmother Cutler's Philosophy About Dirty Laundry

"Members of the family do not show their emotions or their problems to the guests. As far as the guests are concerned, everything is always wonderful here."

The 8 Items of Proper Etiquette Laura Sue Cutler Was Positive Dawn Did Not Know

1. The proper way to greet someone
2. How to curtsy
3. How to look down when given a compliment
4. How to sit at a formal table
5. The proper silverware to use
6. The proper way to eat soup
7. The proper way to butter bread
8. The proper way to reach for things

3 Things That Left Dawn "Floundering in Despair" After She Began to Live at the Cutler Cove Hotel

1. Her father's "bizarre manner"
2. Her grandmother's "unexpected harshness"
3. Her mother's "strange infirmities"

—13—

SECRETS OF THE MORNING
(1991)

There's a land that I heard of
Once in a lullaby.

—E.Y. Harburg, "Over the Rainbow"

CHAPTER LISTING

STORY SYNOPSIS

Secrets of the Morning is the second book in the Cutler series and it begins exactly where *Dawn* ends, with Dawn on her way to New York to study singing. The plane lands and Dawn is immediately a stranger in a strange land. She takes a cab to Agnes Morris's house, the place where she is to live while in New York, and meets her roommate, Trisha Kramer. They become fast friends, and Dawn starts classes at the Bernhardt School. She hears from Jimmy, who has joined the Army. Laura Sue calls but won't tell Dawn the name of her real father. Dawn writes to Ormand; Philip comes to visit. Dawn throws Philip out, and later, Jimmy visits. Dawn and Jimmy stay out past Dawn's curfew, and Dawn is grounded by housemother Agnes for several months. Randolph, Clara Sue, and Laura Sue visit Dawn in New York. Dawn learns that Ormand has remarried. Dawn is accepted into the famous singer Michael Sutton's voice class. Michael seduces Dawn and they end up in bed together; later, Dawn spends the Thanksgiving holiday with Michael in his apartment. Dawn realizes she's pregnant with Michael's child and tells the singer, who leaves immediately for London. When she goes to his apartment and finds him gone, she hysterically runs out into traffic and gets hit by a car. She is then sent to the family plantation, The Meadows, to have her baby under the care of Grandmother Cutler's evil religious fanatic sister, Miss Emily. Miss Emily is horrible and treats Dawn cruelly. While there, Dawn learns that Emily's sister, the simpleminded Charlotte, had also had a baby at one time, but it's gone. After undergoing the tortures of hell, Dawn gives birth to Christie, but the baby is immediately taken from her and given away for adoption (Grandmother Cutler's doing). Jimmy comes and rescues Dawn from The Meadows. Grandmother Cutler dies and no one knows anything about what happened to Christie. At the reading of Grandmother Cutler's will, the truth about Dawn's parentage is revealed, and she inherits a majority interest in Cutler's Cove Hotel. Dawn leaves with Jimmy to find Christie.

THE QUIZZES

1. Multiple Choice

1. What was the complete and correct name of the Bernhardt School?
   - A. The Bernhardt School for the Arts
   - B. The Bernhardt School for Performing Arts
   - C. The Bernhardt Academy of Music, Theater, and Dance
   - D. The Bernhardt Arts Academy

2. What perfume did Dawn see advertised on a huge sign in a corridor in the New York airport after she first arrived in the Big Apple?
   - A. Obsession by Calvin Klein
   - B. Giorgio
   - C. An unnamed perfume by Elizabeth Arden
   - D. Opium

3. What physical ailment did the taxi driver who met Dawn at the airport in New York have every day?
   - A. Heartburn
   - B. Diarrhea
   - C. Constipation
   - D. Migraine headaches

4. What was the one thing the cabbie that picked Dawn up at the airport told her she must never forget about New York City?
   - A. If four guys with earrings in their noses and tattoos on their foreheads approach her on the subway and ask for the time, they are not concerned about being late for an appointment.
   - B. Most street food should come with a Surgeon General's warning.
   - C. Always tip a New York cabbie.
   - D. If her new apartment had a chalk outline on the bedroom floor, look for another apartment.

5. What instrument was Arthur Garwood studying at the Bernhardt School?
   - A. The violin
   - B. The piano

    C. The oboe
    D. The tuba

6. What color was Trisha Kramer's hair?
    A. Dark brown
    B. Black
    C. Blonde
    D. Red

7. What dance step did Trisha Kramer perform in front of Dawn Cutler the first time Dawn met her?
    A. A pirouette
    B. A pas de bourrée
    C. A plié
    D. A grand pas de basque

8. What was Arthur Garwood's nickname in Agnes Morris's house?
    A. Dr. Death
    B. Scarecrow
    C. Bones
    D. Hawkeye

9. What two classes did Trisha Kramer and Dawn Cutler have together?
    A. Biology and History
    B. English and vocal music
    C. Chemistry and Religion
    D. Spanish and Home Economics

10. Where was Trisha Kramer's family from?
    A. Eastern Pennsylvania
    B. Jamaica
    C. Southern Florida
    D. Upstate New York

11. What was Graham Hill studying at the Bernhardt School?
    A. Dancing
    B. Acting
    C. Orchestral conducting
    D. Painting

12. According to Mr. Van Dan, what did Trisha Kramer have a propensity for?
    A. Hyperbole
    B. Hysteria

    C. Stubbornness

    D. Tardiness

13. What Chekhov play did Dawn see a poster for at the Bernhardt School shortly after she met Mr. Van Dan for the first time?

    A. *The Three Sisters*

    B. *The Cherry Orchard*

    C. *The Sea Gull*

    D. *Uncle Vanya*

14. When told by Madame Steichen that she had a natural instinct for music, what did Dawn eat at George's Luncheonette to celebrate?

    A. A cheeseburger with fried onions and a strawberry shake

    B. French fries and gravy

    C. A banana split

    D. A double fudge chocolate sundae

15. What was the only thing Dawn sensed that Arthur Garwood shared with his parents?

    A. Their joie de vivre

    B. Their talent at witty repartée

    C. Their musical abilities

    D. Their dour personalities

16. How did Sanford Littleton die?

    A. He died in an automobile accident.

    B. He committed suicide.

    C. He was shot in battle.

    D. He was stabbed to death by a mugger.

17. What was Ormand Longchamp's job in prison?

    A. He was a maintenance man in the laundry.

    B. He was an orderly in the prison hospital.

    C. He was a guy named Lester's bitch.

    D. He was the warden's assistant.

18. What was the name of the Italian restaurant where Jimmy and Dawn ate during Jimmy's first visit to Dawn in New York?

    A. Angelina's

    B. Armand's

    C. Antonio's

    D. Aniello's

19. What was Dawn's punishment for staying out past curfew with Jimmy when he visited her in New York?
    A. She had to scrub all the toilets in the house for three weeks.
    B. She was grounded for six weeks.
    C. She was restricted to the dorm for six months.
    D. She had to type all of Agnes Morris's voluminous personal correspondence for four months.

20. What game did Arthur Garwood offer to play with Dawn one Saturday night shortly after Jimmy left New York?
    A. Trivial Pursuit
    B. Checkers
    C. Strip poker
    D. Chess

21. What month was Trisha Kramer born?
    A. February
    B. April
    C. December
    D. June

2. True or False

1. The apartment house Dawn lived in upon first arriving in New York was on the West Side.
2. Agnes Morris owned a recording of *Madamn Butterfly.*
3. Agnes Morris once worked with Stanislavsky.
4. Agnes Morris once played Ophelia in *Hamlet,* for which she got horrible reviews.
5. Mr. Van Dan taught math at the Bernhardt School.
6. The gold watch that Trisha Kramer's father gave her had four diamonds, one each at twelve, three, six, and nine.
7. Everyone called Trisha Kramer's boyfriend Victor, Vic.
8. Graham Hill had black hair.
9. The first person in New York to see Dawn naked was Trisha Kramer.
10. Jimmy Longchamp enlisted in the Marines.

11. Growing up, Trisha Kramer went to one public school in a small town.
12. The Bernhardt School had both a basketball and a football team.
13. At the time Dawn Cutler started attending the Bernhardt School, she had never attended a real play.
14. Arthur Garwood's father was short.
15. Arthur Garwood's mother had light blue eyes.
16. Donald Rossi was eighteen years old when Dawn Cutler first met him.
17. The once-a-year, eagerly anticipated Bernhardt School student talent exhibition was known as Sarah's Performance Jamboree.
18. Arthur Garwood was adopted.
19. Michael Sutton's Bernhardt School vocal class had 25 students.
20. Dawn sang Billy Joel's song, "Just the Way You Are," for her audition for Michael Sutton's Bernhardt School vocal class.
21. Michael Sutton's favorite city was Paris.
22. Dawn originally planned on naming her and Michael Sutton's daughter Sally.
23. One of the first things Emily Booth did to Dawn upon her arrival at The Meadows was to give her a brutal internal vaginal examination.
24. The first person to see Dawn naked at The Meadows was Luther.
25. Lillian Cutler's wake was closed coffin.

3. Bonus Questions

1. Who gave Agnes Morris the castanets she kept in a glass case in her apartment?
2. How far was George's Luncheonette from Agnes Morris's house?
3. Who was the only person to whom Arthur Garwood ever revealed his true relationship with his parents?

4. Super Bonus Questions

1. How do you know when you're a New Yorker?
2. Who was Mr. Fairbanks?
3. What color was the linoleum in Agnes Morris's kitchen?
4. Where was Antonio's located?
5. What melody was engraved inside the locket Michael Sutton gave Dawn for their first and only Christmas together?
6. What does Andrew mean?

5. Trick Bonus Question

Where was Johnny Wilson from?

6. Sartorial Bonus Questions

1. What kind of shoes was Agnes Morris wearing the first time Dawn met her?
2. What was Trisha Kramer wearing the first time Dawn Cutler met her?
3. What color sports jacket was Mr. Van Dan wearing the first time Dawn Cutler met him?
4. What was Arthur Garwood's usual outfit?
5. What did Trisha Kramer and Dawn Cutler wear for their audition for Michael Sutton's vocal class?
6. What did Dawn wear to the recital at the Museum of Modern Art?
7. What color jacket was Grandmother Cutler wearing when she visited Dawn in the New York hospital after Dawn's automobile accident?
8. What was Luther wearing the first time Dawn met him?

7. Epistolary Bonus Questions

1. Complete the following plaque inscription: "To the memory of Sarah Bernhardt/Whose bright light lit

up the stage __ __ ____ _____ _____ ___
_____."

2. To whom was the letter from Lillian Cutler addressed that began, "As you know I have enrolled my granddaughter Dawn in the Bernhardt School and asked Mr. Updike to have her housed in your residence"?

3. Provide the line that *precedes* this line of Arthur Garwood's poem "Dawn": "Even the brightest stars can't loosen the hold/The black fingers of night have on the world and on me."

4. Who wrote Dawn the letter that began, "I'm sorry I haven't written to you much, but I've been busy with my new work among other things"?

5. Who wrote Dawn the letter that began, "There's no one else I care to say good-bye to"?

6. Complete the following rope-skipping rhyme: "My mother, your mother, lives across the way, two fourteen East Broadway."

7. Who wrote Dawn the note that began, "Just knowing you're lying back with your head on this pillow makes me feel good"?

8. Who wrote Dawn the letter that began, "Winter here has been very hard"?

9. To whom did Dawn write the letter that began, "By the time you read this, I will be long gone"?

10. Who said the grace that went, "For this and all our other blessings, Dear Lord we thank you. Amen"?

11. To whom did Dawn write the letter that began, "I've been trying to get in touch with you for months, but Grandmother Cutler's horrible sister Emily has kept me from doing so"?

12. Who wrote the letter that began, "This letter is to serve as my final will and testament and is to be read only immediately after the event of my wife Lillian's death"?

8. A Macabre Bonus Question

Who possessed the ashes of Sanford Littleton?

9. The "Punch Line, Please?" Bonus Question

"These two guys were starving to death in the desert when they come upon this dead camel. The first guy says, 'I'm dying for a camel sandwich but I can't get over the smell.' 'Smell?' the second guy says, '__ ____ ____ ____ ____ ____.' "

10. A Euphemistic Bonus Question

What are the wiggles?

11. Who Said It?

1. "Shortly after I was born, I was kidnapped."
2. "Take off your clothes and come stand here by me in the light."
3. "He doesn't want to be here. His parents made him come. Maybe, when you want to put yourself into a depression, you'll get him to read you some of his poetry."
4. "Now that's a honeymoon."
5. *"I don't believe it! I don't! I don't! This can't be happening!"*

A. Miss Emily
B. Trisha Kramer
C. Clara Sue Cutler
D. Michael Sutton
E. Dawn Cutler

LEAFING THROUGH . . .
SECRETS OF THE MORNING

Miriam Levy's Philosophy About New York

"You mustn't be afraid of New York. It's big, but people are friendly once you get to know them."

The Cab Driver's 3 Pieces of Advice to Dawn as to How to Survive in New York City

1. Live and let live.
2. Keep your eyes straight ahead when you walk the streets.
3. Don't listen to anybody.

8 Items of Agnes Morris's Show Business Memorabilia

1. Copies of play
2. Old novels
3. Old play programs
4. Pictures of actors
5. Pictures of actresses
6. Props
7. Glass figurines
8. A pair of castanets from Rudolph Valentino

Agnes Morris's Philosophy About Memories

"[M]emories are more precious than diamonds or gold."

The 10 Rules the Students Had to Abide by in Agnes Morris's House

1. Never violate a single rule.
2. Don't stay out later than ten P.M. on weekdays.
3. Don't stay out later than midnight on weekends.
4. Agnes must know where anyone goes when they go out.
5. There is never to be any excessive noise.
6. No one is to ever be messy.
7. No one is to ever damage or vandalize the home.
8. Everyone has to have his or her bed turned down by ten in the morning at the latest.
9. Everyone has to help with the once-a-week housecleaning.
10. Phone calls are not permitted after seven o'clock at night unless there is an emergency.

The 7 Things Trisha Kramer Swore She Would Do When She Became a Famous Dancer

1. Dress wildly.
2. Have dozens and dozens of boyfriends with shady reputations.
3. Smoke cigarettes in pearl cigarette holders.
4. Be seen in elegant places.
5. Have her picture taken by reporters wherever she went.
6. Wait to marry until she was almost thirty.
7. Marry someone rich and influential.

7 of the Specious "Bad" Things Lillian Cutler Told Agnes Morris About Dawn in a Letter

1. She was the "bad seed" in the family.
2. She was a juvenile delinquent.
3. She was sexually promiscuous.
4. She was sneaky.
5. She lied.
6. She stole.
7. She was a "major problem child."

The 3 Jokes Donald Rossi Told at the Dinner Table the First Time He Ever Ate with Dawn Cutler

1. The one about the starving guys and the dead camel
2. The one about the housewife and the rotten apple
3. The one about the midget who dies and goes to heaven

5 of the "Dismal Subjects" Arthur Garwood's Poems Were About

1. Animals dying
2. Animals being deserted
3. Stars that burned out
4. People dying from horrible diseases
5. A dove that broke its wings

4 of the Questions That Occurred to Dawn Cutler After Being Told by Arthur Garwood That His Parents Never Had Sex

1. "Why would a man and a woman live together as husband and wife if one of them didn't want to touch the other or be touched?"
2. "Wasn't sex a way of bringing yourself as close to another person, a person you loved, as could be?"
3. "And why would a woman be frightened of it?"
4. "Was it just her fear of becoming pregnant?"

"Déjà Vu" Department (Music Subdivision): The 5 Times the Song "Over the Rainbow" Is Mentioned in V. C. Andrews's Novels

1. Cathy Dollanganger in *Flowers in the Attic* knew how to play the song on the guitar.
2. Annie Casteel's music box in *Gates of Paradise* played the song when it was opened.
3. It was Dawn Longchamp's favorite song in *Dawn*.
4. Dawn Cutler sang it when auditioning for Michael Sutton's Bernhardt School vocal class in *Secrets of the Morning*.
5. Dawn Longchamp sang it at her daughter Christie's 16th birthday party in *Midnight Whispers*.

Michael Sutton's Philosophy on Ego Gratification

"Everyone needs to be stroked, to be told he or she is doing well. We all have egos that have to be petted like little kittens."

10 Examples of the Bullshit Michael Sutton Dished Out to Dawn in Order to Get Her into Bed (And 1 Example of His Post-Coital Bullshit)

1. "I feel as if I know you well. If you are like me, you are a passionate person."
2. "You feel everything more deeply than other, ordinary people do, whether it's happiness or sadness, pleasure or pain, and then you are able to translate that experience into song through your beautiful voice."
3. "Remember this, Dawn, passion makes us desperate."
4. "Your talent makes you different, makes it possible for you to be older faster because you are more perceptive, more sensitive."
5. "Like me, you grow with every passing moment and with every experience."
6. "One second I look at you and you are a naive, young girl, and then I blink and your face changes and you become a provocative, seductive woman, a woman who seems to know exactly what she's doing."
7. "Maybe you're not aware of it yourself, aware of your feminine power, the power you have and will have over men."
8. "Some women, women like you, can turn a man into a boy in seconds ... just like that ... and make them beg, plead for a favorable look, a touch, a kiss."
9. "When you sing with me, it will be like making love, making love for the first time each time we sing together."
10. "You can't sing about the ultimate moment of love if you haven't experienced it."
11. "[W]e are special people, linked forever and ever by our talent and music." (Post-coital.)

The End Result of Michael Sutton's Systematic Seductive Bullshitting of Dawn Cutler

"Finally, hot juices spurted forth to warm up my insides pleasantly and then it was all over."

4 of the Changes Dawn Noticed About Herself While Dressing for the Recital at the Museum of Modern Art

1. Her face had lost its childhood plumpness.
2. She had a more mature glint in her eyes.
3. Her neck looked softer.
4. Her cleavage looked deeper.

Madame Steichen's Definition of the Difference Between an Artist and a Performer

"An artist lives for her work. That's the difference between an artist and a performer, who is usually a person infatuated with himself and not with the beauty of what he creates. Fame is often more of a burden than a blessing."

Madame Steichen's Philosophy About America's Attitude Toward Celebrities

"This country is very foolish when it comes to its entertainers, celebrities. They worship them and then suffer when they discover their gods of stage and screen have feet of clay."

The 9 Things Dawn Said Good-Bye to After Michael Sutton Left Her and She Was Told She Had to Go Live with Her Aunts Until After Her Baby Was Born

1. Dreams of singing
2. Dreams of being a stage star
3. The magic of love
4. The magic of romance
5. Believing that fairy tales sometimes come true
6. Being carefree
7. Being young
8. Being hopeful
9. Being energetic

Emily Booth's Philosophy About Childbirth

"Doctors cost money and are unnecessary when it comes to delivering a baby."

Emily Booth's Philosophy About Hardship

"Difficulties and hardships toughen us and allow us to battle the devil and his followers."

Emily Booth's 8 Rules for Dawn at The Meadows

1. Never go to the west wing of the house where Emily and Charlotte lived.
2. Don't bother Luther.
3. Come down to the kitchen every day at six and set the table.
4. Wash and dry all the dishes and polish the silverware every day.
5. Scrub the floor every day.
6. Every third day, wash all the linens.

7. Clean Dawn's entire wing.
8. Wash the first floor windows on Saturdays.

The 3 Names Miss Emily Suggested for Dawn's Baby

1. Chastity
2. Virtue
3. One of the disciples' names

The 7 Things Dawn Said "Good Riddance" to After Being Rescued from The Meadows by Jimmy

1. Miss Emily.
2. Miss Emily's ugly, frustrated, hateful face.
3. Miss Emily's religious hypocrisy.
4. Miss Emily's habit of making everyone feel evil and despicable.
5. Miss Emily's miserly ways.
6. Miss Emily's jealousy of everything soft and beautiful.
7. Miss Emily's pretense of wanting everything clean while she herself lived in a house that Dawn colorfully described as a muck-filled coffin.

—14—

TWILIGHT'S CHILD
(1992)

And dreaming through the twilight
  That doth not rise nor set,
Haply I may remember,
  and haply may forget.

—Christina Rossetti, "Song"

CHAPTER LISTING

Part One

Part Two

STORY SYNOPSIS

Twilight's Child, Book 3 of the Cutler series, begins where *Secrets of the Morning* ends, with Dawn and Jimmy on their way to find Dawn's newborn daughter, Christie. The adoptive parents do not want to return Christie to Dawn but after it is revealed that Dawn did not consent to the adoption, they give up and hand her over. Later, back at the hotel, Clara Sue maliciously steals Christie and hides her in a laundry basket. Meanwhile, Randolph is losing his mind. Dawn meets Bronson Alcott, the guy with whom it is obvious her mother has been having an affair with for years. Jimmy is discharged from the army and he and Dawn plan their wedding. At the wedding, Randolph runs off. It is now clear to Dawn that Philip still wants her. While on their honeymoon, Dawn and Jimmy learn that Randolph has died, and shortly thereafter, Laura Sue and Bronson Alcott announce their engagement. Bronson reveals a secret about Clara Sue to Dawn. Bronson and Laura Sue marry; Philip gets engaged to Betty; Dawn gets pregnant. Clara Sue viciously attacks Dawn, kicks her in the stomach, and causes her to have a miscarriage. Jimmy and Dawn begin building their own home on the hotel grounds. Philip weds Betty, but takes one of Dawn's nightgowns as an erotic fantasy aid for their wedding night. Clara Sue takes Christie for a ride without Dawn's permission. Philip and Betty have twins, and Jimmy decides to go see Daddy Longchamp. Dawn reveals to Jimmy that they have stopped looking for their lost sister, Fern. Philip once again tries to rape Dawn. Jimmy finds Fern, who accuses her adoptive father of sexually abusing her. He denies it, but Fern leaves her adoptive parents to live with Dawn and Jimmy. Fern starts school and is in constant trouble, and she is suspected of stealing from the hotel. Daddy Longchamp, his new wife Edwina, and their son Gavin visit the hotel. Perversely, Fern makes Christie and Gavin undress and look at each other. One day, Michael Sutton calls Dawn and tells her he wants to see his daughter

Christie. Dawn agrees to let him see her, but the truth is that all he wants is money. Michael is taped blackmailing Dawn and agrees to leave her alone. Clara Sue dies in an accident, and Dawn and Jimmy learn that Fern was lying about her adoptive father. Laura Sue goes crazy. Luther from The Meadows calls to tell Dawn that Miss Emily has died, and the truth about Charlotte's parentage is revealed. The story ends with Dawn learning that she is once again pregnant.

THE QUIZZES

1. Multiple Choice

1. What was the name of the Richmond suburb where Sanford and Patricia Compton lived?
   A. Battle Creek
   B. Mayberry Village
   C. Saddle Creek
   D. Castle Rock

2. What was the name of the Cutler's Cove Hotel comptroller?
   A. Mr. Updike
   B. Mr. Dorfman
   C. Mr. Cheever
   D. Mr. Irving

3. What kind of business was Sanford Compton in?
   A. He owned and operated a linen factory.
   B. He ran an X-rated theater.
   C. He owned a Greek restaurant.
   D. He owned and operated a printing plant.

4. What was Christie Longchamp's short-lived adoptive name?
   A. Violet
   B. Pansy
   C. Daisy
   D. Iris

5. What piece of jewelry did Jimmy give Dawn when he left Cutler Cove after the retrieval of Christie?
   A. Ruby earrings
   B. An opal pendant

    C. A diamond engagement ring
    D. A strand of cultured pearls

6. What was Jimmy Longchamp's assignment for his final six months of duty?
    A. Border patrol in Kuwait
    B. Humanitarian duty in Somalia
    C. Guarding the Panama Canal
    D. Embassy duty in Finland

7. What was the "date" of Jimmy and Dawn's wedding?
    A. October 26th
    B. November 1st
    C. September 21st
    D. December 10th

8. Which of Nussbaum's baked goodies did he insist Trisha Kramer try when she first arrived at Cutler's Cove Hotel for Dawn's wedding?
    A. A pecan pie
    B. An eclair
    C. A strudel
    D. A chocolate cake

9. Who was the first person to toast the bride and groom at Dawn and Jimmy's wedding reception?
    A. Bronson Alcott
    B. Philip Cutler
    C. Randolph Cutler
    D. Agnes Morris

10. How and where did Randolph Cutler die?
    A. He shot himself in the mouth with a rifle in his study.
    B. He drowned in the pool at the Cutler's Cove YMCA.
    C. He had heart failure and collapsed over his mother's grave.
    D. He took an overdose of Xanax in his private bathroom.

11. What fairy tale character did Laura Sue Cutler say she felt like following the death of Randolph Cutler?
    A. Little Red Riding Hood
    B. Cinderella

C. Goldilocks

D. Humpty Dumpty

12. What did Alexandria Alcott die from?
    A. Lou Gehrig's disease
    B. A fatal automobile accident
    C. A degenerative bone disease
    D. Lung cancer

13. What was Nussbaum the chef's nationality?
    A. German
    B. Hungarian
    C. Finnish
    D. Danish

14. What after-dinner aperitif did Bronson Alcott serve to his guests the first time Dawn dined at Beulla Woods?
    A. Sherry
    B. Blackberry brandy
    C. Galliano
    D. Sambucco

15. What did Bronson Alcott's father do for a living?
    A. He was the captain of an oil tanker.
    B. He was an animal trainer for the Ringling Brothers and Barnum and Bailey Circus.
    C. He was a jeweler.
    D. He was an investor and a banker.

16. What did Bronson Alcott's mother die from?
    A. Cancer of the brain
    B. Ovarian cancer
    C. A cancer of the blood
    D. Breast cancer

17. Who was Clara Sue Cutler's real father?
    A. Randolph Cutler
    B. Bronson Alcott
    C. Ormand Longchamp
    D. Buster Morris

18. What beverage was drunk at the groundbreaking of Dawn and Jimmy's new house?
    A. Beer
    B. Champagne
    C. Red wine
    D. Brandy

19. How did Betty Ann Monroe mispronounce Dawn's name?
    A. She called her "Dan."
    B. She called her "Don."
    C. She called her "Din."
    D. She called her "Dunn."

20. How many people did the Cutlers invite to Philip Cutler and Betty Ann Monroe's wedding?
    A. Over 500
    B. Almost 200
    C. Over 1,000
    D. Nearly 300

21. How many people did the Monroes invite to Philip Cutler and Betty Ann Monroe's wedding?
    A. Almost 400
    B. Over 600
    C. Close to 500
    D. Not quite 1,000

22. What was the name of the restaurant where Skipper and Clara Sue Cutler took Christie Longchamp without Dawn's permission?
    A. Hoagie's Diner
    B. Eat 'Em & Weep
    C. The Forbes Truckstop
    D. Tipper's Place

23. What was Richard Cutler's middle name?
    A. Tyrone
    B. Wilfred
    C. Stanley
    D. Samuel

24. What was Melanie Cutler's middle name?
    A. Agatha
    B. Rose
    C. Christine
    D. Heaven

25. What did Clayton Osborne do for a living?
    A. He was a surgeon.
    B. He was with the Secret Service.
    C. He was an accountant.
    D. He was an investment broker on Wall Street.

26. What was "Kelly Ann Osborne" 's favorite subject in school?
    A. Chemistry
    B. Gym
    C. English
    D. Algebra

27. What line of work did Michael Sutton tell Christie Longchamp he was in the first time he met her?
    A. He told her he was a lion tamer.
    B. He told her he owned a video arcade.
    C. He told her he was an astronaut.
    D. He told her he was a jewelry salesman.

28. What did Michael Sutton's alleged English wife allegedly die from?
    A. Suicide
    B. A kidney ailment
    C. Drowning
    D. Accidental electrocution (a radio fell into her tub while she was bathing)

2. True or False

1. Sanford and Patricia Compton's house was a three-story colonial.
2. Sanford Compton's butler was Chinese.
3. Sanford Compton had black hair.
4. Judge Powell was a Virginia supreme court justice.
5. Christie Longchamp was wrapped in a pink blanket when Dawn and Jimmy retrieved her from the Comptons.
6. Jimmy Longchamp bought Dawn an engagement ring on Canal Street in New York City.
7. Bronson Alcott had a mustache.
8. Philip Cutler wore a gray three-piece suit to Dawn and Jimmy's wedding.
9. A five-piece band played during the cocktail hour at Dawn and Jimmy's wedding reception.
10. Randolph Cutler was buried beside his mother and father.
11. Beulla Woods was in a valley.

12. Alexandria Alcott's date for her high school prom was her brother, Bronson Alcott.

13. Charlie Goodwin owned a pet store in Tampa, Florida.

14. Claudine and Stuart Monroe had a house in Hyannis Port.

15. Philip Cutler and Betty Ann Monroe's wedding ceremony was held in the ballroom of the Cutler's Cove Hotel.

16. Mr. Parker had once given Christie Longchamp $100 for her birthday.

17. Jason Malamud's science project burned up in the lab.

18. Michael Sutton threateningly asked Dawn to lend him $10,000.

19. Jimmy learned that Dawn was pregnant shortly after Emily Booth's funeral.

3. Bonus Questions

1. Who was in charge of the laundry at the Cutler's Cove Hotel?

2. Who owned the Beulla Woods estate?

3. How old was Christie when she first said, "Momma"?

4. What was Christie Longchamp's nickname for Melanie Rose Cutler?

5. What was the name of the school "Kelly Ann Osborne" attended in Manhattan?

4. Super Bonus Questions

1. What was Patricia and Sanford Compton's street address?

2. Who did Agnes Morris play in *Mary, Queen of Scots*?

3. Name the four passengers of the limousine that carried Dawn to Philip Cutler's graduation.

5. Sartorial Bonus Questions

1. What color dress was Patricia Compton wearing when Dawn first met her?
2. What did Laura Sue Cutler wear to Dawn and Jimmy's wedding?
3. What piece of jewelry did Laura Sue Cutler wear on her left wrist to Dawn and Jimmy's wedding?
4. What did Laura Sue Cutler wear for Dawn's first dinner at Beulla Woods, and what was notable about her outfit?
5. What did Clara Sue Cutler (almost) wear to Philip Cutler's graduation?

6. Epistolary Bonus Questions

1. What was the color of Dawn and Jimmy's wedding invitations?
2. What was written in red and yellow roses on the arch that guests had to pass through to get into the ballroom at Dawn and Jimmy's wedding reception?
3. What was printed on the back of the commemorative makeup mirrors given to women guests at Dawn and Jimmy's wedding reception?
4. What was the first line of the song Dawn sang with the band at her own wedding reception?
5. What did the sign say that was over the door of the seafood restaurant where Dawn and Jimmy ate the first day of their honeymoon?
6. What was the title of the article that included the line, "He did it so often and so casually, I never thought much about it until I was in fourth grade and happened to mention to a friend of mine that my stepfather usually came in while I was taking a bath to make sure I washed the 'important places' "?

7. "Red Alert for Dawn" Bonus Question

What did Betty Ann Monroe do to her hair for her wedding ceremony that shocked and frightened Dawn Longchamp?

8. "Figure It Out" Bonus Question

What was the date Richard and Melanie Cutler were born?

9. Who Said It?

1. "Christie's name has been changed to Violet."
2. "Nobody blows my horn better than she does."
3. "Might I give the bride a congratulatory kiss?"
4. "There will always be something making life miserable for us, turning everything sweet into something sour."
5. "A boy in eleventh grade shouldn't be interested in a girl your age."

A. Bronson Alcott
B. Jimmy Longchamp
C. Dawn Longchamp
D. Sanford Compton
E. Ormand Longchamp

LEAFING THROUGH . . . TWILIGHT'S CHILD

5 of the Items in Patricia Compton's Curio Case

1. Glass figures of animals.
2. Figurines of hand-painted Chinese men
3. Figurines of hand-painted Chinese women
4. Hand-painted figures of children with mothers
5. Hand-painted figures of children with animals

The 1 Covenant in the Adoption Agreement of Christie Longchamp That the Comptons' Attorney Tried to Use as a Defense Against Dawn and Jimmy's Attempt to "Reclaim" Christie

"Mr. and Mrs. Sanford Compton of 12 Hardy Drive accept full responsibility for the health and welfare of said infant from the date of delivery and agree not to make any additional demands on the Cutler family concerning the said infant, to wit the life and limb of said infant will from this day forward remain their sole responsibility."

Mrs. Boston's Philosophy About Birth and Death

"The birth of a child washes away the shadows Death leaves behind when he visits a house."

Laura Sue Cutler's Philosophy About Love

"Love. That's such a ridiculous word. A romantic notion drummed up in novels, but not something for real life. Love someone who can give you what you need and deserve. All love really is, anyway, is fulfilling a need. Believe me."

The 5 Questions Dawn Asked Herself While Gazing at Her Real Father's Portrait

1. "[W]hat, if anything . . . [had I] inherited from this man[?]
2. "Would I now become as ambitious as he was?"
3. "Would I live up to the responsibilities placed on my shoulders and develop into a good administrator?"
4. "Did I have his charm when it came to pleasing guests?"

5. "Had he been fair with the help and liked by them, and would I be?"

Even One More "Gone with the Wind" Reference

"I saw that Bronson wasn't going to sit down until I did. He was the quintessential Southern gentleman who easily made every woman feel a little like Scarlett O'Hara."

"Déjà Vu" Department

In *Twilight's Child,* Christie thought of her mother moving through the hotel "[l]ooking like an animated, hand-painted Dresden doll." In Book 1, *Flowers in the Attic,* Jim Johnston's affectionate nickname for the Dollanganger children was "the Dresden dolls."

3 of Randolph Cutler's "Post-Lillian's Death" Obsessions

1. He counted boxes of paper clips to see if they were short any.
2. He reviewed butcher's receipts to see if they were getting the bulk discount they were entitled to.
3. He wanted to count the screws and nails in the hotel workshop.

5 Bad Things Clara Sue Cutler Did in School

1. She was failing all her subjects.
2. She was very disruptive in class.
3. She violated curfews.
4. She was caught smoking in her room.
5. She was caught drinking in her room.

Gaffe Alert

On page 57 of *Twilight's Child,* Dawn and Jimmy Longchamp's wedding invitation is reprinted. It states that the date of their wedding is October 26th. Then, on page 76 of the same book, we are told about Trisha Kramer's arrival at Cutler's Cove Hotel for Dawn's wedding. "She had arrived on one of our warmest early *spring* [emphasis added] days." Since the seasonal references throughout the remainder of the novel concur with this reference to spring, it's obvious that the use of the month October on the invitation was an error that slipped through.

The 3 Commemorative Mementos Given to Guests at Dawn and Jimmy's Wedding Reception

1. Gold-trimmed matchbooks with "Dawn and James" printed on them.
2. Real leather bookmarks with the bride and groom's name embossed.
3. Small makeup mirrors for the women.

3 Toasts

1. Bronson Alcott to Dawn and Jimmy at their wedding reception: "The people of Cutler's Cove joyfully welcome Mr. and Mrs. James Gary Longchamp to our community and wish them health, happiness and success. May you two have a long and wonderful marriage and be blessed from this day forward. To James and Dawn."
2. Jimmy Longchamp at the groundbreaking of his and Dawn's house: "To our house. May it be the home of love and happiness forever and ever."
3. Philip Cutler to Dawn and Jimmy Longchamp: "To Jimmy and Dawn's new home. May it be the place where dreams come true."

The 7 Courses of the Meal Served at Dawn and Jimmy's Wedding Reception

1. Fresh melon
2. Salad
3. Soup
4. Filet mignon
5. Baked potatoes
6. Stir-fried vegetables
7. Bread shaped like wedding bells

The Best Excuse for Looking at Naked Breasts Ever Uttered

As an explanation for not being able to take his eyes off Dawn's naked breasts when they were younger and they both thought they were brother and sister, Jimmy later told Dawn, "[Y]ou were like a magnet, and my head was like iron."

The 4 Characteristics of the World Laura Sue Cutler Came from, According to Bronson Alcott

1. Illusion
2. Deceit
3. Distrust
4. Betrayal

The 4 Acts of "Miscarriage-Causing" Violence Clara Sue Cutler Committed Against Dawn Longchamp After Learning That Dawn Had Moved Her Things to Beulla Woods Without Telling Her

1. First she punched Dawn on the side of her head with her right fist.
2. Then she kicked Dawn hard in the stomach.
3. Then she kicked Dawn repeatedly in the side.
4. Then she randomly punched her several times.

6 of the Things Dawn Found Wrong with Philip Cutler's Fiancée, Betty Ann

1. Her mouth was too small.
2. Her eyes were too close.
3. Her pale complexion looked sickly.
4. Her hair was brushed too far back.
5. Her forehead was too wide.
6. She didn't know how to dress.

Laura Sue Cutler's Philosophy About Whatever Gets You Through the Night

"Everyone accepts a certain amount of deception and illusion. It's the price we pay for what little happiness we can achieve."

4 of the Weird and Leering Questions Philip Cutler Asked Jimmy Longchamp About the Bedroom in Jimmy and Dawn's Newly Built House

1. Where exactly would the bed be located in the bedroom?
2. What side did Jimmy sleep on?
3. Which closet was Jimmy's?
4. Which closet was Dawn's?

The 6 Items Christie Longchamp Packed All by Herself in Her Suitcase for the Move from the Hotel to Her Own New House

1. A hairbrush
2. A rag doll
3. Another rag doll
4. A pair of blue cotton socks
5. A summer dress
6. A book of nursery rhymes

4 of the Things Dawn Wanted That No One Could Provide

1. To heal the scars of years of painful living.
2. To bury her sad and bitter memories.
3. To gain new courage.
4. To be able to face the ghosts and drive them back into the shadows.

—15—

MIDNIGHT WHISPERS
(1992)

But God has a few of us whom he whispers in the ear;
The rest may reason and welcome; 'tis we musicians
know.

—Robert Browning, "Abt Vogler"

CHAPTER LISTING

Prologue

Epilogue

STORY SYNOPSIS

Midnight Whispers is the fourth book in the Cutler series; it begins nine years after the end of *Twilight's Child*. Dawn and Jimmy's son Jefferson is now nine years old. Christie, now sixteen, is very close with Daddy Longchamp's son, Gavin. Laura Sue Cutler is completely gone, mentally, and Dawn, sometimes feeling in some way cursed, still runs the very successful Cutler's Cove Hotel. The story begins with Christie's sweet-sixteen birthday party. Uncle Philip, who once gave Dawn so many problems, has devolved into an outright lech. Trisha, Fern, Gavin, Ormand, and Edwina Longchamp arrive for the party. Uncle Philip's 12-year-old twins are arrogant and obnoxious. Dawn tells Christie the truth about her father, Michael Sutton. Gavin and Christie kiss: They're clearly an "item." Unimaginable tragedy befalls Cutler's Cove Hotel *and* Dawn and Jimmy. Philip and his family move into Christie's house and take over. Trouble brews, and Christie must acknowledge to herself that Uncle Philip "wants" her. Big time. Christie visits Bronson and confides her pain. Christie learns that Melanie, one of Philip and Bet's twins, has been stealing her letters to Gavin, reading them, and throwing them away. Laura Sue dies. Uncle Philip rapes Christie. Christie and Jefferson run away to New York to visit Michael Sutton, but Michael is a useless has-been and wants nothing to do with his daughter. Gavin comes to New York and he, Christie, and Jefferson travel to The Meadows, the place where Christie was born. Miss Emily's sister, Charlotte, tells Christie about her son who was taken away, and then Luther reveals the truth about this missing boy. Gavin and Christie make love. The cruel and heartless Fern shows up at The Meadows and begins inflicting all kinds of torture on everyone there. Jefferson almost dies from a tetanus infection. Philip arrives and Fern flees. Back at the hotel, Philip tries to rape Christie (thinking of her as Dawn). Christie once again turns to Bronson, and Philip is arrested and taken away, but by now his mind is shattered. Jefferson recovers from tetanus and he and Christie decide to live with Bronson. Christie eventually becomes a concert pianist and she and Gavin end up together.

THE QUIZZES

1. Multiple Choice

1. What was the nickname Christie Longchamp's classmates teasingly called her?
    A. Bitch
    B. Princess
    C. Pea-Brain
    D. Scarlett

2. During Christie Longchamp's childhood "Alice in Wonderland" fantasy game, what animal was Nussbaum the chef?
    A. A lion
    B. A giraffe
    C. An owl
    D. A rabbit

3. What animal was Leon, Nussbaum's assistant?
    A. A lion
    B. A giraffe
    C. An owl
    D. A rabbit

4. What animal was Mr. Dorfman?
    A. A lion
    B. A giraffe
    C. An owl
    D. A rabbit

5. During Christie Longchamp's childhood "Alice in Wonderland" fantasy game, what was Grandmother Cutler?
    A. Scarlett O'Hara
    B. The Evil Stepsister
    C. The Big, Bad Wolf
    D. The Wicked Witch

6. What cartoon character did Christie's brother Jefferson remind her of?
    A. Archie
    B. Beetle Bailey
    C. Dennis the Menace
    D. Charlie Brown

7. What birthday gift did Dawn and Jimmy give to Christie at breakfast on the morning of her 16th birthday?
   A. Diamond earrings
   B. A gold watch
   C. A new Rolls-Royce
   D. A book of Emily Dickinson's poems and a video of *The Prince of Tides*

8. What game did Melanie and Richard Cutler play with some of the Cutler's Cove Hotel's guest children after breakfast on Christie's 16th birthday?
   A. Post office
   B. Trivial Pursuit
   C. Monopoly
   D. Parcheesi

9. What erotic book did Aunt Fern give Christie for her 16th birthday?
   A. A novelization of *Deep Throat*
   B. Henry Miller's *Sexus*
   C. *Justine* by the Marquis de Sade
   D. *Lady Chatterley's Lover* by D. H. Lawrence

10. How did Ormand Longchamp wear his hair?
    A. Short on top and a ponytail in the back.
    B. He shaved his head bald twice a month.
    C. Brushed back on the sides and flat on top.
    D. Parted in the middle on top and almost down to his waist in back.

11. What historical figure did Ormand Longchamp remind Christie of?
    A. Abraham Lincoln
    B. George Washington
    C. Mark Twain
    D. Truman Capote

12. How did Gavin Longchamp describe his trip to Cutler's Cove for Christie's 16th birthday party?
    A. "Hot and tiresome."
    B. "Long and boring."
    C. "Lots of fun."
    D. "A drag."

13. What did Pauline Bradley do as a nervous habit when she talked to people?
    A. Blink and squint repeatedly
    B. Scratch the tip of her left breast
    C. Pull on her right earlobe
    D. Twirl her hair with her forefinger

14. Which of the following images did Dawn use to describe Michael Sutton to Christie?
    A. An "oily, despicable snake."
    B. A "vulture of love."
    C. The "Prince of fucking Darkness."
    D. The "biggest loser who ever lived."

15. What ailment forced Laura Sue Alcott to use a wheelchair?
    A. Arthritis
    B. Bursitis
    C. Rheumatism
    D. Multiple sclerosis

16. What was the first song Dawn Longchamp sang at Christie's 16th birthday party?
    A. "Over the Rainbow"
    B. "High Hopes"
    C. "The Way You Look Tonight"
    D. "Because"

17. What was Gavin Longchamp's middle name?
    A. Steven
    B. Stephen
    C. Sebastian
    D. Sidney

18. What did Gavin Longchamp give Christie for her 16th birthday?
    A. A ruby and diamond ring
    B. A paperback of *Lady Chatterley's Lover*
    C. A leather jacket
    D. A gold identification bracelet

19. How did the Cutler's Cove Hotel fire start?
    A. A guest fell asleep smoking a cigarette.
    B. Two guest children were playing with matches.
    C. A boiler in the basement blew up.
    D. The kitchen dishwasher short-circuited.

20. What animal did Dr. Stanley remind Christie of?
    A. A giraffe
    B. A poodle
    C. A tiger
    D. An elephant

21. What prank did Gavin Longchamp tell Jefferson Longchamp to pull on Richard Cutler every morning?
    A. Tie his socks together.
    B. Put salt on his breakfast cereal.
    C. Put his underwear in the toilet.
    D. Sprinkle red pepper on his toast instead of cinnamon.

22. How many apologies did Philip Cutler offer to Dawn as she lay in her grave?
    A. 1
    B. 100
    C. 1,000
    D. 1,000,000

23. Where did Mrs. Boston's sister Lou Ann live?
    A. Georgia
    B. Connecticut
    C. Arkansas
    D. Texas

24. What musical piece did Christie perform for the Cutlers prior to the "honey-vandalization" of her piano?
    A. A Beethoven sonata
    B. A Scott Joplin rag
    C. A Chopin nocturne
    D. A Mozart rondo

2. True or False

1. At the age of 16, Christie Longchamp was still sleeping with a night-light on.
2. Christie Longchamp's bed had a yellow polka-dotted canopy.
3. Mr. Wittleman wanted Christie to audition for Juilliard.

4. By the time he was nine, Jefferson Cutler had seen his cousin Melanie Cutler topless.

5. Melanie and Richard Cutler both wore glasses.

6. Christie called Ormand Longchamp "Granddaddy" Longchamp because he was Jimmy Longchamp's father.

7. Gavin liked to tease Christie that she had to call him "Granddaddy" because of their familial relationship.

8. Christie's father was the first person to ask her to dance at her 16th birthday party.

9. Christie Longchamp's 16th birthday cake was baked in the shape of a violin.

10. Christie Longchamp blew out all the candles on her 16th birthday cake on the first try.

11. Gavin and Christie saw a Cutler's Cove Hotel bell-hop kissing Fern Longchamp's breasts during Christie's 16th birthday party.

12. Aunt Trisha was the last person to leave Cutler's Cove Hotel following Christie's 16th birthday party.

13. Sunday was always a big checkout day at Cutler's Cove Hotel.

14. Dawn and Jimmy Longchamp died in each other's arms.

15. Jimmy Longchamp often used the dining room in his house as a second office.

16. After Dawn and Jimmy's death, Aunt Fern asked Christie if she could borrow the diamond pendant they had given Christie for her 16th birthday.

17. Aunt Bet's breakfast regimen included an eight o'clock (precisely) start time.

18. Shortly after Christie saw Uncle Philip talking to Dawn's grave, Richard and Melanie Cutler both came down with either food poisoning or some kind of stomach virus.

19. Gavin Longchamp sold his valuable coin collection in order to get enough money to be able to visit Christie in Virginia a week earlier than scheduled.

20. When Uncle Philip raped Christie, he wore a condom.

21. Aunt Charlotte called the room in The Meadows

where Dawn stayed when she was pregnant, The Bad Room.
22. Morton Atwood's sport was hockey.
23. In the summer of her 19th year, Christie Longchamp went on a three-week concert tour of Paris and Vienna.
24. Christie believed in the fish.

3. Bonus Questions

1. What was the Cutler family's code words for *Top Secret*?
2. How did Richard Cutler "segregate" his clothes from Jefferson's after he moved into Jefferson's room?
3. Who was the only member of the Cutler's Cove Hotel's staff to remain on salary after the fire?
4. What room at The Meadows did Aunt Fern maliciously decide to sleep in during her visit?

4. Super Bonus Questions

1. What type of music did Mr. Wittleman choose for Christie to practice on "dark, cloudy" days?
2. What type of music did Mr. Wittleman choose for Christie to practice on sunny days?
3. What did the Hammersteins give Christie Longchamp for her 16th birthday?
4. What did the Malamuds give Christie Longchamp for her 16th birthday?
5. What were Jefferson Longchamp's grades on his "worst report card ever"?
6. How much did the Booth family pay for Darcy?
7. How did Aunt Fern get to The Meadows?

5. Epistolary Bonus Questions

1. To whom did Christie write the letter that began, "I'm so happy you will be able to attend my Sweet Sixteen party"?
2. What did the banner hung in the Cutler's Cove Hotel ballroom for Christie's 16th birthday party say?
3. On what piece of jewelry given to Christie Longchamp for her 16th birthday was engraved, "With Love, Forever, Gavin"?
4. To whom was the letter written that contained the line, "But no matter what Aunt Bet says about the twins, to me they are nothing more than some two-headed monster"?
5. To whom did Christie once write a letter that she signed with four X's?

6. Sartorial Bonus Questions

1. What did Christie Cutler wear to her sweet-sixteen birthday party?
2. What was Aunt Trisha wearing when she arrived at the hotel for Dawn's 16th birthday?
3. What was Fern wearing when she arrived at the hotel for Dawn's 16th birthday?
4. What scandalous outfit did Aunt Fern wear to Christie's 16th birthday party?
5. What was Aunt Fern's "post-birthday party" hang-over outfit?
6. What was Gavin Longchamp wearing when he arrived in New York City to "rescue" Christie and Jefferson Longchamp?
7. What did Philip Cutler wear the second time he tried to rape Christie Longchamp?

7. Literary Bonus Question

What was so special about Chapter 10 of *Lady Chatterley's Lover*? And why did Aunt Fern want Christie to read it?

8. Funereal Bonus Questions

1. How did Fluffy die?
2. In Christie's "Grandmother Cutler/Lost in the Graveyard" nightmare, what did Christie see on Grandmother Cutler's tombstone?

9. Disgusting Bonus Question

What kind of pie did Mrs. Boston give Jefferson Longchamp after he rebelliously spit his food out onto the dinner table?

10. Prurient Interest Bonus Questions

1. How old was Aunt Fern when she lost her virginity?
2. What items of clothing did Christie take off as "partial payment" for losing a hand of strip poker?

11. Who Said It?

1. "The fire shot up the stairways and through the heat and air ducts. It popped out of every grate and the floor in the card room collapsed."
2. "You two take off any six pieces you want. I gotta take off nine. Oh, that will leave me stark naked."
3. *"Fern! You're drunk and disgusting!"*
4. "How old was your baby before ... before the devil took him, Aunt Charlotte?"
5. "Can you believe in the fish, Christie? Can you believe in the magic?"

A. Aunt Fern
B. Gavin Longchamp
C. Philip Cutler
D. Dawn Longchamp
E. Christie Longchamp

LEAFING THROUGH . . .
MIDNIGHT WHISPERS

2 Rare Verbalizations of the Subtext Implicit in Every V. C. Andrews Novel

1. "I can't help feeling there's something terrible waiting for me, too, a dark shadow just waiting to cast itself over me." (Thought by Christie Longchamp.)
2. "[N]o matter what everyone says, I can't help believing there is a dreadful curse on our heads."

The Tradition Continues . . .

Philip Cutler's children, Richard and Melanie, who were twins, thought nothing of getting dressed and undressed in front of each other when they were twelve years old.

The 3 Questions Jefferson Cutler Asked About Dawn's Gold Watch

1. "Does it have an alarm?"
2. "Does something pop up?"
3. "Is it waterproof?"

6 "Uncle Philip" Early Warning Signs Dawn Noticed

1. "He embraced me and pulled me to him and then pressed his lips to my forehead, softly at first and then, surprising me by continuing his kiss down the side of my head to my cheek."
2. "The intimacy of his arms around me and his breath on my face made me squirm a little. I thought everyone must be looking at us and wondering why a man Uncle Philip's age would dance with his niece so closely."
3. Uncle Philip held her the longest and kissed her

twice after she blew out the candles on her 16th-birthday cake.

4. After the Cutler's Cove Hotel fire, Philip said to Christie, "Dawn, you're all right. Thank God."
5. To seal their "pact," Uncle Philip closed his eyes and kissed her on the cheek, but his lips "accidentally" touched her mouth.
6. After her parents' death, Uncle Philip once walked in on Christie while she was taking a bath and offered to scrub her back. He then gave her a see-through nightgown of which Christie thought to herself, "What sort of gift was this for an uncle to buy his niece?"

Dawn Longchamp's Advice About Love and Caution to Christie

"Don't be afraid to love someone with all your heart, but don't give your heart freely. A little skepticism is a good thing, a necessary thing, and if a man really loves you, truly loves you, he will understand your fears and your hesitation and never try to move too quickly."

Dawn Longchamp's Philosophy About Men

"Men are babies. Remember that. Even the strongest and toughest are more sensitive than they care to admit.

3 Wheelchair-Bound V. C. Andrews Characters

1. Jory Sheffield (Books 2, 3)
2. Annie Stonewall (Books 9, 11)
3. Laura Sue Cutler Alcott (Books 14, 15)

2 More "Gone with the Wind" References

1. At her 16th-birthday party, Christie thought to herself that Bronson Alcott had a "Clark Gable mustache."
2. When all dressed up in antique clothes for the dinner party at The Meadows, Christie postured "like Scarlett O'Hara" when saying good night to Charlotte and Luther.

Christie Longchamp's Philosophy About Men

"Men are more afraid to believe in someone. They steal hearts so often, they're terrified of giving their own sincerely."

The Order of the 7 People Who Kissed and Hugged Christie After She Blew out the Candles on Her 16th Birthday Cake

1. Her mother, Dawn
2. Her father, Jimmy
3. Aunt Trisha Kramer
4. Granddaddy (Ormand) Longchamp
5. Edwina Longchamp
6. Aunt Bet Cutler
7. Uncle Philip Cutler

Momma Longchamp's Philosophy About Personality Types

"[S]ome cows are just born to give sour milk, no matter how sweet the grass they feed on."

The 3 Things Jefferson Longchamp Promised to Do After Receiving His "Worst Report Card Ever"

1. Clean up his room
2. Pick up his clothes
3. Never leave the front door open

The 2 Things About Her Parents Christie Did Not Want Aunt Fern to Tell Her

1. That Dawn and Jimmy used to sleep together in their underwear when they thought they were brother and sister.
2. That Dawn French-kissed Philip Cutler before she knew he was her brother.

Aunt Bet's Philosophy About Cleanliness

"Neatness and cleanliness are the twin sisters of a healthy, happy life."

5 of the Revolting "Non-Brother and Sister"-Type Things Richard and Melanie Cutler Did Together

1. They brushed each other's hair.
2. They used the same toothbrush.
3. They cut each other's toenails.

4. They consulted with each other about wardrobe.
5. They bathed together.

The 3 Provisions of the Pact Uncle Philip Talked Christie into Making with Him

1. To "trust and depend on each other from this day forward."
2. To "tell each other things we wouldn't tell anyone else."
3. To "work hard at making everyone happy and safe."

"Déjà Vu" Department

In the Casteel family series, Tony Tatterton once walked in on Annie while she was taking a bath, stared at her, and offered to scrub her back. In *Midnight Whispers,* part of the Cutler family series, Christie's Uncle Philip walks in on her while she's in the tub, stares at her, and offers to scrub her back.

Christie's 7 Complaints to Bronson Alcott About Aunt Bet

1. She was horrible to her and Jefferson.
2. She fired Mrs. Boston.
3. She was always yelling at Jefferson for being too messy.
4. She wanted Christie and Jefferson to take their shoes off before they entered the house.
5. She moved Richard into Jefferson's room.
6. She moved Dawn's things into the attic.
7. She kept some of Dawn's jewelry.

Laura Sue Alcott's Philosophy About Wrinkles

"Wrinkles! They are a slow death for a beautiful woman."

3 of the Things Richard and Melanie Cutler Did for "Recreation" (Besides Bathing Together)

1. They played chess.
2. They played Scrabble.
3. They listened to educational tapes.

The 4 Things Aunt Bet "Took Over" After Dawn and Jimmy's Deaths

1. Christie's life
2. Jefferson's life
3. The family's home
4. The family's possessions

The 7 Things Uncle Philip Did to Christie While Generously Offering to Answer Her Questions About Sex

1. He rubbed her stomach.
2. He put his hand over her breast.
3. He moved his hand from one breast to another.
4. He touched one of her nipples.
5. He put his hand on her knee.
6. He patted her on the thigh.
7. He kissed her on the cheek.

The 6 Things Christie Remembered Hearing as She and Jefferson Ran Away from Cutler's Cove

1. Her Daddy's laughter.
2. Her Mommy's laughter.
3. Her piano.
4. Her mother's beautiful voice.
5. Mrs. Boston calling everyone to dinner.
6. Her father calling to Jefferson upon his arrival home from work.

6 of the Things Jefferson Longchamp Noticed About New York When He and Christie First Arrived There

1. The street vendors
2. The taxicabs
3. The policemen on horseback
4. People begging
5. People sleeping in entryways
6. Many fancily dressed people

"Same Building, Different Floor?" Department

Michael Sutton's sublet apartment when he was teaching at the Bernhardt School was 4B. When Christie visited him in New York 16 years later, his apartment number was 3B.

Dawn Longchamp's Definition of the Difference Between Making Love and Having Sex

"There's a sense of fulfillment. Your heart and soul join in a wonderful and magical way . . ."

Dawn Longchamp's Attitude About Promiscuity

"Girls who give their bodies to men for the pleasure of the moment don't value themselves; they don't even value sex. They've choked and suffocated the best part of themselves; they've closed the doorway to the soul and to love."

5 of the Book Collections in the Library in The Meadows (and 1 Favorite Novel)

1. Dickens
2. Guy de Maupassant
3. Tolstoy
4. Dostoyevski
5. Mark Twain
6. *The Secret Garden*

The 5 Childish Things Aunt Fern and Mort did at The Meadows While Drinking Brandy and Waiting for Christie and Gavin to Clean Her Room

1. Giggle
2. Knock things over
3. Ring the old dinner bells
4. Flick lights on and off
5. Chase each other through the rooms of the house

The 5 Times Fern Longchamp Let Herself Be Seen Naked While Staying at The Meadows

1. She let her blanket fall while Gavin was in the room.
2. She got out of bed and strode naked into the bathroom in front of Christie and Mort.
3. She made Christie paint her toenails while she sat naked in a tub.
4. She undressed in front of Mort, Gavin, and Christie after losing a hand of strip poker.
5. She came to her bedroom door stark naked when Christie woke her up after Jefferson got sick.

The 6 Acts of Vandalism Richard and Melanie Cutler Committed Against Christie's Stuff When She Was Away at The Meadows

1. They sliced her sweet-sixteen dress in two.
2. They put dead worms and clumps of mud on her panties.
3. Some of her perfumes and colognes had been mixed together.
4. They put skin cream in her shoes.
5. They smeared lipstick on her blouses.
6. They poured water into one of her jewelry boxes.

UPDATE: DARKEST HOUR
(1993)

"Just before the *Dawn* comes the *Darkest Hour*."

—Cover blurb for *Darkest Hour*

Prologue

Part One

Part Two

STORY SYNOPSIS

Darkest Hour is the prequel to the Cutler series and tells the story of Lillian Booth Cutler, "Grandmother Cutler" from the later books. Lillian lives with her Mamma, Papa, and her sisters Emily and Eugenia at The Meadows, a glorious old Southern plantation that thrives on its tobacco crops. Eugenia has cystic fibrosis and is usually bedridden, and Emily, the horrid "Miss Emily" from Book 13, *Secrets of the Morning,* is a grim, Scripture-spouting premature harridan who hates not only Lillian, but all that is happy and light. We learn the reason behind Emily's loathsome treatment of Lillian: They are not really sisters and thus Emily believes that Lillian has been cursed by the devil himself. Emily kills Lillian's kitten and traps Lillian in a barn with a skunk, necessitating the cutting off of Lillian's hair (sound familiar, V. C. fans?). Lillian, though, tries to maintain a normal life, and finds love with the handsome Niles Thompson. Tragedy strikes twice, however, and Lillian is left alone. Meanwhile, Papa Booth, Lillian's "father," gambles, drinks, and carouses. One night he breaks a leg in a drunken stupor and ends up bedridden. He drafts Lillian as his nurse and it isn't long before he uses her as a "bed warmer" and commits the ultimate violation. Lillian gives birth to Charlotte from this obscene moment, and she must pretend that Charlotte is not her daughter. Because of the loss of her youngest daughter, Eugenia, Mamma retreats into herself and becomes fatally ill. With a vengeance, Papa seeks solace in his vices and in one disastrous card game loses The Meadows to wealthy hotel owner, Bill Cutler. Bill makes Papa an offer: Arrange his marriage to Lillian, (whom he lusts after), and Papa can keep the plantation. Papa agrees and Lillian ends up Mrs. Cutler, the new mistress of Cutler's Cove Hotel.

An interesting element of *Darkest Hour* is its conscious references to and modeling upon the classic Southern novel of all time, *Gone with the Wind.* Some of the story elements and *Gone with the Wind* nods in *Darkest Hour* include:

- The Meadows, like Tara, survived the Civil War fairly intact.
- Louella's mama had been a slave cook at the *Wilkes* plantation, which was not far from The Meadows. (Louella was the cook at The Meadows.)
- Lillian and Emily's classmates included Lila *Calvert* and Caroline *O'Hara.*

- The Booths often had huge barbecues and parties which were eagerly anticipated and attended by all the neighboring plantation families.
- A favorite expletive of Captain Booth's was "God's Teeth!" Gerald O'Hara was particularly fond of "God's Nightgown!"

[NOTE: The inside cover of *Darkest Hour* announced the forthcoming publication of *Ruby*, the first novel of a brand new V. C. Andrews series.]

—16—

THE FINAL AND ULTIMATE
V. C. ANDREWS QUIZ
QUESTION

This "ultimate" question isn't really a question.

Here's the deal: Somewhere in the *Leafing Through . . .* lists in *The V. C. Andrews Trivia and Quiz Book* is a minor, intentional error.

It could be a list item that doesn't belong in the list; it could be in the "title" of the list.

For instance, there might be a list that says something like "The 5 Items of the Meal Served at Corrine's 16th Birthday Party" when the party was for Cathy, not Corrine. Or the contents of a jewelry box could be listed and there might be a pair of pearl earrings included that are not mentioned in the text. (I'm making these examples up: They are not real lists.)

The admitted purpose of this "question" is to drive you crazy checking the trivia items against the novels—but I guarantee that it will be a lot of fun to go back and track stuff down.

A Hint: To make your quest a tad easier, I offer this clue. Now, at first glance, this "hint" may only appear to muddy the waters, but with a little thought (thought that should allow serendipity to take you where it may, by the way), it is actually quite revealing and not abstruse at all.

Remember the words of the poet Stephen Spender, from his elegaic poem, "The Living Values":

> *Their collected*
> *Hearts wound up with love, like little watch springs.*

And consider them along with this verse from T. S. Eliot's magnificent "Rhapsody on a Windy Night":

> *Midnight shakes the memory*
> *As a madman shakes a dead geranium.*

Now you've got it, right?
No?
Well, if you *really* can't find it and you *absolutely* give up, the answer to this "Final and Ultimate" question can be found in the *Answers* section, complete with book citation explanation, and page number.

—17—

THE V. C. ANDREWS
CROSSWORD PUZZLE

This puzzle is meant to serve as a refreshing break from the hundreds of text questions you just answered. (You did answer all those quiz questions it took me months to write, now, didn't you!?) The clues for this puzzle are drawn from book titles, chapter titles, and general information found in V. C. Andrews's novels.

Happy Puzzling!

ACROSS

2. Dr. Paul _____
6. Carrie's twin
8. _____ Secrets
9. A _____ Life
10. _____ in the Attic
12. Color All Days Blue, But Save One for _____
14. V. C.'s first name
17. My Sweet _____
20. Cathy's older brother
22. _____ on the Wind
24. Bart's favorite uncle
25. _____ Hearts

28. Paul and Cathy's son
31. Christie Longchamp's mother
32. _____ Leigh Casteel
33. The _____ It Used to Be
35. Web of _____
37. Tales of _____
41. Seeds of _____
43. Ever Since _____
44. The _____ Saga
45. _____ of the Morning

DOWN

1. Malcolm _____
2. The Last _____ of the Web
3. The Spider and the _____
4. Labyrinth of _____
5. The Reluctant _____
7. Malcolm's _____
11. Birthday _____
13. Twilight's _____
15. Cory's twin
16. Christopher _____ Foxworth
18. Judgment _____
19. Dark _____
20. Chris's sister and wife
21. Corrine's mother
22. Gates of _____
23. Garden of _____
25. The second chapter in Book 12
26. Arden _____
27. Color All Days Blue, But Save _____ for Black
29. If There Be _____
30. A Piece of the _____
34. Cathy's firstborn
36. Cindy's boyfriend
38. Good-_____, Pa
39. Here Comes the _____
40. _____ of Dilemma
42. An _____ on the Roof

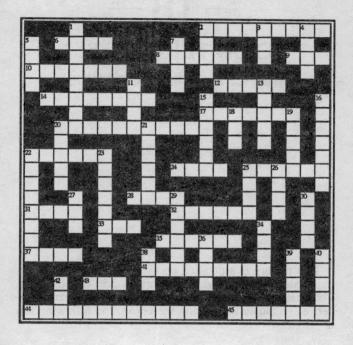

―18―

CHAPTER FACTS:
A V. C. Andrews Checklist

This feature is a detailed breakdown of elements common to over 130 of V. C. Andrews's 356 chapter titles. The chapters are listed within the lists in alphabetical order; as an aid to identifying the books, the following key is provided.

1. *Flowers in the Attic*
2. *Petals on the Wind*
3. *If There Be Thorns*
4. *My Sweet Audrina*
5. *Seeds of Yesterday*
6. *Heaven*
7. *Dark Angel*
8. *Garden of Shadows*
9. *Fallen Hearts*
10. *Gates of Paradise*
11. *Web of Dreams*
12. *Dawn*
13. *Secrets of the Morning*
14. *Twilight's Child*
15. *Midnight Whispers*

V. C. Andrews's novels contain . . .

- 3 "Birthday" Chapters:
  - √ "Aunt Fanny's Birthday Party": Book 10, Chapter 4
  - √ "A Birthday Gift": Book 2, Chapter 12
  - √ "Birthday Gifts": Book 10, Chapter 2

- 3 "Bitter" Chapters:,
  - √ "Bitter Fruit": Book 13, Chapter 10
  - √ "Bitter Season": Book 6, Chapter 5
  - √ "Carrie's Bittersweet Romance": Book 2, Chapter 28

- 4 "Christmas" Chapters:
  - √ "Christmas": Book 5, Chapter 16
  - √ "Christmas Gift": Book 6, Chapter 9; Book 8, Chapter 13
  - √ "The Christmas Party": Book 1, Chapter 10

- 12 "Day" Chapters:
  - √ "Again Upon a Rainy Day": Book 4, Chapter 22
  - √ "The Blackest Day": Book 8, Chapter 15
  - √ "Color All Days Blue, But Save One for Black": Book 1, Chapter 20
  - √ "Days Colored Black": Book 8, Chapter 9
  - √ "Days of Happiness, Days of Sorrow": Book 14, Chapter 11
  - √ "Days of Passion": Book 8, Chapter 8
  - √ "Judgment Day": Book 3, Chapter 32
  - √ "A Long Day's Journey": Book 4, Chapter 17
  - √ "My Wedding Day": Book 14, Chapter 4
  - √ "The Nightmare in Daylight": Book 4, Chapter 9
  - √ "School Days Renewed": Book 2, Chapter 6
  - √ "Tuesday Teatime": Book 4, Chapter 4

- 5 "Dream" Chapters (and 1 "Dream" Title):
  - √ "Dream Chasers": Book 7, Chapter 16
  - √ "Dreams Come True": Book 2, Chapter 21; Book 7, Chapter 22
  - √ "Fevered Dreamer": Book 6, Chapter 13
  - √ "Papa's Dream": Book 4, Chapter 3
  - √ "Winter Dreams": Book 2, Chapter 17
  - √ *Web of Dreams:* Book 11

- 7 "Epilogues":
  - √ Books 1, 3, 5, 11, 12, 14, and 15

- 8 "Prologues":
  - √ Books 1, 3, 6, 8, 10, 11, 13, and 15

- 5 "Family" Chapters:

√ "Family Affairs": Book 13, Chapter 5; Book 14, Chapter 10
√ "Family Secrets": Book 10, Chapter 1
√ "Family Support": Book 7, Chapter 15
√ "Winnerrow Family": Book 6, Chapter 18

- 3 "Fern" Chapters:
  √ "Fern": Book 12, Chapter 2
  √ "Fern's True Colors": Book 14, Chapter 16
  √ "Seeing Fern Again": Book 14, Chapter 13

- 2 "Gathering" Chapters:
  √ "Gathering Darkness": Book 3, Chapter 15
  √ "Gathering Shadows": Book 2, Chapter 22

- 3 "Ghosts" Chapters:
  √ "Ghosts": Book 9, Chapter 5
  √ "Ghosts in the House": Book 10, Chapter 12
  √ "The Ghosts of the Past": Book 8, Chapter 4

- 2 "So Long, Pop" Chapters:
  √ "Good-bye, Pa": Book 9, Chapter 12
  √ "Good-bye, Daddy": Book 1, Chapter 1

- 2 "Grandmother" Chapters:
  √ "The Grandmother's House": Book 1, Chapter 3
  √ "The Grandmother, Revisited": Book 2, Chapter 32

- 3 "Holiday" Chapters:
  √ "Holiday Joys": Book 5, Chapter 15
  √ "Holidays": Book 1, Chapter 9
  √ "Holidays, Lonely Days": Book 7, Chapter 11

- 3 "Homecoming" Chapters:
  √ "Homecoming": Book 3, Chapter 12; Book 5, Chapter 12; Book 10, Chapter 21

- 2 "Honeymoon" Chapters:
  √ "Honeymoon Heartache": Book 14, Chapter 5
  √ "The Honeymoon's Over": Book 11, Chapter 10

- 7 "Last" Chapters:
  √ "At Last, Momma": Book 1, Chapter 17
  √ "Free, at Last!": Book 2, Chapter 1
  √ "The Last Dance": Book 3, Chapter 17
  √ "Last Rites": Book 4, Chapter 23

√ "The Last Spin of the Web": Book 4, Chapter 27
√ "The Last Supper": Book 3, Chapter 30
√ "My Prince, at Last": Book 10, Chapter 24

- 3 "Life" Chapters:
  √ "Life and Death": Book 9, Chapter 11
  √ "Life Goes On": Book 14, Chapter 9
  √ "Life's Second Chance": Book 2, Chapter 3

- 4 "Malcolm" Chapters:
  √ "Malcolm Has His Way": Book 8, Chapter 10
  √ "Malcolm's Rage": Book 3, Chapter 16
  √ "Malcolm's Stepmother": Book 8, Chapter 7
  √ "Malcolm's Way, My Way": Book 8, Chapter 11

- 18 "My" Chapters (which includes 3 "First" Chapters; 2 "Mother" Chapters; 3 "Father" Chapters"; and 3 "Wedding" Chapters):
  √ "My Attic Souvenirs": Book 3, Chapter 26
  √ "My Brother's Keeper": Book 12, Chapter 5
  √ "My Choice": Book 6, Chapter 11
  √ "My First Date": Book 2, Chapter 8
  √ "My First Son": Book 5, Chapter 5
  √ "My Heart's Desire": Book 3, Chapter 6
  √ "My Knight in Shining Armor": Book 13, Chapter 16
  √ "My Mother's Room": Book 10, Chapter 10
  √ "My Mother, My Father": Book 7, Chapter 20
  √ "My New Life": Book 12, Chapter 9
  √ "My Prince, at Last": Book 10, Chapter 24
  √ "My Savior, "My Father": Book 6, Chapter 16
  √ "My Second Son": Book 5, Chapter 4
  √ "My Stepfather": Book 1, Chapter 19
  √ "My Sweet Small Prince": Book 2, Chapter 25
  √ "My Wedding": Book 8, Chapter 2
  √ "My Wedding Day": Book 14, Chapter 4
  √ "My Wedding Party": Book 8, Chapter 5

- 10 "New" Chapters (which includes 2 "A New Home" Chapters):
  √ "Another New Place": Book 12, Chapter 1
  √ "My New Life": Book 12, Chapter 9
  √ "A New Adventure, A New Friend": Book 13, Chapter 1
  √ "A New Best Friend": Book 11, Chapter 6

√ "A New Brother, A Lost Love": Book 12, Chapter 10
√ "A New Home": Book 2, Chapter 2
√ "A New Home": Book 6, Chapter 12
√ "The New Lovers": Book 5, Chapter 21
√ "New York, New York": Book 2, Chapter 15
√ "Old and New Lives": Book 9, Chapter 9

- 2 "Opening" Chapters:
  √ "Opening Gambit": Book 2, Chapter 26
  √ "Opening Night": Book 12, Chapter 6

- 2 "Papa" Chapters:
  √ "Papa's Dream": Book 4, Chapter 3
  √ "Papa's Story": Book 4, Chapter 26

- 2 "Prisoner" Chapters:
  √ "The Prisoner and the Warden": Book 8, Chapter 12
  √ "A Prisoner's Escape": Book 10, Chapter 20

- 3 "Private" Chapters:
  √ "Private Conversations": Book 12, Chapter 16
  √ "Private Lessons": Book 13, Chapter 7
  √ "A Very Private Place": Book 11, Chapter 3

- 2 "Promises" Chapters:
  √ "Promises": Book 7, Chapter 10
  √ "Promises of Spring": Book 9, Chapter 1

- 3 "School" Chapters:
  √ "Exploring the Bernhardt School": Book 13, Chapter 2
  √ "School and Church": Book 6, Chapter 2
  √ "School Days Renewed": Book 2, Chapter 6

- 7 "Secret" Chapters (and 1 "Secret" Title):
  √ "Family Secrets": Book 10, Chapter 1
  √ "More Secrets from the Past": Book 14, Chapter 7
  √ "Secret Lovers": Book 13, Chapter 9
  √ "The Secret of the Cottage": Book 10, Chapter 23
  √ "The Secret of the Wind Chimes": Book 4, Chapter 24
  √ "Secrets": Book 15, Chapter 7

√ "Secrets Revealed": Book 12, Chapter 15
√ *Secrets of the Morning:* Book 13

- 6 "Shadow" Chapters (and 1 "Shadow" Title):
    √ "Gathering Shadows": Book 2, Chapter 22
    √ "Momma's Shadow": Book 2, Chapter 11
    √ "Shadows": Book 3, Chapter 7
    √ "Shadows and Light": Book 8, Chapter 16
    √ "The Shadows Deepen": Book 15, Chapter 16
    √ "Shadows Fade Away": Book 5, Chapter 19
    √ *Garden of Shadows:* Book 8

- 3 "Sin" Chapters:
    √ "Sin and Sinners": Book 7, Chapter 12
    √ "The Sins of My Father": Book 9, Chapter 13
    √ "The Wages of Sin": Book 8, Chapter 18

- 2 "Ugly" Chapters:
    √ "The Ugly Duckling and the Swan": Book 8, Chapter 3
    √ "Ugly Realities": Book 13, Chapter 13

- 3 "Visit" Chapters:
    √ "The Grandmother, Revisited": Book 2, Chapter 32
    √ "A Visit to a Circus": Book 11, Chapter 19
    √ "A Visit with Jimmy": Book 13, Chapter 4

- 2 "Winterhaven" Chapters:
    √ "Winterhaven": Book 7, Chapter 5; Book 11, Chapter 11

PART III

The "Flowers in the Attic" Film

—19—

FLOWER FACTS:
A DETAILED LOOK AT THE
FLOWERS IN THE ATTIC
MOVIE

(New World Pictures, 1987)
Color; 92 minutes; PG-13

This feature is a scene-by-scene look at the *Flowers in the Attic* film, with commentary and interesting bits of trivia thrown in for good measure. I also make an attempt here to point up the differences between the book and the film—changes that effectively illustrate the process a 400-page novel goes through as it is shoved through a funnel to make a coherent and entertaining 92-minute movie.

- The film adaptation of *Flowers in the Attic* opens with the following voice-over narration by Cathy:

  Grandmother's house. Though it's been many years since I last saw it, I'll always remember that even my first impression was one of fear . . . and wonder. My childhood was soon to be lost, my innocence shattered. All our dreams destroyed by what we would find within.

- The film's credits roll, as Cathy's monologue continues:

My mother and father were the center of my universe when I was young. And I always wanted to grow up to be just like Mom.

- The first scene shows the children hiding behind the sofa waiting for Daddy to come home. We are told that Cathy was his favorite. We see Daddy giving Cathy the ballerina music box that will figure prominently later in the film.
- The family prepares for Daddy's birthday party. When presented with the problem of how to arrange Daddy's 36 birthday candles, Cathy chooses six rows of six, effectively foreshadowing a later scene that takes place in the bathroom of the children's Foxworth Hall bedroom. After Corrine shows the children her bleeding, whipped back, Cathy and Christopher tend to her in the bathroom in front of a huge frosted multipane window made up of 36 panes of glass, in *six rows of six*.
- Back at the house, though, Daddy is late. Two policemen come to deliver the bad news: He is dead, killed in an automobile accident. Daddy's favorite, Cathy, screams in grief upon hearing the news.
- It is many days, perhaps weeks later. The house is now empty. Corrine, who is wearing her signature strand of cultured pearls, has had to give up the house. They all take a bus to the grandparents' house. Corrine explains her plan to win back her father's love and become the heiress she could have been before her parents severed all ties with her many years earlier. We don't yet know why they cut her off and cast her out. During the bus ride, Cathy tells Chris that she is angry that they never had a pet. If they had, she reasons, then they would have learned about death when the animal died.
- Upon their early-morning arrival at Foxworth Hall, the family is "greeted" by three vicious dogs. The first actual person they see is the bearded caretaker who calls off the barking canines. Carrie is carrying a doll; the others, suitcases. John the butler opens the door to Corrine and her four children. The Grandmother appears. She is stern of face, dressed in black, and as cold as ice. Her first words are, "Leave

all the bags with John, Corrine, and bring the children upstairs."

- They all troop upstairs to the room where the children will "live." John carries the bags. *Difference:* In the film, John the butler and the caretaker know about the children. In the novel, John is not present when they arrive, and even though he may suspect or even secretly know what's going on, it isn't actually confirmed that he's aware of them until later.
- The Grandmother tells the children why Corrine was disowned seventeen years earlier. Her marriage to their father, she tells them, was "unholy," a "sacrilege," and an "abomination." She reveals to them that their father was Corrine's uncle. *Difference:* In the novel, Christopher is Corrine's *half*-uncle, but this was changed for the film to just plain uncle.
- The children attempt to settle in, but it's clear they are upset with the situation.
- Downstairs we see Corrine undressing in front of her father and then her mother whipping her repeatedly with a nasty-looking bullwhip.
- *The Fight Scene:* After the whipping, Corrine and her mother visit the children locked away upstairs in the room in the north wing. Corrine is crying, but the kids are happy to see her. The Grandmother shrieks at them for making noise. Carrie screams on purpose, and The Grandmother picks her up by the hair. Cory runs over and bites The Grandmother on the leg. The Grandmother kicks the little boy and then slaps him.
- Corrine is then made to show the children the 17 bloody lashes on her back. They are told that she received one lash for each year she lived in sin with their father. *Difference:* In the book, Corrine received 48 lashes: one for each year of her age, and fifteen extra for each year she "lived in sin" with Christopher. (See the feature on Wes Craven's shelved *Flowers in the Attic* script for details on Craven's treatment of this element of the story.)
- We later see The Grandmother kneeling and praying with her hair down, a scene not in the book.
- Corrine tells Chris and Cathy about the closet stairway to the attic.

- We see a hand sprinkling "powdered sugar" on cookies. We don't know who's doing the sprinkling. *Difference:* In the book, it's doughnuts, not cookies.
- Grandmother gives the children their list of rules and tells them they must never be seen by anyone in the house.
- The children go upstairs into the attic and explore the dusty, cavernous place. Symbolically, Cathy opens a window in the attic in an attempt to let in light and air, suggesting that she and her siblings hope to be able to fly free from their prison one day soon.
- We hear Cathy's voice-over narration:

Grandmother's rules weren't rules—they were cruel punishments. We were trapped. And the only way we could even feel the sunlight was to look out a barred window. Our mother must have been desperate to have come back. We were all going to pay the price.

- We see Corrine's father, The Grandfather, lying in bed as Corrine plays the piano for him.
- The children clean up the attic. They try on old clothes they find. Chris finds a bar suitable for Cathy to use as a ballet barre and puts it up on a mirror.
- Cathy's voice-over continues:

As the weeks became months, our memories of our real home began to fade, but we clung to our dreams. Chris wanted to go to medical school someday. And I wanted to be a dancer.

- We see Cathy practicing dance steps in front of the mirror.
- Scenes of attic "family" life: Chris puts up a swing for Cory. Cathy combs Carrie's hair. Chris bathes Cory. Time passes—too *much* time locked in a room.
- Cathy's voice-over continues:

Mother's visits became fewer and fewer. And then stopped altogether. We imagined that something horrible had happened to her. Or had we been forgotten? There seemed to be no way to escape. But soon, very soon, we'd have to find a way past Grandmother to find and to help Mother . . . if we could.

- More time passes: Cory, Carrie, and Cathy cut paper flowers. Cory makes his paper snail. Chris gives his "tubular intestines" speech about snails. Cathy explains to the twins that God took all the grass to Heaven for Daddy. Ominously, Cory says he's itchy. Carrie wants TV, ice cream, and to be able to play with her friends and go outside. In an attempt at quieting the complaining twins, Chris gives a very "biblical"-type speech about there being a time for everything.
- Later, Chris goes into the bathroom while Cathy is taking a bath and washes her back. He is worried that something has happened to Mother. Illness? Imprisonment? Cathy doesn't believe it. Chris says he has a plan.
- The next morning The Grandmother, catching Cathy and Chris in one bed, and the twins together in the other, freaks. She knocks Cathy's music box—the one given to her by her father—off the mantel and breaks it. Cathy is devastated.
- Cathy and Chris discuss Chris's plan: That evening, they will escape, find their mother, and tell her what's been going on.
- Cathy chisels open one of the bedroom windows. They take out one window bar and crawl out onto the roof. Chris climbs alone down a rope, but four dogs sense his presence and run to where he's touched down on the grounds. Cathy starts down the rope. The caretaker puts on the outdoor floodlights. While Cathy is halfway down the rope, Chris begins to climb back up. The dogs are biting at his feet. A storm starts. The rope breaks as Chris nears the top. Chris dangles off the roof. The caretaker appears on the ground with a gun. Chris throws the end of the broken rope up to Cathy and manages to climb up onto the roof. The caretaker sees the rope being pulled up onto the roof and the broken floodlights on the ground. The escape attempt has failed.
- *V. C. Andrews's cameo:* It is the next morning. In a scene that occurs 44 minutes into the film, (with 48

minutes remaining), the camera pans across a maid cleaning an upstairs window. The maid is played by V. C. Andrews, and the scene is exactly 2.5 seconds long. In the script, this is Scene 62A.

- The same morning. Corrine brings the children their breakfast. They take her into the attic. They question her: Where have you been? Cathy scolds her mother about the twins' health. Corrine claims The Grandfather is on the way out. The children agree to wait a little longer.
- Cory catches a mouse and names him Fred.
- Corrine reads to her father. He strokes her hair. She kisses his hand. The Grandmother watches.
- The twins call Christopher: There are more bars on the attic windows.
- Cathy takes a bath. We hear her thoughts:

I found a way to escape, even if it was only to a hot bath and my fantasies. Fantasies of a life filled with dancing, friends, and maybe even romance. Fantasies that might never come true.

- Chris stands at the door while Cathy's bathing and asks her if she's mad at him for siding with Mother. The Grandmother comes up from behind and yells, "Sinners!" Chris castigates The Grandmother. He tells her they laugh at her and then he throws her out of the room. Cathy is frightened.
- Later: Cory is gone. They all rush up to the attic calling his name. They search the attic and find Cory hiding in an open wicker trunk. *Difference:* In the book, Cory is trapped in a trunk that accidentally closes shut as he's hiding in it during hide-and-seek.
- Cathy goes downstairs to the bedroom after the search. The Grandmother pushes her down onto the floor and locks the twins and Chris in the attic. The Grandmother then slaps Cathy and hacks off her hair. *Difference:* In the book, The Grandmother puts hot tar in Cathy's hair while she's sleeping.
- Chris trims and shapes what's left of Cathy's hair. He tries to convince her that their mother could not have known about what The Grandmother did to her.
- We see John wheeling The Grandfather in to dinner.

In the attic, Chris fixes the music box. The Grandmother stops bringing the children food.

- The Grandfather buys Corrine a beautiful dress. Bart Winslow arrives at the mansion with flowers for Corrine.

- Upstairs, the children are being slowly starved. Cory gets sick. Chris sterilizes a razor, wraps a belt around his arm, and slits open his arm at the elbow. He feeds Cory with his blood. *Difference:* In the book, Chris slits his wrist.

- Chris hammers out the bedroom's door hinges. He and Cathy leave the room. They go downstairs and sneak into their mother's bedroom. Cathy goes through her closet. She finds tons of clothes (but *not* the pornographic picture book, as in the novel). They roam the house, going into The Grandfather's room. The old man opens his eyes as they're looking at him, grabs Cathy around the neck, and says, "I always loved you the best, Corrine." They flee, bumping into John at the door but managing to make it back upstairs to the bedroom. Cathy gets in the bathtub fully clothed. Chris sits on the bathroom windowsill. Chris defends Corrine. Cathy reminds him that the twins are sick. Cathy wants to leave; Chris says no. Cory comes into the bathroom. He has to throw up.

- We see a cupboard being opened. The children are to be fed now. More "powdered sugar" is sprinkled on the children's cookies. We still don't know who's doing the sprinkling.

- Cathy has a nightmare that her mother comes into their room wearing a hood, but when the hood is pulled off, it's really The Grandmother.

- Carrie takes down the paper flowers in the attic because it is now winter. Chris is trying to diagnose Cory's illness from medical books. Corrine comes in. She's been away. She tells them that The Grandfather was in a hospital. Carrie cuts the heads off the paper flowers as her mother speaks. She tells the children that The Grandfather is giving her a party that evening because he loves her so much now. He wants to reintroduce her to society. Tomorrow he's having his attorney, Bart Winslow (whom Corrine is dating, of course, a little tidbit Corrine conveniently forgets to tell the children), change the will and put her back in. Cathy's not buying any of it and confronts her mother with the facts of the twins' illness and their nightmarish situation. Corrine responds, "When you are ready to treat me with love, I'll be back."

- Chris and Cathy decide to escape once again to go see the party. They hide behind what looks like a heating duct. *Difference:* In the novel, it is some type of chest. We see Corrine and Bart dancing. Bart gives Corrine an engagement ring. They kiss. Back in the room Chris embraces Cathy.

- The next morning The Grandmother and Corrine find the children all still in their nightclothes. Cory is desperately sick. Cathy yells at her mother to bring Cory to a hospital. Corrine slaps her. Cathy slaps her back. The Grandmother tells John to take Cory downstairs. John picks Cory up and Cory says, "Hello, John." John is as impassive as ever and does not respond to the little boy's touching greeting.

- We see the caretaker digging a grave. Carrie dances with her doll in the attic. They wait and pace. Corrine returns and tells them that Cory had pneumonia and that the doctors did all they could. There won't be a funeral, they're told. Cory has already been buried.

- We see the caretaker filling in a grave, but now we see three empty graves next to Cory's.

- Cory's pet mouse, Fred, dies. Chris finds a piece of "sugar" cookie in his cage. He studies his medical books and determines that the mouse died from arsenic poisoning. He realizes that they are all slowly being poisoned to death by the "powdered sugar" on their cookies, which he now knows has been arsenic all along. He decides to steal money or jewelry from their mother and escape.

- Chris sneaks downstairs and overhears Corrine and Bart talking about getting married tomorrow. Chris decides that they are not going to sneak away: They're going out through the front door.

- We see more "cookie sprinkling," but this time the

camera pulls back and we see who has been doing the poisoning: It is Corrine.

- The children hide in a closet in the bedroom and when The Grandmother comes in, Chris hits her with a bedpost and knocks her out. They run downstairs. Cathy won't leave until she tells The Grandfather the truth. But The Grandfather's room is empty: He's dead. And it's obvious that he has been for quite some time.

- Meanwhile, Corrine decides she will wait no longer for her mother (who, thanks to Chris, is lying unconscious in the children's room). They start the wedding ceremony without her.

- Back in The Grandfather's room, Cathy finds a copy of the wedding invitation. The wedding is today, April 23rd. Chris finds a copy of the old man's will. It states that if it's ever proven that Corrine had children from her first marriage—even after he's dead— she will be disinherited. We now know that Corrine *must* kill her children. If they live, then she stands to lose all of her father's riches.

- We see Corrine in a bridal gown at the altar with Bart. Chris, Cathy, and Carrie slowly walk down the aisle behind her. When they reach the front of the room, Cathy yells out, "Mother!" and Corrine spins around, but she pretends she doesn't know them. Chris and Cathy tell all the guests the truth, including Corrine's scheme to poison her own children. Bart believes them and begins to back away from Corrine in horror and revulsion. Cathy tries to force the lying Corrine to eat the cookie. They struggle. Corrine falls off a balcony and hangs herself on the train of her bridal gown. *Difference:* In the novel, Corrine does not die.

- We see the three surviving children walking away from Foxworth Hall. As The Grandmother watches from a window, we hear Cathy's final words:

We finally got our real revenge. We managed to make it on our own. I got a job to help put Chris through medical school. Little Carrie grew up, but she was never truly healthy. I even started dancing again. We left the past behind—all except the mem-

ories of Mother, Grandmother, and the attic. I sometimes wonder if Grandmother's still alive, still pre-
siding over Foxworth Hall, still awaiting my return.

• Fade to black and roll credits.
                    —The End—

Cast

Louise Fletcher (Grandmother); Victoria Tennant (Mother);
Kristy Swanson (Cathy); Jeb Stuart Adams (Chris); Ben
Granger (Cory); Lindsay Parker (Carrie); Marshall Colt (Fa-
ther); Nathan Davies (Grandfather); Brooke Fries (Flower
Girl); Alex Koba (John Hall); Leonard Mann (Bart Wins-
low); Bruce Neckels (Minister); Gus Peters (Caretaker);
Clare C. Peck (Narrator); V. C. Andrews (Maid).

Production Credits

Director: Jeffrey Bloom; Producers: Sy Levin and
Thomas Fries; Executive Producers: Charles Fries and
Mike Rosenfeld; Screenplay: Jeffrey Bloom; Based on
the Novel by: V. C. Andrews; Directors of Photography:
Frank Byers, Gil Hubbs; Production Designer: John
Muto; Casting: Penny Perry; Music: Christopher Young;
Film Editor: Gregory F. Plotts; Executive Production
Manager: William P. Owens; Unit Production Manager:
William Hole; First Assistant Director: Peter S. Gries;
Second Assistant Director: Douglas F. Dean III; Camera
Operator: Frank Byers; First Assistant Cameraman: Lex
DuPont; Second Assistant Cameraman: Rick Osborn;
Gaffer: Bobby Ferrara; Script Supervisor: Jill Gurr; Loca-
tion Manager: Pavel Cerny; Costume Designer: Ann
Somers Major; Makeup: Robin Neal; Hairstylists: Cathy
Estocin, Robert Hallowell; Set Director: Michele
Starbuck.

V. C. SPEAKS:
The *Publishers Weekly* Interview with V.C. Andrews on the Making of *Flowers in the Attic*

On Location with *Flowers in the Attic:*
V.C. Andrews Bestseller to Be a Movie*
by William Goldstein

"It's thrilling to see my characters come alive, to see actors and actresses playing them," says V. C. Andrews, who was the center of attention as she spent a mid-October day observing the transformation of her bestselling novel, *Flowers in the Attic,* into a Fries Entertainment–New World Pictures film, directed by Jeffrey Bloom, to be released in March 1987.

Most of the interiors for the film had already been shot in California, but for exterior shots, the location switched to the Crane House in Ipswich, Massachusetts, a sprawling mansion set atop Castle Hill, about a 45-minute drive outside of Boston. The broad expanse of sculptured lawns, used for open-air concerts in the summer, rolls literally in waves from the top of the hill to the shore of the

Atlantic Ocean. The ocean is at low tide at midday, and wide rings of beige sand are visible beyond the green lawns as V. C. Andrews, up with her mother from where they live in Virginia Beach, Virginia, contemplates the view through the massive windows of the house's chilly library.

The author, in a white fur hat and beige cashmere cape, sits by a crackling fire and admits that the Crane House (built during the first part of this century by bathroom-fixture king Robert Crane) is the very image of her own Foxworth Hall, the fictional Virginia home where the Dollanganger children were kept locked in the attic by their dastardly grandmother. Her books, *Flowers in the Attic* and its three sequels (*Petals on the Wind, If There Be Thorns, Seeds of Yesterday*), have more than 14 million copies in print since they were published beginning in 1979 by Pocket Books. (Andrews's seven books, including *My Sweet Audrina, Heaven* and the current *Dark Angel,* have a total of more than 24 million copies in print.)

But because, as Andrews says, "No other book gives you the thrill that the first one does," it is particularly exciting, she feels, that the first movie to be based on any of her books is this one, her first published novel. "I did picture the movie in the back of my mind when I was writing it," Andrews explains. The movie tie-in edition of *Flowers* ($4.50) will have a one-million-copy first printing and a new cover featuring the film's cast.

Andrews, who uses a wheelchair but can walk on crutches, is resting up for her 4 p.m. call. She is to film a cameo appearance as a maid in Scene 62A, and in her movie debut will be seen washing a window. The screenplay (written by director Bloom) calls for the camera, positioned outside, to zoom in on the maid scrubbing the window. The shot signifies that a nighttime rainstorm midway through the picture is over, and that a new and terrible day for the Dollanganger children has dawned.

"The camera will skim over me," demurs Andrews, whose first name is Virginia. "If you blink you'll probably miss me, but I'll have my best window washing hand out." Not quite seriously echoing the sometimes purplish prose of Andrews's books, Ann Patty, the author's editor at Pocket Books (she is also Poseidon Press editor-in-chief), believes there is romantic significance in the director giving the role of a maid to the author, and she spins out a metaphor as she sits by the author's side. "The writer is a person who wipes the window clean so that the reader can clearly see into the lives of the characters," Patty says.

This is not only a red-letter day for Andrews—today is the day they are filming the important scene where the mother sprinkles the children's cookies with arsenic. In the book, the grandmother sprinkles arsenic on powdered doughnuts, but in the movie, the mother sprinkles arsenic on a plate of cookies. The change makes the mother much more evil, everyone agrees, including, somewhat reluctantly, Andrews herself. Victoria Tennant, who was Pamela in *The Winds of War* and Steve Martin's girlfriend in *All of Me,* plays Corrine, the blonde-haired mother of the imprisoned children.

In *Flowers in the Attic,* Corrine, recently widowed (she was married and had four children by a distant cousin), returns to Foxworth Hall, her wealthy parents' home, to charm her way back into her father's will. The religious Foxworth grandparents are not happy that Corrine has had four children by an incestuous marriage, and the grandmother requires that the children hide in the attic while their mother works her magic with their grandfather. Of course, the grandmother has ulterior motives—she wants to kill the children.

"Louise Fletcher, who plays the grandmother, called Virginia up one night," begins Lillian Andrews, the petite, pixie-ish mother of the author, wearing a hat and coat that, like her daughter, she doesn't take off all day. But mother is immediately interrupted by her daughter (they interrupt each other all day, and no anecdote is recounted without an addition or aside from the other).

"And she said she wanted to get inside the grandmother," the author continues, since Fletcher called her, after all. "She said, 'It's hard for me to play a role without understanding the motivation of the character,' and I told her that she [the grandmother] considers the children should never have been born, they shouldn't exist. So the natural love she'd have for her own grandchildren, she stops. She just stops." In the movie, the grandchildren—Cathy, Chris, Cory and Carrie—are played by newcomers

Kristy Swanson, Jeb Adams, Ben Granger and Lindsay Parker.

Andrews has long been concerned with how her book makes it to the screen, as her mother tells the clerk from the hotel gift shop, who was invited to the set when she said she was a V. C. Andrews fan. "One of the very first letters Virginia received," recalls Lillian, "was from a man in Texas, and he said, 'It was a wonderful book, and it will make a wonderful movie—if they do it right.'" Andrews demanded and got script approval when she sold the film rights to producers Thomas Fries and Sy Levin.

"I turned down five scripts before this one," she says. "I was upset at the beginning, when there were changes from the book," Andrews explains, "till I began to see their point." When she objected to changes and cuts the producers suggested, "they changed everything I objected to," the author says. "They had really horrible things in there," she continues. "I kept thinking, 'You idiots, you don't know what you're doing.'" And she was vocal, she says.

"But my film agent told me, 'Virginia, you say that in such a nice way, they want to do what you say.' I kept writing them letters, blasting away at all the gross things they had in there. Like when Cathy [the oldest child] is kissing Bart [her mother's second husband, whom she spies sleeping and kisses lovingly in one scene in the book] they had him wake up and go into action, and I said, 'You can't have him do that!'" (Leonard Mann plays Bart in the film.)

On the whole, Andrews says, "They wanted to make it more gothic—they even had Dobermans nipping at the escaping children's heels," she reveals, hinting at the movie's ending, which is different from the ending in the book.

Ann Patty believes the script of the movie is "darker" than the book upon which it is based, but says it is faithful to the mood of the novel. Nevertheless, with two murders in the mixture (the murders do not occur in the book), the movie's ending does not leave as much room for a sequel as the book did—at least not a sequel along the lines that Andrews herself envisioned when she wrote her three follow-up Dollanganger books. At her editor's suggestion, Andrews is about to begin work on a "prequel" to *Flowers in the Attic*.

As for other future books, Patty predicts "two or three more books in the Heaven series," (Andrews's current *Dark Angel,* a November Pocket Books release, is the second book of that series). Andrews, however, says, "I haven't thought much about a third book in the Heaven series," and Patty advises, "I definitely think the prequel to *Flowers* is an easier book to write."

Andrews writes in the afternoon, she says, "because I don't feel as super-duper as I used to." She suffers from a debilitating arthritis (though the story of what has crippled her varies with each retelling) and, Andrews says, "It's sort of worn itself out and just left me stiff. It's not painful." Her preferred writing time is "at night. I do my best writing when the phone isn't ringing. It's quiet; that's when I really move into it."

"Sometimes she'll be up at midnight or one in the morning," Lillian interjects, "and I just have to say, 'Enough.' " "I get totally involved in the story," Andrews admits, offering an excuse to her mother and a reason to the rest of her listeners. "If I can laugh or cry, get emotionally caught up, then it's good. If I can't, then it isn't." Her passionately devoted readers, predominantly teenagers, evidently like "my way of taking the reader into the story," she says, "because their letters tell me they don't feel like they're reading, they feel like they're living, experiencing. Then when they finish the book, they start it over to live it again."

The author says her readers' reactions reflect her own attitude toward her novels. Part of what she writes "is autobiographical. Bits and pieces, though, no, I won't tell you which bits and pieces! Whenever I read about myself in my books, I cry. And I cry in all my books." Andrews says she also talks out loud to get dialogue, "and I do both sides!"

But she put all writing briefly aside as she prepares for appearances on behalf of *Dark Angel,* at the same time eagerly anticipating the spring 1987 release of the movie *Flowers in the Attic*—and any other film from the Flowers or Heaven series producers want to make. No, the author doesn't care about reviews, even if movie producers and performers do. Andrews knows that a writer can sell

24 million copies with either bad reviews (as she has) or none (as she has also done).

"When I first started to write," the former commercial artist remembers, "I just wanted to be published. I wrote nine novels before *Flowers*. I thought, 'If they'd only accept this!' Then when it becomes a bestseller, you're overwhelmed. And grateful." With the cast and crew working around her to make her book come to life, she says, "It's kind of incredible being in the middle of all this."

Andrews's nurse, Margaret Sullivan, nearby throughout the day, rises to escort her into the makeup and costume area, which is in a wood-and-marble bathroom just off the front entrance. The author finally takes off her hat and coat, puts her jewelry aside and emerges in a black-and-white maid's uniform. She moves to the tape that marks her place by the first floor window where the camera is set up. Producer Levin, who all day has been making sure Andrews and her mother are comfortable, moves into camera range, squirts out a lot of Windex, and quickly jumps away from the window. The director says, "We're rolling," and Andrews starts scrubbing. Fifteen seconds later, when it is all over, the author smiles brightly through the newly clean window.

—21—

BUFFY BLOOMS:

An Interview with the Star of *Flowers in the Attic,* Kristy Swanson

> I've been fortunate—
> I've been able to play
> quite a variety
> of characters in my career.
> I've played the girl
> you bring home to Mom,
> the killer,
> the victim,
> the hooker,
> the bitch.
>
> Kristy Swanson,
> January 1993

Introduction:
Cinema Girl

V. C. Andrews once told Kristy Swanson that she was exactly how she had envisioned Cathy Dollanganger when she originally created the *Flowers in the Attic* character. Could there be higher praise for an actor?

Buffy the Vampire Slayer director Fran Rubel Kuzui has described Kristy as part "Lucille Ball" and part "Linda Hamilton." Appropriately, then, in *Buffy,* Kristy gets to emote as both personas: Her "Valley Girl" mentality is hilarious (she was born with the Mark of the Slayer, but had it removed); and at the same time (and in the *same movie*) her kickboxing vampire slayer moves are killer.

Born six days before Christmas in 1969, Kristy

Swanson's first appearance before the cameras was her acting debut at the age of nine in a dollhouse commercial.

Her first starring role in a feature film was as a reanimated computer-chip-in-her-head killer teenage zombie in horrormeister Wes Craven's *Deadly Friend*. She then moved on to star as Cathy Dollanganger in V. C. Andrews's *Flowers in the Attic*.

Prior to *Deadly Friend*, she had a bit part in *Ferris Bueller's Day Off*, as the airhead Economics student Simone, the girl who told the teacher that Ferris had been seen at an ice cream parlor the previous night. When the teacher thanked her, Simone smiled and said, "No problem whatsoever." It was a tiny part, but Kristy hit a home run with it. You might even say that Simone could be considered the artistic harbinger of Kristy's later character, mall maven Buffy the Vampire Slayer. Kristy also later appeared in *Pretty in Pink* (she was one of the students at the prom), and a Disney Movie-Of-The-Week, *Mr. Boogedy*.

Kristy has since appeared in the sports movie *Diving In;* the sci-fi film *Dream Trap* (of which Kristy has said, "I don't know what I was thinking of when I made that movie." It went straight to video.); the *Mannequin* sequel *Mannequin Two: On the Move;* the *Airplane*-like *Hot Shots: An Important Movie!* (she was Kowalski, the only female fighter pilot); the sci-fi horror flick, *Highway to Hell* (she had to be rescued from Hell); and the vampire spoof *Buffy the Vampire Slayer*. Her latest film is *The Program*, a football movie with *Misery* star James Caan, Craig Sheffer, and Halle Berry. (Kristy also appeared in director William Friedkin's 1985 film, *To Live and Die in L.A.* when she was 14 years old but her part ended up on the cutting room floor.)

Kristy has also done a great deal of TV work, including episodes of "Alfred Hitchcock Presents"; "Cagney and Lacey"; "Valerie"; "Knots Landing"; "B. L. Stryker"; "O'Hara"; and "It's Your Move." She has won two Youth in Film Awards: one for best actress guest-starring in a television series for her appearance in "Cagney and Lacey"; and one for best actress in a motion picture for her performance in *Flowers in the Attic*.

I would not be revealing a state secret if I acknowledge

that Kristy Swanson is astonishingly beautiful (*USA Today* said she had "hotcha looks").

But she is also talented, charming, and genuinely ingenuous. She brings to all of her performances better acting than the roles sometimes deserve. She is both a gifted dramatic *and* comedic actress and *USA Today* also rightly acknowledged that Kristy's performance in *Buffy the Vampire Slayer* was the most humorous part of the film.

Kristy Swanson can act. Perhaps the day will come when she gets to do it in something other than a leotard or leather miniskirt.

Now don't get me wrong: There's nothing wrong with being drop-dead gorgeous, but it shouldn't blind producers, directors, and casting agents to talent that goes beyond "hotcha" looks.

There is hope in Hollywood, though. Remember: Michelle Pfeiffer had to don a slinky gown (fire-engine red, no less) and crawl around erotically on a piano in *The Fabulous Baker Boys* before she was "allowed" (both by Hollywood *and* her audience) to take on the role of the no-makeup, almost-unattractive waitress in *Frankie and Johnny* three years later. (I say "almost" because let's face it: we *are* talking about Michelle Pfeiffer here!)

For now, Hollywood wants to see Kristy Swanson in tube tops and hot pants. Fine. But let's hope that we soon get to see her in a film project that is noted more for its dialogue than its wardrobe.

Kristy currently lives in California, where she drives around in a Ford Taurus station wagon.

Really.

She recently told *Entertainment Weekly* magazine, "I had a little sports car, but it got me into trouble."

Here's my talk with a young woman who is sure to be one of the outstanding actresses of the 1990s.

BUFFY BLOOMS: THE INTERVIEW

Call Me Cathy

Steve Spignesi: How did you get the part of Cathy in *Flowers in the Attic*?

Kristy Swanson: Basically I just went in and auditioned.

Actually I auditioned seven times for it. Normally you don't need to audition that much. The reason why it took so long was that they needed to match up four kids to look alike and so they had me reading with a lot of different guys and then they would take pictures of us together, and then separately, trying to match up the cast so that we all looked like brother and sister. And then it just happened, you know?

Wes Craven's "Flowers" Screenplay

SS: I know your first starring role was in *Deadly Friend,* which was directed by *Nightmare on Elm Street*'s Wes Craven. Did you know at the time that Wes himself had written a *Flowers in the Attic* screenplay?

KS: No, not really. It's kind of strange. I had just done *Deadly Friend* with Wes and it turned out that a while before that Wes himself had written a draft screenplay of *Flowers in the Attic*. [See the feature on Wes Craven's *Flowers in the Attic* script in this volume.] One day when we were doing reshoots on *Deadly Friend* I mentioned to Wes that I was auditioning for this movie *Flowers in the Attic* and he told me that he had wanted to do that. He told me that he had written a script for it and that he wanted to direct it, but that they just weren't getting it off the ground. So he took *Deadly Friend* instead and did that. He was kind of bummed about the whole thing. I think there were probably ten different scripts written but Jeffrey Bloom's script ended up being the one chosen and Jeffrey also got picked to direct it.

SS: Had you read Wes Craven's script or V. C.'s novel before you auditioned?

KS: No, I hadn't read either of them. In fact, I have not read *any* of V. C.'s books. I had read Jeffrey Bloom's script and then after I got the part, everybody was telling me, well, now you've *got* to read the book.

At this point I was very familiar with the novel *Flowers in the Attic* because in grade school and junior high, so many of my girlfriends had read it. *Flowers in the Attic* was *huge*. In the younger grades, the really popular book was *Are You There God? It's Me, Marga-*

ret. But then as we got a little older, *Flowers in the Attic* was the big rage.

But *I* never read it because I've always been a bad reader and it was such a thick book that it scared me. I always figured I would never get through it. And so after I got the part when I was 16 and everyone was telling me to read the book, I said, I think I'm just gonna stick with the script. Because at that time I really didn't want to confuse myself. I just felt more comfortable working only with Jeffrey's script.

What Mom and Dad Thought

SS: Had your parents read the novel?

KS: Yes, my mom and dad read the book when I was auditioning for the part.

SS: What did they think?

KS: My parents read the book *and* the script and they told me that it was *based* on the book but that there was no possible way that a movie could include everything in the book. The story extends over such a long period of time in the book and it is, after all, only a two-hour movie. So I decided to just play the character from the script.

Meet My Coworkers: Nurse Ratchet and Mrs. Steve Martin

SS: I think you did a terrific job in capturing Cathy, so it's apparent that Jeffrey Bloom's script really worked in communicating her character to you. The film did leave out a lot of story, but in terms of pushing the novel through a funnel and getting the bare bones narrative, it worked. Louise Fletcher was marvelous, as was Victoria Tennant. What was it like working with Louise and Victoria, the two actors who were probably the two biggest names on the set?

KS: Yes, they were the two most well-known actors on the set. They were great. Victoria was lovely—a really lovely lady and I adored working with her. Victoria is a very sweet woman. She was struggling a bit with her British accent, though. They wanted her to have an

American accent so she was always saying, "How do you say this?" She had a difficult time with the word "children" so I tried to help her with that. It was funny, you know? (Laughs) She was just a quiet lady and real nice and pleasant.

SS: How about Louise Fletcher?

KS: Louise was great. She didn't make me feel intimidated by her in any way and I genuinely enjoyed working with her. She, too, was a really sweet lady. And strong. She was just so cool. And *real* hip.

SS: She wasn't as scary as say, Nurse Ratchet, in *One Flew Over the Cuckoo's Nest*?

KS: (Laughs) Oh, no, not at all, not at all. Totally the opposite.

A Visit with V. C.

SS: V. C. Andrews had a small cameo appearance in the film. [See the *Publishers Weekly* interview with V. C. about filming *Flowers in the Attic* in this volume.] Did you get a chance to meet her?

KS: Yes, I did, and she attended a dinner with the whole cast as well.

We shot the majority of the film in Los Angeles. The entire Foxworth Hall attic was in L. A. on a soundstage. It took up an entire stage and the set was loaded with antiques and all sorts of old furniture and was a really neat set.

But we also went to Boston for about three or four weeks of location shooting. We went to shoot all the exteriors of the big mansion and V. C. came out there to meet all of us and to do this little cameo.

I remember going to a restaurant to have dinner with the whole group and she was there in a wheelchair and she was kind of reclined in the chair and she couldn't really move her head around. Her mother was there taking care of her. At that point I didn't know that she had been in a wheelchair all her life.

SS: Did you get a chance to talk to her?

KS: Yes, I did. I spoke to her, and she said to me, "You're exactly as I picture Cathy." And I was unbelievably flattered. I imagine it's very hard for a writer to see an actor playing one of their characters and realize that the actor is not like what was in her mind when she wrote the book. So it was really cool that she saw that in me. And later, after she passed on, I was sorry she was not able to see the finished movie, but at least she got to see it being made and also be in it.

SS: Did she seem to be in pain?

KS: She did not look comfortable.

SS: Apparently it was pretty draining for her to appear in the movie.

KS: Yeah, it was. She was usually in a wheelchair, but she supported herself on crutches for the one scene she was in. She played one of the housekeepers.

SS: How much total time did you get to spend with her and her mother?

KS: Just for dinner on location in Boston.

SS: From what you know of her stories, what do you think is her huge appeal?

KS: I think it's because V. C. writes her books like they're true stories. Like I said, when I was in grade school, *Flowers in the Attic* was enormously popular.

Ch-Ch-Ch-Changes

SS: Have you seen the *Flowers in the Attic* book with the picture from the film on the cover?

KS: Yes, and it was very strange what they did for the poster and the cover of the film tie-in edition of the book. I always thought that the original book cover was really neat. It had the girl's face in a little circle, and then you open it up and you see the whole family. But then Pocket Books redesigned the window cover to look like our video jacket and the poster of the film. On the cover of one of the film editions, there's a photo of Louise, and there's also a photo of four kids, but the kids are not us.

SS: Really? How do you feel about them using models instead of the real actors?

KS: I think I would have preferred the poster, the video sleeve, and the book to have had the four of us kids and not models. They actually did a photo session with four kids and dressed them up like us. I think New World Pictures did that because they would have had to pay us to come in that day—and it would have been more than they had to pay these other kids. So they photo-doubled us. They do that all the time now. On the jacket of my movie, *Highway to Hell,* for instance. That's not my body. It's my head, but it's not my body. And it's not Chad Lowe's body either. It's our heads stuck on other people's bodies. The girl looks like she's six feet tall! And the guy they used for Chad's body is huge, and Chad's got a very thin frame! If you ask me, I would call this false advertising.

SS: They did that with Bette Midler and Woody Allen's bodies for the *Scenes from a Mall* poster.

KS: Speaking of Woody, I was just nuts about *Husbands and Wives.*

Husbands and Wives

SS: Yeah, me too. I thought it was terrific. I was sorry it came out too late for me to include in my *Woody Allen Companion.*

KS: The first scene kind of threw me because I didn't realize it was all hand-held camera. I actually got a little motion sick because the camera was moving around so much and it was such a long scene. I was enjoying the conversation that was going on but I wasn't used to seeing so much camera movement. But then I got used to it. I just loved that film. I call that movie the bitter truth. Judy Davis was awesome. Did you know that I was up for the Juliette Lewis role?

SS: No, I didn't. How did that come about?

KS: Apparently Woody saw my screen test for *Machine Gun Kelly* and asked to meet with me for *Husbands and Wives.*

Auditioning for Woody

SS: What's auditioning for the Woodman like?

KS: Well, I went to New York and everybody kept telling me not to get offended because Woody doesn't have long meetings. I was told that I'd probably be in and out in less than five minutes. He's not a big conversationalist when it comes to auditioning, I was told, and he's really shy and so most of his auditions literally last under five minutes.

A *lot* of people told me that, so that's pretty much what I was expecting.

Well, I walked in and said, hi, nice to meet you, and Woody *was* kind of nervous and shy at first. Then he says, "You're from California?" And I said, yeah, and he asked me if I was having a nice time in New York, and I told him, yeah, I love it. And then he asked me to read something for him, and he tells me that it won't take long, and that I could take the material into another room and spend as much time as I want with it and then come back into the editing room when I was ready. So he gives me the sides and it's five pages of dialogue with big paragraphs in it! (Laughs) And I'm not a great reader! So, I'm thinking, oh shit, I really have to cram for this one. (Laughs)

I go into another room and when I look over the material, I realize that there's big words in there that I don't know how to pronounce. I've got to find a dictionary, I decide. So I start looking everywhere for one and finally I ask this guy for a dictionary and he brings me one. Now I'm cramming and getting familiar with the dialogue but then I suddenly realize, hey, this is Woody Allen. I'm not gonna have to say it perfectly, because his style is to have his characters talk like normal people talk. They forget what they're talking about in the middle of a conversation or they say things wrong, and everybody's really pretty natural.

So I relaxed a bit and realized that I didn't have to know the dialogue word for word. When I felt ready, I walked in and did the scene and then he just stared at me until finally he said, "Would you do another one for me?" I said sure, and did another scene. So I ended up being there almost an hour. (Laughs) It was pretty funny.

SS: So what happened?

KS: It came down to me and Emily Lloyd. And the way the part was written, the character was a very upper-class, very sophisticated, kind of "poised" young woman. And Emily Lloyd is British and she has that kind of quality about her. So she got the part and then, after two weeks of filming, Woody replaced her with Juliette Lewis. I felt bad for Emily, but Juliette was unbelievable in the role.

SS: What'd you think of Woody?

KS: I really liked Woody a lot. I thought he was really cool.

SS: And I guess you liked Juliette's performance?

KS: Oh, yeah. She was great, just great. I thought she was really good.

SS: Speaking of actors, are there any actors or actresses whose work you particularly admire?

KS: I think Meryl Streep is awesome. Totally awesome. I also really like Judy Davis and Donald Sutherland. I worked with Donald in *Buffy the Vampire Slayer*.

The Climb

SS: Of all the films you've been in, is there one that's your favorite?

KS: Not really. Believe it or not, when I watch my films, I don't really watch them for entertainment. I watch them with more of a critical eye, like what take of a particular shot they used, or how the edited version compares with the way we shot it. Generally, I look upon each of my movies as another rung on the ladder of my career.

SS: I know you paint. Do you do any writing yourself?

KS: Mostly journal/diary-type of writing and some poetry.

SS: Do you ever see yourself doing your own scripts?

KS: Right now I don't think I could sit down and turn out a complete script. But I do have creative ideas that I'd like to develop someday and I would like to possibly contribute to the writing of scripts.

SS: Do you keep in touch with any of the other *Flowers in the Attic* cast members?

KS: Yeah, I still keep in touch with Lindsay Parker, the little girl who played my sister, Carrie. Lindsay is now twelve years old and still in the business. She was six when we made the film.

Hot Stuff

SS: Were there any "memorable moments" on the set during the shooting of *Flowers in the Attic*?

KS: Well, I do remember setting myself on fire. (Laughs) We were shooting in Boston and I was really sick. I had the flu, and my mom had come out from California and was taking care of me.

We were all on the set and it was freezing cold. It was October in Boston, and it was freezing! And I am *definitely* not used to that kind of weather!

I was wearing this skirt that Cathy wears in the movie when all of us first arrive at the mansion. We were on our lunch break and we were in this barn with the caterers, eating our lunch, and I was so cold that I was standing by one of those portable propane heaters to warm up before I walked to the trailers.

So I'm standing there, and I'm rubbing my hands together and blowing in my hands trying to get warm and all of a sudden my skirt catches on fire. And we only had one skirt! (Laughs) Apparently, they hadn't doubled it.

Everybody was patting me down trying to put out the fire. I didn't get burned at all, but the skirt was a mess.

The wardrobe people had to pull the skirt together and cut another seam and get the burn marks out of it. (Laughs)

SS: That's funny. We're glad you didn't get hurt.

KS: Yeah, me too.

Friday the 13th . . . NOT!

SS: Are you a horror fan?

KS: I like some horror movies. I enjoy more "haunting"-type stories.

One of the reasons why I really like *Flowers in the Attic* is because I never really considered it a horror story or movie at all. I've always considered it more of a psychological thriller—very haunting and strange.

I speak to a lot of people, and they go, "*You* were in *Flowers in the Attic*?" and I'm talking about *Teamsters,* guys in their forties. And they're like, "God, that movie, I just couldn't watch it. It was too spooky. It was just awful, with these kids being locked up in an attic." (Laughs)

It seems as though a lot of people consider it a horror film, but it was never a horror movie to me. It was more sad and spooky. It was definitely not a slasher movie, for sure.

Except Neil Diamond, Right?

SS: What kind of music do you like?

KS: I have quite a variety of taste in music. I like big band music, rock and roll, heavy metal, country-western, classical. I like everything. I've always had a great appreciation for music. I grew up with it around me so I'm really fond of everything.

Seen Scenes

SS: Have you seen any movies lately that you really liked?

KS: I just last week rented Lasse Hallstrom's *My Life as a Dog* and I loved it.

SS: Do you spend a lot of your free time watching movies?

KS: Yeah, I do. I've got four here now that I need to watch.

SS: What are they?

KS: *Kansas, Little Man Tate, Europa, Europa,* and *Fried Green Tomatoes*.

SS: Have you seen *Sister Act*?

KS: Yeah, that was really great. I loved Whoopi Goldberg in that.

SS: By the way, was that your hair in *Mannequin 2*?

KS: No, it was a fall. It was mine in the front, though.

SS: Yeah, that's exactly what my wife said.

KS: (Laughs) We girls know these things.

The Sequel That Never Was

SS: Has there been any talk of more V. C. Andrews movies?

KS: Yes, actually. I was sent a script of *Petals on the Wind,* but it never took off.

SS: The same cast?

KS: Yes. I remember running into Louise Fletcher in Santa Barbara about four years ago. She asked me if I had gotten the *Petals on the Wind* script, which I had, and she wanted to know if I had read it.

I told her I had and that they had called me about it. I was interested but then I didn't hear from them anymore. And apparently the same thing happened with her. It's like they wanted to do it but they couldn't get it off the ground.

So it was never done. They came kind of close, though.

SS: What'd you think of the script?

KS: When I read the script, I wasn't too thrilled with it. I know Cathy goes through a lot in the next book, and the script was a real "sexfest." She gets pregnant and has so many affairs. There's her brother, Christopher, and then she has an affair with Julian, the dancer, and there's Paul, the doctor.

I was actually kind of wondering if I should even *do* a sequel, you know? I just didn't know if it should be done.

SS: Was the *Petals* script as toned-down sexually as the *Flowers in the Attic* adaptation?

KS: The *Petals on the Wind* script was just *all* sex. I would have had to discuss it with them.

SS: Was it a Jeffrey Bloom script?

KS: No, it wasn't. I don't remember who wrote it, but nothing ever came of it.

Curtain Call

SS: To conclude, here's a basic, generic, Barbara Walters-type interview question, Kristy. Where do you see yourself in twenty years?

KS: In twenty years I see myself at the age of 43. (Laughs)

SS: (Laughs) And that is *definitely* not your basic, cli-
ched, Barbara Walters-type answer. I thank you for
your sense of humor, and for your participation.

KS: It was my pleasure, Steve, and good luck with the
book.

[AUTHOR'S NOTE: Kristy Swanson was extremely helpful to me with
The V. C. Andrews Trivia and Quiz Book. She granted me an interview when
she was busy filming *The Program,* she lent me several pictures from her
personal collection, she dug up a *Flowers in the Attic* press kit for me to use
in the book, and she just really went out of her way to be as accommodating
as possible. She has my sincerest thanks and appreciation.]

—22—

A KRISTY SWANSON FILMOGRAPHY

FILMS

1985: *To Live and Die in L.A.* (cut from final version)
1986: *Ferris Bueller's Day Off*
      Pretty in Pink
      Deadly Friend (first starring role)
1987: *Flowers in the Attic*
1990: *Diving In*
      Dream Trap (straight to video)
      Highway to Hell (1992 release)
1991: *Mannequin Two: On the Move*
      Hot Shots: An Important Movie!
      The Chili Con Carne Club (short film for the American Film Institute)
1992: *Buffy the Vampire Slayer*
1993: *The Program*
1994: *The Chase*

TV WORK

"Archie Bunker's Place"
Dreamfinders (Disney TV-movie)
Call to Glory (TV-movie; pilot episode for "Call to Glory" series)
Miracle of the Heart: A Boys Town Story (Made-for-TV sequel to *Boys Town*)
Mr. Boogedy (Disney TV-movie)
"Cagney and Lacey"
"Alfred Hitchcock Presents"
"It's Your Move"
"Valerie"
"Growing Pains"
"Juarez"
"The Loner"
"Knots Landing"
"O'Hara"
"Nightingales"
"B. L. Stryker"

—23—

A LOST GARDEN:

A Look at Wes Craven's Shelved *Flowers in the Attic* Script

Horrormeister Wes Craven, the father of the Freddy Krueger *Nightmare on Elm Street* films, almost directed the film version of V. C. Andrews's novel, *Flowers in the Attic.* (See my interview with Kristy Swanson, who worked for Craven in *Deadly Friend,* for details on Craven's involvement with the V. C. novel.)

Craven did his own screenplay for *Flowers,* and this feature offers a rundown on what the movie might have looked like if Craven had directed it using his own script.

If filmed as written, the main difference in the two films would probably have been the rating. Craven's script is raunchier than Bloom's (it has necessary profanity—see "Cathy's Nude Scene" below) and has scenes of full nudity by Kristy Swanson's character, Cathy, and Jeb Adams's character, Chris, as well as scenes of semi-nudity by both of them also.

The script also contains one scene of torture that, if presented with the classic Wes Craven "touch," would have been quite graphic and horrifying. Craven's script is also much more violent than Bloom's version.

All of these scenes, plus the conscious inclusion of the incestuous element of Cathy and Chris's relationship (complete with a sex scene that could have been done either suggestively or graphically), would have easily garnered the film an R rating instead of the PG-13 that Bloom's version was given. I believe that these differences, and the fact that an actual V. C. Andrews script written by horror legend Craven exists, warrants a detailed look at the *Flowers in the Attic* movie that never was.

The script I used for this feature was the 117-page, second draft of the screenplay, dated March 28, 1985. Here is a look at a "Lost Garden": the unseen Wes Craven *Flowers in the Attic* script.

- The children's family in this script is named Chapman. The first scene shows Chris and Cathy bathing the twins. We then see the birthday party during which two police officers come to the house to tell Corine (which is how Craven spells "Corrine" throughout) that her husband, Christopher, is dead.
- The main titles begin. (The children's father has died before the opening credits.)
- A cemetery scene plays as the credits continue. We see a moving van in front of the house. Cathy opens a gift: It is a "silver box" with a ballerina on top. She cries. Everything has been repossessed. Corine tells Cathy that she and her father "were in hock up to our ears."
- The train to Virginia scene. Corine tells the children they're all going to be rich. She reveals to the children that she was cut off from her parents and their money because they didn't approve of her marriage to their father. No one meets them at the train station. They walk to Foxworth Hall. As they walk up the long drive, they all sing "Three Blind Mice." Christopher "rewrites" the lyrics as follows:

  Observe how they ambulate, observe how they ambulate. They all pursued an agriculturist's spouse, she amputated their appendages with a culinary cleaver, did you . . . [page 12]

- When they reach the front door, Chris is violently, physically attacked by a huge wolfhound dog. The dogs are called off by a "watchman" whom Cathy calls an "asshole."

- The Grandmother "greets" them. Her first words are, "He's my watchman, Doberman, and he was just doing his job."
- After The Grandmother brings them to their room, Cathy faces off to her early. The Grandmother says, "I smell arrogance here." There is a Hieronymus Bosch painting of sexual depravity on the wall in their room. Chris pukes. Corine leaves to pretend she's arriving for the first time the next day.
- In the room, Cathy and Chris sprawl on the bed together:

  Cathy (to Chris): Did you cut one?
  Chris: Must've been one of the twins.
  Cathy: Gross.

- Chris reads one of Cathy's "Nancy Drew" mysteries. Cathy tells him who the killer was. Chris describes his puke to Cathy:

  Chris: Okay, I threw up. Big green globs of slime, too.
  Cathy: Gross me out, why don't you?
  Chris: No, really. And some weird pink spongey stuff with greenish pustules hanging off it, and an old meat ball from last Tuesday.
  Cathy: Dis-*gust*-ing!
  Chris: They had turned green too. Except for the worms, of course. Those were red.

- The next morning, The Grandmother catches Chris and Cathy in bed together. She grabs Cathy by the hair and pulls her out of the bed. She is also pissed off that they haven't memorized her "Rules" yet, which she considerately reads aloud to them. Later she brings them food and warns Cathy not to clench her fists in her presence and also cautions them all not to try to win her friendship.
- Corrine returns to Foxworth Hall to see her father. Later, Corrine and The Grandmother visit the children's room. The screaming Carrie/biting Cory scene is the same as in Bloom's version.
- The Grandmother makes Corrine remove her blouse to show the children her whipped back, but in this version, Corrine has been lashed 48 times, as in the

novel. Later, Cathy bathes her mother and Corrine tells them she is enrolling in secretarial school, also as in the novel.

- Corrine shows them the attic. She tells them:

I thought it would give you a place to stretch your legs. You deserve that, my little flowers. Flowers in the attic. [page 35]

- In the classroom in the attic, Corrine tells them the story of her family. In this script, the children's father was Corrine's *half*-uncle, as in the book. Later, Chris and Cathy discuss whether they're truly evil because they are the product of a possibly incestuous marriage.
- Corrine brings gifts. The Grandmother makes them recite their biblical scriptures. Chris recites Psalm 25:19. In the novel, the passages are Genesis 44:4; Job 28:12; Job 31:35; and Job 32:9.
- The children are brought a tray of powdered sugar *doughnuts,* as in the novel. Later, Chris and Cathy have a discussion of Chris's fondness for burping and farting.
- *Scenes from the Attic:* Chris reveals he stole back Cathy's ballerina music box from the repossessors and also shows her a Victrola in the attic. They put on music and Cathy dances. They all make paper flowers. Mother pops in and then disappears for a long time.
- *The Cory in the Trunk Scene:* As in the novel, Cory gets trapped in a trunk when the cover closes accidentally.
- *Christmas.* Corrine brings gifts.
- *The Party Scene:* Chris and Cathy hide in a chest, as in the book. They watch the dancing. Two guests talk about their missing champagne glasses. Chris stole them—also as in the book. Later, Chris sneaks out of the room dressed in old clothes and does a Groucho Marx move for Cathy, as he does in the novel.
- Chris goes into the Trophy Room. Two party guests come in. Chris hides, and then trips one. The guy remarks, "Damn, I believe I've cracked my Rolex."

- Chris goes into her mother's bedroom and sees the Swan Bed. He sees his paper bird Christmas gift to his mother in the wastebasket. Corrine and Bart show up. Corrine sees her son. Chris flees and is attacked by Doberman the caretaker. Doberman is about to slit Chris's throat when Corrine stops him. The Grandmother appears and tells Doberman that he can kill the "rats in the attic" if he ever sees them again. Back in the room, Corrine slaps Chris. And Cathy is missing.

- The "Torture of Cathy" Scene: In a scene not in the book, Cathy is found in the bathroom. But she's not putting on makeup or taking a bath. Here's what Chris found in the bathroom:

INT. BATHROOM

She's half-naked, bound by tape hand and foot, and silenced by it as well—a broad band of it runs around her head and through her mouth again and again. She's been laid across the toilet, back down, head hanging off into space. Her legs are taped at the knee to the faucets of the tub, and from the calves on down she's under the boiling water of the brimfilled tub, water that rolls up steam as if it had been poured from a witch's cauldron.

Cathy twists around, seeing Chris run in, her face deep purple, her eyes glazed with agony.

Chris lets out a cry of rage and pain, tearing at the tape on her legs, trying to break it and not being able to. He lets out a scream of frustration and panic, flings open the medicine cabinet looking for a blade—then, not finding anything—drives his fist into the mirror of the thing, plunging into the bowl of the sink for the biggest shard of glass he can find, flying back to his sister.

He saws at the tape like a madman, sobbing, his fingers bleeding until she's free. He pulls her away, gasping and cursing and wild-eyed, lifting her up and taking her out of there as fast as his shaking legs can carry him. [page 71]

- Later, Cathy tries to dance on her excruciating feet. We see transition scenes as Cathy continues to heal and rehearse her dance moves.

- Spring. Cathy and Chris are getting older and more mature physically. Cory, however, constantly wets the bed, and Carrie has chronic diarrhea.
- Corrine brings more gifts. She's been to Europe. She tells them the will's been changed and that she will inherit her father's riches, but then she also reveals to them the clause that states that if it's ever learned that she had children from her first marriage, then she will disinherit everything.
- Later that night: Chris and Cathy climb down from the roof of the *south* wing of the house. (They are in the north wing, but they have access to the whole house from the attic.)
- As in the book, they go swimming in a nearby lake, Cathy in her nightgown (that hides *nothing*) and Chris in his jockey shorts. They talk about escaping, but Chris can't help but notice his sister's sexy body and he gets an erection that embarrasses him. Cathy stares at his groin:

  Cathy: Ewww, that's weird. How you *doing* that? [page 86]

- As they're climbing back up to the roof, they're attacked by Doberman and his dogs. Doberman actually begins climbing up the rope after them, but they make it back to the attic.
- We learn that Chris has pulled bricks out of the chimney and can hear his mother talking in her room. The next morning, Chris throws up.
- The next night: Chris fashions a key for the door to their room. Cathy steals money from her mother and finds a pornographic picture book called *Swedish Ecstasy*. She also suddenly realizes that Bart Winslow is in the room, asleep on the bed. (In the book, he was in a chair.) She kisses him. He awakens, but she is hiding. She returns to the room and tells Chris she only stole $15.23. Chris realizes that Cathy found—and looked at—*Swedish Ecstasy*.
- *Cathy's Nude Scene:* Later, Cathy, now quite curious about sex, completely undresses and looks at herself in a full-length mirror:

She walks naked in front of the mirror and looks at herself. Swallows. She's really quite beautiful, even she can see it.

She smiles, shakes her new breasts. Turns and looks at herself over her shoulder. Likes that too.

CLOSER, ON HER FACE—as she assumes a variety of poses—sultry, mysterious, vampish, the ingenue.

WIDE AGAIN—she closes her eyes and wraps her arms about herself, bending her head back for a kiss from an invisible, beautiful lover. It's about then that Chris barges in from the attic. [pages 96–97]

[Whew! Okay, America. Are we hot yet?] The Grandmother catches Cathy naked and Chris standing there watching her and pandemonium ensues. The Grandmother grabs Cathy by the arm and raises her hand to strike. Chris picks up a chair:

Chris: You touch her and I swear to God I'll break this fucking chair over your head! [page 97]

- The Grandmother does not hit Cathy but she forces Chris to undress and bend over the tub, where she whips him with a cane. (The reason Chris acquiesces to the whipping is because if he hadn't, The Grandmother threatened to let Doberman do whatever he wanted with Cathy.) After Chris, The Grandmother whips Cathy.
- The Grandmother stops bringing food. Chris and Cathy lay naked and wounded from the caning. The proximity of each other's nude bodies is too much to resist and they make love. Later, they feel guilty.
- Cory is in bad shape. Chris slits open a wrist (as in the novel) and feeds him with his own blood. Food finally comes—and powdered doughnuts are included. The door is now padlocked from the outside. Chris climbs down the inside of the chimney to listen to his mother. He overhears a woman tell Corrine that it's a good thing she never had children. Chris sneaks into The Grandfather's room. It's empty. It's obvious that he's been dead for quite a while. Cory's mouse, Mickey, is also dead. Chris comes upon an old servant who believes that Chris is a chimney

sweep. The servant tells Chris that "the daughter" has been putting arsenic in the food she's been leaving for "the rats" in the north wing.

- Cory dies.
- *The Wedding Day:* The Grandmother sics Doberman on Cathy, who escapes out the window. Chris interrupts the wedding as Cathy fights with Doberman on the roof. On the roof, Cathy yells down to the wedding guests that they are Corrine's children. Cathy stabs Doberman in the chest with a lightning rod. He falls off the roof and lands on The Grandmother, killing her instantly. Chris screams at his mother, "You imprisoned us! Poisoned us! But you couldn't kill us, Mother!" The sounds of sirens get nearer. Corine denies they're her children. Bart backs away from her because it's clear Chris is telling the truth. Chris, Carrie, and Cathy embrace. The picture freezes on the children.
- Roll credits.

—The End—

[If you'd like to read Wes Craven's script for yourself, copies for study and entertainment (NOT for publication) are available from HOLLYWOOD SCRIPTS, 5514 Satsuma Avenue, North Hollywood, California 91607. Their phone number is (818) 980-3545 and they have always been extremely helpful to me with my research needs. Tell 'em Steve sent ya.]